TELITA SNYCKERS

DIRTY TOBACCO

SPIES, LIES AND MEGA-PROFITS

TAFELBERG

Tafelberg
An imprint of NB Publishers, a Division of Media24 Boeke (Pty) Ltd
40 Heerengracht, Cape Town
www.tafelberg.com

Text © Telita Snyckers (2020)

All rights reserved.
No part of this book may be reproduced or transmitted
in any form or by any electronic or mechanical means, including photocopying
and recording, or by any information storage or retrieval system,
without written permission from the publisher.

Cover design: Simon Richardson
Book design: Nazli Jacobs
Editing: Albert Weideman
Proofreading: Kelly Norwood-Young
Index: Telita Snyckers

Printed and bound by CTP Printers, Cape Town

First edition, first impression 2020

ISBN: 978-0-624-08893-6
Epub: 978-0-624-08894-3
Mobi: 978-0-624-08895-0

Contents

Foreword by Rob Rose 7
Acronyms 12
Prologue 13

PART 1: Smuggling 101 19
1. The birth of big tobacco 21
2. The competition: 'Cheap and nasty' 27
3. 'Bigger than drugs' 35
4. Dead easy to cheat 42
5. Smuggling: A rogue's gallery 48
6. Jam on their face and still they do nothing 56
7. They play a weak defense 64
8. Toothpaste, fish and fig leaves 69
9. A playbook for profit 82

PART 2: Controlling what we think 87
10. Merchants of disinformation 89
11. Astroturf, ghost writers and bots 101
12. Hashtags, headlines and Ipsos 114
13. Lipstick on a pig 118

PART 3: Spies, hitmen and a silent coup 123
14. Captured 125
15. Political patronage 135
16. Victims and saviours 144
17. Sex, lies and videotape 150
18. From taxman to hitman 168
19. Unholy alliances and friends in even higher places 176
20. BAT's Christmas present to the underworld? 180

PART 4: Quo Vadis? 191
21. Avoidance, evasion and glass houses 193
22. Blowing smoke 202
23. Inconvenient truths 208
24. Pebbles for government's David 213
25. Too big to fail? 219

Conclusion 223
Addendum 1: What Project Honey Badger was investigating 225
Addendum 2: Where the quoted internal industry documents come from 230
Addendum 3: Counterfeits 232
Addendum 4: Illicit whites 234
Addendum 5: A short history of tobacco smuggling 236
Addendum 6: Selected extracts from the BBC Panorama's story: 'The secret bribes of big tobacco' 240
Addendum 7: Big tobacco's rogue's gallery – additional detail 242
Addendum 8: Email from JTI manager on doing nothing 255
Addendum 9: Extracts from affidavits on BAT's espionage ring in South Africa 257
Index 300
About the author 304

Foreword
by Rob Rose

A devastating playbook dating back decades

What you'll read in these pages is nothing less than an indispensable part of the canon of work that explains the secretive role that tobacco played in warping South African society over the most traumatic decade in its post-apartheid era.

Written with meticulous care and absorbing detail, Telita Snyckers' devastatingly blunt chronicle deserves to be read alongside Johann van Loggerenberg's *Rogue* and *Tobacco Wars*, and Jacques Pauw's *The President's Keepers*.

Telita points out that the strategy of tobacco multinationals to neuter South Africa's tax authority, the SA Revenue Service (SARS), is nothing especially novel. Almost from the 15th century, when tobacco was first discovered by European explorers in North America, merchants have been doing their damnedest to find loopholes in the rules: be it through rampant smuggling, dodging taxes or bribing politicians. Governments fought back in, at times, pretty draconian ways (in 1692 five Spanish friars were found smoking during a church service and put to death).

The reality is, almost since the day Buck Duke began mass-producing cigarettes in 1887, authorities have been a step behind. As this book meticulously chronicles, the large tobacco companies have often been actively involved in smuggling to boost their margins for decades, not to mention more ingenious methods of nimble side-stepping of tax services.

Along the way, as Telita deftly sketches it here, tobacco barons became virtuosos in propaganda. Bending the facts to support their narrative has become such an ingrained tactic, it's now part of their DNA. Don't tell Donald Trump, but tobacco merchants were the original fake news.

Take the example of a Lucky Strike advert from 1929, featuring the original poster girl, Rosalie Adele Nelson. Staring out seductively at the reader, above a tagline that reads 'I'm a Lucky girl', Nelson says: 'I've found a new way to keep my figure trim – whenever the desire for a sweet tempts me, I light up a Lucky Strike.'

Another advert, from 1960, is of a successful businessman, staring meaningfully at the audience as he lights a cigarette, under a banner which read: 'More scientists and educators smoke Kent with the micronite filter.' What Kent hadn't told anyone is that for years, those micronite filters were made with asbestos.

With such an effortlessly Machiavellian pursuit of profit, and blinding ethical agnosticism, is it any wonder that South Africa, already untethering from its moral centre under the Jacob Zuma presidency, was so comprehensively manipulated by tobacco interests?

It's been a bracing reality-check for South Africa. Still basking in the glow of being an exciting and favoured emerging market, we were, after all, a more naive, trusting country at the turn of the last decade.

Just like the rest of the world, we had no idea how British American Tobacco (BAT), alongside a bubbling cauldron of illicit tobacco dealers, and an unofficial army of former mercenaries operating in the shadows, were playing journalists, regulators and the public like marionettes on a string.

Many of us were duped. I, for one, vastly underestimated how skilful and coordinated this really was.

Back in 2014 when I was working at *Business Times*, Van Loggerenberg put me in touch with a lawyer, Belinda Walter, whom he said had a wild, scarcely-believable tale of how BAT was not only spying on rivals, it was also operating a secret network of spies it was paying illegally. Of course, the tobacco giant had a lot to lose at the time: it was facing a wide-ranging probe into its tax practices that ultimately led to a R2 billion assessment against it. Walter, and others on BAT's payroll, soon turned on Van Loggerenberg, dramatically weakening SARS in the process.

There are many who have fought for BAT to account for its role in this saga, none more so than Van Loggerenberg. But they've been resoundingly ignored. And instead, big tobacco has used its time-tested wiles to shift the focus to how it was 'illicit tobacco' that has destroyed the country.

Telita's gripping narrative deftly slices through the spin, connecting the dots in a devastating critique of the industry – both legal and illicit. And she runs a red pen over the glaring contradictions, all over the place.

How, for example, do you reconcile the fact that the Tobacco Institute of South Africa claims its members – BAT, Japan Tobacco International and Philip Morris – manufactured 19 billion cigarette sticks in 2017/2018, yet tax was only paid on 15,3 billion cigarettes that year?

How do you reconcile the fact that big tobacco claims 72 000 people stand to lose their jobs in South Africa due to illicit tobacco, when BAT (which controls 72% of the market) only employs a grand total of 2 187 people?

The bottom line, as she points out, is that when tobacco companies pay less than their fair share of tax, thanks to some ham-fisted smuggling effort or a sophisticated profit-shifting scheme, 'the result is the same: you and I pay more tax than we should'.

If there's one person who can tell the story from an insider's vantage point, it is Telita Snyckers. Between 1999 and 2010, she worked in several critical roles at SARS, including being part of the creation of its special compliance unit, later heading up its criminal investigations across the country, and working as a policy advisor in the Commissioner's office.

You may not have seen her name much before, but it was because of Telita, and people like Telita, that SARS hit its high watermark. Before, obviously, the rapacious grip of rent-seekers in 2014 led to its unravelling under Commissioner Tom Moyane.

Since leaving SARS, she has worked in 25 countries across the world, including such far-flung places as Serbia, Ethiopia, Jordan and Kosovo, as an expert on tax and customs reform for clients that include the International Monetary Fund (IMF).

Before joining SARS, Telita was a public prosecutor and commercial litigation lawyer. Those skills are on full display in these pages, as she methodically dismantles the façade that big tobacco has built around itself. I'd hate to have come up against her in court.

Which makes this an indispensable, and global, view of how the bending of South Africa's national interest to suit the tobacco companies, with such devastating precision, wasn't some aberration: it was just part of a playbook stretching back centuries.

'They control what we read; they control what our politicians do; they control where our law enforcement agencies look; and they'll do anything to ensure that their supply chains remain opaque,' she writes.

You've been warned.

'One comes to the conclusion that you are either crooks or you are stupid, and you do not look very stupid.'

— *George Osborne, a member of the UK Parliament's Public Accounts Committee, during questioning of the CEO of Imperial Tobacco.*[1]

Acronyms

BAT – British American Tobacco

DNP – Duty not paid; also referred to as 'GT – general trade'; 'free markets' or 'border trade' (short-hand for contraband or black-market cigarettes)

FCTC – Framework Convention on Tobacco Control, the World Health Organization's instrument which seeks to curb the illicit trade in tobacco

FSS – Forensic Security Services, contracted by BAT

FITA – Fair Trade Independent Tobacco Association, whose members include the smaller independent tobacco manufacturers in South Africa

Imperial – Imperial Tobacco

JTI – Japan Tobacco International

OLAF – European Anti-Fraud Office

PMI – Philip Morris International

SARS – South African Revenue Service

SSA – State Security Agency (South Africa)

TISA – Tobacco Institute of Southern Africa, whose members include BAT, PMI, JTI (now defunct)

Prologue

Globally, big tobacco controls more than 80% of the world's tobacco market. An estimated 98% of all illicit cigarettes is believed to come from legal, licensed manufacturing facilities,[2] and around one third of all exported cigarettes go missing somewhere along the supply chain.[3]

You do the math.

Indeed, British American Tobacco's *own* documents, which date from the early 1990s, suggest that the company may historically have been involved in smuggling in around 30 countries; and suggest that, at the time, as much as 25% of BAT's profits may have come from selling contraband in China.[4]

The tobacco trade has been dirty for centuries, effectively breeding an industry that I believe has criminality embedded in its DNA. (Mind you, I'm not suggesting that tobacco is *all* bad: there was a time when tobacco smoke could reportedly be applied – by way of an enema – to resuscitate drowning victims.)

I had initially written a simple thesis on the instances where big tobacco had been caught smuggling. It was meant to be a moderately academic discourse that really would have just preached to the choir – more boring than brave.

But once you start connecting the dots, you realise that there is far more to the story than just smuggling – there is an entire playbook of strategies, rhetoric and tactics behind the façade that big tobacco puts up, one that seeks to secure its continued success, the demise of its competitors and the downfall of those who stand in its way. A playbook that may, perhaps, be aimed at positioning big tobacco as too big to fail.

Just ask the team of tax investigators that tried to take on the tobacco industry in South Africa.

They faced the wrath of an industry willing to go to almost any lengths to protect its profits. When the pressure became too much, the tobacco industry played a role in the demise of those in power at the South African Revenue Service who could oppose them or expose them. The subsequent implosion at SARS can't be blamed entirely on them, but their agents lit the match that burnt the SARS house down.

I spent most of my early career at SARS, and since then have had work assignments in more than 25 countries – mostly on tax and customs modernisation initiatives. Using this experience, I wanted to place the events in South Africa in a broader global context. And, so, while much of this story details what happened in SARS' efforts to take on the illicit trade in tobacco, this is not a South African story – it is a story about how big tobacco acts with impunity, wherever it operates.

By 2011, tax evasion in the tobacco industry was costing SARS around R3 billion ($203 million) a year. With laundering and corruption rife, SARS launched Project Honey Badger, targeting various tobacco industry players – including British American Tobacco (BAT).[5] (See addendum 1 for an extract of the letter SARS sent to the industry, where they set out in some detail what they were investigating.)

Honey Badger had the potential to make history as one of SARS' most effective industry-wide investigations ever. Thanks in large part to Honey Badger, contraband tobacco had dropped from around 26% of the total market in 2013 to 17% in 2014.

Then, as the project's wings were clipped, illicit trade spiked upwards, and markedly so: By 2017 – the last year for which sound estimates are available – the share of illicit cigarettes in the market had shot up to somewhere between 30-35%,[6] and in the space of only two years there was a steep drop of 26% in the quantities of cigarettes declared to the taxman.[7]

It's all too easy for our eyes to glaze over when bombarded with figures like these. What does '35% of the market is illicit' translate to in real monetary terms? It means South Africa was losing out on tax revenue of an estimated R7 billion ($350 million) a year. That's the equivalent of 74 000 new homes that government could have subsidised; 66 500 new policemen that could have been appointed; 277 777 pension grants that could have been paid out; or 400 000 electrical connections that could have been installed.[8] But for which there now was no funding, because somebody hadn't paid the taxes on a pack of smokes.

The data tells a story of how Project Honey Badger made a significant difference, only to lose traction once SARS came under attack, in what one might call big tobacco's Christmas present to the underworld.

With 15 different criminal cases against tobacco manufacturers and importers ready to be prosecuted, the fiscus should have netted an extra R3 billion (roughly $200 million). But Honey Badger had come too close to the truth, and people like tax detective Johann van Loggerenberg and others had to go. To be fair, they had made enemies far beyond just the tobacco industry. All of them had both the incentive and the power to engineer their demise, but tobacco was the thin end of the wedge that pried open the door for their departure.

To fully grasp how their downfall came about, one needs to understand the power of big tobacco globally. 'Big tobacco' commonly refers to multinational companies that control more than 80% of the world's market, including: British American Tobacco, Philip Morris International, Japan Tobacco International, Imperial, Reynolds. (China Tobacco controls most of the Chinese market and is a book all on its own.)

In an older internal corporate affairs presentation, one of the big tobacco companies – Japan Tobacco International – talks about the importance of 'finding allies that cannot be ignored', of 'building allies across ministries'. It talks about the importance of 'building complete political power maps' and how 'roadblocks are as important as solutions'.[9] And it talks about having 'the best expertise on our side: door-openers, strategists, spin doctors'.[10]

And in an older quote, one of RJ Reynolds Tobacco Company's lawyers explains how they win cases: not by spending all of their money, but 'by making the other son of a bitch spend all of his'.[11]

And so, when SARS had started digging a bit too close to the tobacco dung heap, it came as little surprise that the industry was ready to retaliate. Because big tobacco had, indeed, found allies that could not be ignored, and had built networks across ministries, and had the best door-openers on its side.

What happened in South Africa is simply part of a bigger story – not an isolated example of the tobacco industry gone rogue. It is a problem that plagues countries the world over, from advanced nations in Europe to those least able to defend themselves in the developing world.

I had started out with the simple hypothesis that much of the illicit trade we see in tobacco is not attributable just to tattooed gangsters, but to big, established, reputable tobacco companies, who are only too happy to pin the rise of illicit tobacco on smaller competitors. Along the way, I discovered a few things that are far, far more interesting, that lets me tell a story that goes beyond a bland academic discourse on the interpretation of rebate item 624.10 in the Customs and Excise Act or an exposition on what a 'secure stamp' means.

You're here to consider the evidence that proves, in my view, just how dirty tobacco's hands are. To test my hypothesis in the 'real world', I rounded up some of the biggest, baddest cigarette smugglers I could find.

And so, while much of what I'm about to tell you comes from decades of peer-reviewed research, from investigative journalists and from NGOs, and much of it from big tobacco's own documents (either leaked or forcibly disclosed as a result of court orders, from a time when they were far more brazen about documenting their goings-on), some of it comes straight from the mouths of smugglers, and some from an incriminating thumb drive that was slipped to me in Rosebank, Johannesburg.

I should point out at the get-go, that much of the big tobacco documentation comes from the early 1990s, a time when big tobacco appears to have been much less careful in the way it recorded its activities internally.

The majority of the internal industry documents we now have access to, relate mostly to BAT, simply because PMI and other tobacco companies responded more narrowly to the courts' disclosure orders. As a result, while the examples quoted may create the impression that BAT may have been particularly active in establishing a contraband network, this may not be an accurate reflection and conceivably understates the involvement of other tobacco companies. Indeed, PMI had to pay a lot more in EU settlements than BAT did. (Addendum 2 has more details on where the internal industry documents that are quoted extensively throughout the book come from.)

Here is why I largely believe what was on that thumb drive and what the smugglers I spoke to told me: because there is a common thread in all of their stories; because of the many lines where their allegations intersect; because they reference details that can be verified; because of the sheer volume of evidence; and because much of it simply validates tactics that are explicitly discussed in the tobacco industry's own internal documents.

I believe it because it overlaps with serious allegations that many others have uncovered in other parts of the world, including the International Consortium of Investigative Journalists, which asked: '[Tobacco] executives meeting with criminals in Niagara Falls to discuss smuggling into Canada, or BAT executives in Hong Kong taking bribes to feed a Triad-backed smuggling ring, or Mafia bosses in Italy with a seemingly endless supply of Marlboros, all raise serious questions about international corporate participation in a conspiracy to defraud governments.

Have BAT, Philip Morris, Reynolds, and Japan Tobacco become mafia-like organisations involved in massive illegal operations?'[12]

At the heart of this book sits a disturbing thought: big tobacco may just be too big to fail. Based on my research, I believe it thrives because its very own products end up on the black market, their packs being sold tax free. And they have managed to get away with it because they influence what we think by controlling the narratives and rhetoric we are fed. They get away with it because they influence the policy positions our governments take. They get away with it because of the political patronage networks they have established. They get away with it because they spy on their competitors and use our enforcement agencies as economic hitmen to put pressure on the smaller players making cheaper cigarettes.

If you only remember one thing from this book, make it this quote from George Osborne, a member of the UK Parliament's Select Committee on Public Accounts, after hearing evidence from the big tobacco companies – because this sits at the heart of our story: 'One comes to the conclusion that you are either crooks or you are stupid, and you do not look very stupid'.[13]

PART 1

Smuggling 101

1. The birth of big tobacco

If you've ever been to Geneva or Lausanne, you'll know what it smells like. It smells like money. Not *nouveau riche*, flashy mobster money – old money.

In the quaint university town of Lausanne, just down the Rue de Lausanne, are the grandiose offices of British American Tobacco (BAT), Philip Morris International (PMI) and Japan Tobacco International (JTI), who have chosen one of the world's most private and secretive corporate environments in which to base their global operations and house their massive profits. The setting stands in stark contrast to the addiction, devastation and ruin that their products dispense to the world with Swiss-like efficiency.

The industry has come a long way since the invention of the paper-rolled cigarette in Turkey in 1832. During the siege of Acre, an Egyptian artilleryman's crew improved their rate of fire by rolling the gunpowder in paper tubes and were rewarded with a pound of tobacco. Their only pipe was broken, so they rolled the pipe tobacco in the same paper – giving the world its first paper-rolled cigarettes.[1]

Somewhere between the birth of hand-rolled Turkish cigarettes and PMI, BAT, JTI and Imperial dominating the scene today, lies the story of James Bonsack and Buck Duke.

Buck Duke's father owned a US-based tobacco company, which he took over in the 1880s, over time earning himself the moniker of 'robber baron'. He is often referred to as the 'father of the modern cigarette'.

At the time, the cigarette market was small – cigarettes were expensive and hand-rolled by 'cigarette girls'. In 1881, James Bonsack created a machine that was capable of rolling cigarettes 13 times faster than a cigarette girl could. But the industry wasn't interested. Because the market for cigarettes was so small, they didn't see the benefit of investing in a machine that produced more than they believed the market could consume.[2]

Buck Duke – who at that stage controlled a modest 1,5% of the tobacco market in America – seized his chance. He signed an agreement with Bonsack, giving him exclusive rights to use the machines (and paying very little by way of royalties).

He now had the capacity to produce millions of cigarettes but needed to create a market for them. He did so using spectacular promotions and advertising campaigns, spending an unheard of $800 000 in billboard and newspaper advertising (making Duke and Bonsack not only the godfathers of the industrialised cigarette trade but also of modern mass-market advertising and promotion). By 1887, Duke and Bonsack had refined the machines, and could easily produce 120 000 cigarettes in 10 hours.

With the power of both mass production and mass marketing behind him, Duke set out to conquer the tobacco market. He bought out Ligget&Myers; took over RJ Reynolds; absorbed Lorillard; and over time took over more than 200 other rival firms. So began the American Tobacco Company. He controlled 90% of the American tobacco market; and his company became one of the original 12 members of the Dow Jones Industrial Average, which is used to measure the performance of the stock market.

Not content with dominating just one side of the Atlantic, Duke set his sights on the British tobacco market. To avoid being gobbled up as part of Duke's expansion plans, four smaller British manufacturers joined forces to create Imperial Tobacco.

Eventually, Duke and Imperial struck a deal: Duke would control the market in America; Imperial the market in British territories; and the rest of the world would be controlled by a new joint venture set up between them: British American Tobacco.

The American Tobacco Company was ultimately charged with breaking anti-trust legislation, and in 1911 the US Supreme Court dissolved the company as a monopoly, freeing RJ Reynolds and others from the American Tobacco stable.

With that, the tobacco wars really started.

Long before Duke started trading – as far back as 1847 – a gentleman named Philip Morris had opened a shop on London's Bond Street, selling tobacco and hand-rolled Turkish cigarettes. It became the centre of the retail tobacco trade in Britain. Morris died in 1873, but his namesake company lived on.[3]

By 1901, when Queen Victoria – who passionately hated cigarettes – died, her successor, Edward VII, gathered friends in a large drawing room at Buckingham Palace and announced, 'Gentlemen, you may smoke.' By royal warrant, he appointed Philip Morris as tobacconist to the King.

Philip Morris had its next seminal moment when RJ Reynolds decided to hike cigarette prices at the start of the Great Depression in 1930, leaving a perfect opening for Philip Morris to counter with low-priced brands, in the process painting Reynolds as greedy and opportunistic.

By the time Duke's monopoly was disbanded in 1911, Philip Morris was well-established, mainly off the back of brands like Marlboro, which initially targeted women.

Philip Morris embarked on a quest for world domination: buying out not just countless other tobacco companies but also the Miller Brewing Company (then the 7th largest brewery), most of the Seven-Up Company, General Foods and Kraft, a share in Brazil's leading chocolate company, and Nabisco Holdings Corp for $18,9 billion – making it the world's second-biggest food company (only trailing Switzerland's Nestlé).

Aside from expanding its business empire beyond tobacco, PMI also made another strategic move: it began to establish a series of structures aimed at managing the public discourse around tobacco, setting up the Tobacco Research Centre in 1973 and the Tobacco Institute in 1978.

In 2001 Philip Morris decided to split its corporate identity: Altria (predominantly housing Miller Beer and Kraft Foods), and the two cigarette branches, Philip Morris USA and Philip Morris International. (At the time of writing, there were rumours that PMI and Altria are talking about a merger.)

As an aside, this book does not dwell on tobacco in China, because it warrants an entire book by itself. China has its own version of big tobacco, the China National Tobacco Corporation. It's a state-owned monopoly, producing 2,5 trillion cigarettes a year – 43% of global output. It makes more money than BAT, PMI and Altria combined, and is responsible for somewhere between 7% and 11% of China's government revenues every year.[4]

South Africa – where much of this book plays out – has its own tobacco-related rags-to-riches story (which ultimately ends up circling back to Lausanne decades later). In the 1940s a small tobacco farmer, Anton Rupert, noted that even the depression did not seem to decrease people's consumption of tobacco and liquor, and started manufacturing cigarettes in his garage with an initial investment of £10,[5] which he eventually built into the tobacco and industrial conglomerate Rembrandt Group. He has been credited with innovations ranging from king-size filter cigarettes, foil-wrapped packs and menthol filters, and the international hit brand Peter Stuyvesant.

In 1988, Rupert's Rembrandt group founded the Swiss luxury goods company Richemont, effectively turning his earlier £10 investment into a company with annual net sales of $10 billion. In 1995, Rembrandt and Richemont consolidated their tobacco interests into Rothmans International (at the time controlling 93% of the legal tobacco market in South Africa). Their market share was ultimately ceded to BAT, handing over what was a virtual monopoly,⁶ and setting BAT up for dominance in the local market for decades to come.

Today, BAT is estimated to control around 74% of the local licit market, followed by JTI with 9% and PMI with 8%. This dominance, combined with the high excise tax on cigarettes, makes BAT one of the largest contributors to the fiscus.⁷

Whether it's South Africa or America or mostly anywhere, the story almost always plays out the same way: a man makes some cigarettes; he finds a faster and cheaper way to make more cigarettes; he expands into other products; he gets bought up by a larger company; that big company merges with another conglomerate.

Oligopolies that started in somebody's garage.

In recent years, a confluence of events has started putting pressure on what was previously a seemingly invincible industry. And industries under pressure bring out the big guns and the dirty tricks.

The first reason why big tobacco has been forced into a defensive posture has to do with simple market dynamics: smaller, local, low-cost manufacturers who are making inroads into its market share.

The second dynamic is a general increase in the awareness of big tobacco's chequered past, resulting in more efforts around the world to regulate its business practices more effectively (especially in places like Western Europe).

The third is an obligation imposed under an Illicit Trade Protocol in the World Health Organization's Framework Convention on Tobacco Control⁸ to introduce a track-and-trace system for cigarettes, so that cigarettes end up where they are supposed to, and packs that do make their way to the black market can be traced back to their manufacturer.

A fourth problem facing the industry is that governments are increasingly being pressured to introduce higher tax rates, as an incentive for people to stop smoking. Quite understandably, this is the last thing the tobacco industry needs.

Make no mistake: Impressive bottom lines notwithstanding, big tobacco is under pressure.

Which perhaps in part explains why it feels the need to take out the competition that is mercilessly chipping away at their market share. While the focus of this book is on big tobacco, it helps to understand the upcoming crop of independent manufacturers who are giving the big boys a run for their money.

2. The competition: 'Cheap and nasty'

'The magician must expect the exposure of his tricks sooner or later, and see what it has required long months of study and time to perfect dissolved in an hour. The very best illusions of the best magicians of a few years ago are now the common property of travelling showmen at country fairs.'
　– French magician Alexander Herrmann

In the simplest terms, there are three circles in the tobacco manufacturing industry: multinational big tobacco companies with their globally-known big brand names; smaller, independent manufacturers who typically make cheaper – but still legal – cigarettes (sometimes called 'cheapies' or value brands); and the guys who manufacture specifically for the contraband market, making counterfeits (addendum 3) or what are called 'illicit whites' or 'cheap whites' (addendum 4).

In an interview Johann van Loggerenberg, the tax sleuth and author of books like *Rogue*, *Death and Taxes*, and *Tobacco Wars*, describes them as bank robbers, bag snatchers and muggers respectively.[1]

The big guys, the little guys, the purely criminal guys, they all have three things in common: they all try in some way to minimise their tax liabilities; their products all – to a lesser or greater degree – seem to find their way on to the black market; and they all, in the end, will likely kill half of their customers.[2]

Increasingly, big tobacco is under material pressure from smaller, local low-cost manufacturers who are making inroads into its market share.[3] For instance, South Africa's Carnilinx sells its value brand for R17 (just over $1 at the time of writing) a pack. BAT's most popular Peter Stuyvesant packs sell for around R44 (roughly $3).[4] How can a Carnilinx pack sell for so much more cheaply than one from BAT does? They could be evading taxes, but not necessarily so: on average, it costs less than R1,50 to make a pack of cigarettes, and these smaller, low-cost companies do not have to send royalty payments, management fees and IT charges to an offshore parent company like BAT has to. And because what you're allowed to put into cigarettes is reasonably well regulated, their product is at least in some way comparable to what big tobacco makes. For cash-strapped consumers it's an obvious choice.

As Yusuf Kajee of Amalgamated Tobacco South Africa puts it: 'It's like people having a choice between Prada and Gucci [meaning the big tobacco companies] and then Mr Price [a value clothing and homewares brand in South Africa]. That's all we are doing – offering a lower-priced cigarette to the ordinary man on the street.'[5]

In 2002, when the illicit cigarette trade was just beginning to pick up pace, BAT's market share in South Africa stood at between 86% and 95%; it now sits at around 74%.[6] Here's why: In 1999, 27% of South Africans smoked. Big tobacco held more than 80% of that market, equating to some 4,6 million smokers buying their brands. By 2015, in large part because of targeted anti-smoking campaigns, only 11% of South Africans were smoking. Where big tobacco previously had a potential pool of 4,6 million smokers to target, they were now down to a pool of 2,7 million smokers[7] – many of whom were now more price conscious. So, in the space of six years, big tobacco in South Africa had effectively lost 1,9 million smokers – close to half their market.

With fewer potential smokers to sell their products to, the entrance of competitors who sell what are essentially the same products more cheaply would be the last thing big tobacco needs.

What big tobacco instead appears to have done, is to effectively suggest that there are only *two* classes of tobacco manufacturers: big multinational corporations, and criminals. It's a tactic that works well – by attempting to paint all of its competitors as inherently criminal, big tobacco plays to our collective sympathies and fears. In South Africa, big tobacco has claimed that the local market is being flooded with illicit cigarettes and seemingly lays the blame squarely at the feet of smaller, local low-cost manufacturers like Gold Leaf Tobacco and Carnilinx, portraying them as the veritable axis of evil.

2. The competition: 'Cheap and nasty'   29

Painting them as entirely criminal is not borne out by the facts. So, for instance, media reports suggest that in 2018 South Africa earned around R17 billion (more than $1 billion) from excise duties and VAT on tobacco products. R4 billion of that is reported to have come from local independent manufacturers of cheapie brands.[8] If these reports are correct, it would suggest that almost a quarter of the tobacco tax being collected comes from value-brand manufacturers. Labelling them as intrinsically criminal just doesn't add up: they seem to be paying at least *some* taxes, although they have also been implicated in allegations of unlawful behaviour.

Indeed, illicit cigarette sales are on the increase in South Africa as they are in many parts of the world, and they do put our tax offices under greater pressure. They may well come from smaller, low-cost manufacturers like Gold Leaf, Savanna, Amalgamated Tobacco and Carnilinx. Or they might not. Let me be very clear – I don't pretend that these new kids on the block are squeaky clean.

Globally, we've seen how smaller manufacturers – who don't have as many sophisticated tax avoidance mechanisms at their disposal as multinationals do – cheat the system a bit differently: they might post[9] illicit cigarettes, because small, high-frequency smuggling by post goes largely undetected;[10] hang gliders take off from Ukraine and drop as many as 100 cartons of contraband cigarettes per flight in Hungary;[11] a drone was caught smuggling cigarettes from Lithuania to Russia – it cost $10 to build, could carry up to 500 packs of cigarettes per trip, and was fitted with a GPS device allowing it to make drops at pre-determined waypoints, making $1 300 profit per trip;[12] a 700-metre-long tunnel between the Ukraine and Slovakia was fitted with an electric railway which was used to smuggle contraband cigarettes;[13] and on the border between Russia and Estonia, consignments of illicit cigarettes are simply dropped at a strategic point along a river bank in Russia, where it drifts along the current and is promptly deposited on the Estonian side, with nobody needing to carry the packs across any borders.[14]

(It's easy enough to set up a back-yard operation. Want to make your own commercial batch of illicit cigarettes? Order a manufacturing machine off Alibaba,[15] buy bulk loose tobacco and filters without a licence – none of which are actually illegal in many countries – and you're in business.)

Where did they learn how to smuggle? One of the smugglers I spoke to was explicit: 'Initially, we bought our tobacco from the big guys, but we soon realised that we could make far more profit making our own cigarettes, initially in places like Dubai, and later here in South Africa, and just play the same games they always have, but this time with all the profit going to us.'[16]

He went on to claim: 'Of course big tobacco supplies the local illicit market. But they do it the same way I do it. We're not stupid enough to do the smuggling ourselves – we pay agents to do it for us. That is why I have never been caught, and that is why they have never been caught here.' (In fairness, he has his own motivations for speaking out against big tobacco, and so I don't expect you to take his word for it – read the rest of this book and decide for yourself.)

To be clear – I was not a member of the Project Honey Badger team, and I don't know what evidence they found. I have not personally investigated any of the names now being bandied about as the sources of illicit cigarettes in South Africa – I left SARS before they became players in this saga. I am certainly not suggesting that these independent manufacturers of what are loosely referred to as 'cheapies' are innocents – there are allegations about them being associated with cocaine dealers, wanted by Interpol, and linked to apartheid assassins and arms traders, after all – just that their potential role in the abuses of tobacco is but one dimension of a bigger story.

More information about these smaller players, and the allegations that they face, can be found in Van Loggerenberg's books, and in Jacques Pauw's *The President's Keepers*.

I should also mention that the Fair Trade Independent Tobacco

2. The competition: 'Cheap and nasty'

Association (FITA), which represent many of these smaller players, and is predictably at loggerheads with TISA, has denied that any of its members are involved in illegal activities, and has pledged to take action against any of their members found to be contravening the laws of the country.

For what it's worth – it's not just smaller competitors who are fuelling the illicit trade in cigarettes. Many politicians are doing the same, doing more than just giving tobacco room to breathe, but actively getting into the black market themselves.

As far back as the 1730s in France, we see examples where those in power got their hands dirty. Local churches exploited the niche market, hiding hundreds of pounds of contraband tobacco in their buildings – the *Couvent de la Trinité* was widely known as a reliable source of cheap tobacco, and over time various religious orders were found guilty of smuggling.

In eighteenth-century France, convicted smugglers were frequently ordered to join the army instead of being sent to the galleys, bringing with them both their proclivities and black-market skills. As soldiers they had access to two sources of cheap tobacco: troops only paid half price for tobacco; and they had easy access to cheap tobacco from neighbouring countries from their border patrols, allowing them to buy cheaply, and still make a profit on-selling on the black market.

It's a trend that continues to this day:[17] The ex-president of Paraguay reportedly owned the company that produced the majority of smuggled cigarettes in Latin America, although he frequently denied this accusation.[18] The Montenegrin Prime Minister was accused by Italian prosecutors of having run a cigarette smuggling operation worth more than $1 billion – but he could not be prosecuted because he had diplomatic immunity.[19] Belarus, which only has two state-owned tobacco manufacturers, has been the largest single identifiable source of contraband cigarettes smuggled into the EU.[20] Seven Gambian diplomats were convicted for dealing in illicit tobacco, defrauding the UK

Treasury of £4,7 million.[21] North Korean diplomats at the Stockholm Embassy were involved in contraband tobacco and alcohol sales as far back as 1976, and more recently were again caught smuggling cigarettes into Sweden in 2009.[22]

In China some local governments are so zealous about defending the tobacco industry that at some point, officials in Hubei were reportedly required to smoke a collective 230 000 packs of regional brands a year.[23]

In the last two years alone we saw government officials really get their hands dirty: In Jordan politicians have reportedly been involved in an illicit tobacco manufacturing scheme resulting in an estimated $100 million in evaded taxes and duties.[24] In Montenegro a journalist was shot following a series of allegations of senior policemen being involved in a counterfeit cigarette syndicate.[25] Greece disbanded a contraband cigarette syndicate headed by an ex-policeman. In the US, three military veterans were charged with cigarette smuggling. In one of the Balkan countries illicit tobacco largely comes from two factories in the country – both of them rumoured to be run by the state security agency.[26]

Not all government complicity takes the form of corruption, though. Sometimes governments' complicity may be unintentional: The Indian government resells some of the smuggled cigarettes it seizes in special customs shops. However, a BAT document reveals how it viewed these shops as a new marketing opportunity: cigarettes were being smuggled directly to the shops, where they were illegally sold under the cover of the shops' legal sales of seized cigarettes.[27]

Other politicians actively encourage illicit trade and smuggling as an act of patriotism. Former Australian senator David Leyonhjelm praised tobacco smugglers, calling them patriots. He said people dealing in illicit tobacco were simply avoiding unreasonable taxes, arguing that the government is only getting away with harsh new measures to target tobacco smugglers because 'smokers are sneered at by the elites of society.'[28]

2. The competition: 'Cheap and nasty'

Of course, the illicit trade in tobacco frequently involves crime syndicates. In Europe alone, organised crime groups rake in at least €9,4 billion a year from illicit cigarettes. Illicit tobacco in France yields more than €2 billion a year. In Canada, an estimated 105 crime syndicates are involved in the illicit tobacco trade.[29] At one point, illicit tobacco in Ireland was generating up to €3 million a *week*.[30]

And some reports suggest that illicit tobacco may be funding extremist organisations who are increasingly turning to cigarette smuggling as a high-profit, low-risk way to finance their operations. It's an extremely lucrative business, earning the Real IRA an estimated $100 million over a five-year period. It also provided the bulk of the financing for AQIM, formerly backed by Osama bin Laden; constituted the second biggest source of funding for the Taliban (after heroin); and – together with oil – earned Saddam Hussein as much as $2,7 billion annually.[31]

Where do syndicates get the cigarettes from? The smaller independent manufacturers may be fuelling some of it, but a study by a US-based think-tank claims that they simply may not have the capacity to produce those kinds of volumes by themselves.[32] The smaller independent manufacturers are an indisputable problem – but they are certainly not the whole problem.

Whether we're dealing with the new crop of smaller independent manufacturers, or senior politicians, or crime syndicates, the road was paved by big tobacco. What big tobacco did – globally – was perhaps to perfect the trick of making tons of cigarettes disappear. An illusion that was subsequently adopted by smaller competitors, who can operate even more obscurely than big tobacco can, but using the same supply lines and facilitators and tactics as the ones originally perfected by big tobacco. They have mastered the art of infiltrating illicit products into the legal supply chain, making it more and more difficult to distinguish between licit and illicit products on the market.[33]

It's clear that between the explosion in illicit cigarettes, the rise of legitimate independent cigarette manufacturers, and the growing regulatory framework, big tobacco is increasingly under pressure. And a business under pressure is a business with an incentive to play dirty.

Big tobacco needs governments to focus their efforts somewhere else. Why? For two key reasons, which we explore in the rest of the book: to get our law enforcement agencies to get rid of the competition that is eating into its market share, and because big tobacco appears to have had its own hand in the cookie jar.

Smoke. Mirrors. Obfuscation.

3. 'Bigger than drugs'

Jacques Pauw's bombshell book *The President's Keepers* includes a revealing quote from Glenn Agliotti – one of South Africa's best-known crime bosses (in turn described as a fixer, drug dealer and gangster, sometimes called The Landlord): 'I have been smuggling cigarettes for thirty years. I am a fucking gangster. Cigarette game is bigger than drugs.'[1]

The picture he paints of smugglers fits in with the perception many people have: 'We terrible. We gangsters. I believe in the AGE. A in AGE stands for Arrogance. Most of us, we are arrogant. G for greed. E for Ego.'[2]

This is part of the problem, of course: We have a certain picture of what a cigarette smuggler looks like. Tough, a bit rough around the edges, enigmatic, crew-cut hair, bad grammar.

Part of the challenge in telling the story of how big tobacco smuggles is that the 'optics' are wrong – in essence, how things *look*, how they seem from the outside. Big tobacco doesn't *look* like a smuggler, and so we believe it isn't one.

Having worked in more than 25 countries around the world – from Singapore to Serbia; from Cape Town to Canberra – I can assure you: smugglers don't have a 'look'. They may be burly musclemen with gold chains and chunky rings, or skinny boys with flipflops and haunted eyes, or men wearing tight Armani shirts and Rolex watches in shiny Porsches. They may be good people simply trying to put food on the table, or they may be fraudsters or mobsters or all-round bad guys.

They may carry boxes across a border for a pittance, or they may be living it up in luxury villas and Instagram-worthy offices with plush carpets. They may be dads who take their kids to football practice on Saturdays. They may well live in a temple with pig sties. They're all smugglers.

But the really *good* smugglers? They do have a look. They're suave, smart, well-spoken. They're generally quite likeable. And they're always – always – powerful.

When I first started toying with the idea of writing this book – and in subsequent conversations about it – virtually every person I spoke to met the notion that a big, listed company could be smuggling its own products with incredulity.

The risks to the company would be too big. There would be no incentive to do so. They would never get away with it. Illicit cigarettes are made by criminals, not by large listed companies with shareholders to account to. Right?

To tell you the truth, until a few years ago, it is most likely what my reaction would have been, too. Because, while I've long known that big companies have no qualms playing both sides of that thin line between evasion and avoidance, the very idea that a company like BAT or PMI or JTI would stuff packs of cigarettes into containers destined for the black market just seemed anathema to their very business model. Surely illicit trade was harming them – not being perpetrated by them? Surely big companies stick to white collar tax evasion, leaving criminals to sell dirty cigarettes in dark alleys?

Surely, if there are illicit cigarettes being sold anywhere, they must all come from smaller companies like Gold Leaf, Savanna, Amalgamated Tobacco, Carnilinx or perhaps from Zimbabwe or China or the United Arab Emirates – but most certainly not from the big tobacco companies?

There is also another factor that drives public scepticism of the notion that big tobacco's hands may be dirty: most of the industry's tax

3. 'Bigger than drugs'

troubles – for both the big players and the smaller independent manufacturers – are hidden from sight under a veil of legislated confidentiality and secrecy. It is relatively easy to compile a dossier with examples of instances where tobacco companies defrauded us with respect to the supposed safety of tobacco products. It is far more difficult to compile a list of examples where tobacco companies defrauded the tax man, simply because tax and customs agencies are invariably subject to secrecy clauses. We tend to only know about the complicity of established, licensed tobacco companies in criminality where a case is referred to court and becomes a matter of public record and where they are no longer subject to the secrecy clauses imposed by legislation. Consequently, much of the criminality on the part of the tobacco industry – including that of the bigger tobacco companies – goes unreported and under-exposed publicly.

Against this backdrop, it is entirely natural to initially be sceptical of claims that big tobacco companies smuggle their own products or in some way supply the illicit market. The optics are all wrong. Why would any company potentially undercut the sales of their own legal products? And indeed, by conventional wisdom, why would a listed company potentially put its reputation at risk?

The answer in a capitalist system is simple: profit. For the most part, tobacco companies effectively make the same profit per pack on smuggled cigarettes as they do on legally sold ones. Smuggling allows tobacco companies to sell their cigarettes in countries that they would otherwise not be able to do business in because of import bans, sanctions and government monopolies. In many countries, smuggling may be the only way for a cigarette company to get their product on the market. In Somalia, documents suggest BAT had a strategy to continue selling its cigarettes in spite of warnings by fundamentalist group Al-Shabaab that it would punish those who sold them under Sharia law. A slide from an internal BAT PowerPoint presentation – revealed in an article by *The Guardian* – notes 'The No-Smoking ultimatum made by Al-Shabaab now in effect. Cigarettes are now a black-market commodity. Distribution is being made in black paper bags.'[3]

Evidence suggests that smuggling also makes it possible for cigarettes to be sold in countries where tax rates and duties would otherwise make legal imports too expensive compared to cheaper domestic brands. Indeed, often the contraband market seems to have been so profitable that it discouraged the companies from entering the legal market, as appears to have been the case for BAT in China: 'On China, a visit by the Chairman to Beijing in October might actually be counterproductive if he was under pressure to commit to investment . . . why are we looking at joint ventures rather than a continuation of transit [smuggling]?'[4]

But smuggling could also simply be a matter of undercutting competitors and maintaining market share. In Colombia PMI had exclusive rights to sell the Belmont brand. BAT continued to make Belmont cigarettes elsewhere, and reportedly simply smuggled them into Colombia, cannibalising PMI's market share.[5]

In Canada, Imperial blatantly noted: 'Although we agreed to support the Federal government's effort to reduce smuggling by limiting our exports to the USA, our competitors did not. Subsequently, we have decided to remove the limits on our exports to regain our share of Canadian smokers. Until the smuggling issue is resolved, an increasing volume of our domestic sales in Canada will be exported, then smuggled back for sale here.'[6]

Smuggled cigarettes, of course, are also inherently cheaper than their legal cousins, giving them a competitive advantage against legally sold cigarettes. By helping to keep overall cigarette prices down, tobacco companies get to retain more price-conscious smokers who otherwise may have quit, which helps to increase overall sales.[7]

The simple fact is that tobacco companies benefit from cigarettes that end up in the hands of smugglers. They sell them at the same prices that they would to legal wholesalers.

3. 'Bigger than drugs'

As South Africa's Dr Yussuf Saloojee (the Executive Director of the National Council Against Smoking) succinctly says: 'The industry worldwide has been found guilty of aiding smuggling, for the simple reason that they get the same amount of money whether they sell to a legal buyer or a smuggler.'[8]

Still sceptical?

I can't point to any publicly available information that proves that a company like BAT has been caught with its hand in the proverbial contraband cookie jar in South Africa in particular.

Well, aside from that eye-watering assessment for R214 million (around $15 million) that SARS issued against BAT towards the end of 2018. It related to apparent mismatches between their export declarations and what was actually in the containers, and some other apparent abuses around rebates.[9]

Or the additional income tax assessments SARS issued against BAT to the value of $124 million for aggressive tax planning using debt financing structures (the single biggest dispute on record between SARS and a taxpayer.)

Or that affidavit, filed as part of a High Court case against BAT, by an ex-employee of their security company that alleged the company bribed police officers and tax officials, including allegations that this was intended to secure a blind eye to BAT's 'tax evasion' and 'money laundering' in South Africa.[10] At the time, BAT said it had appointed an independent law firm to investigate whether there were any illegalities in the way the security firm had done its work.

I asked BAT for comment. They never got back to me.

There is also the small problem of the Tobacco Institute of Southern Africa's missing billions. In Johann van Loggerenberg's *Tobacco Wars*, there is this little nugget: TISA apparently said that its members – BAT, JTI and PMI – had manufactured around 19 billion sticks of cigarettes during 2017/18. But for the same fiscal year, only 15,3 billion sticks of cigarettes were reportedly declared to the taxman (at least some of which must have come from the independent manufacturers). Just on big tobacco's own numbers that's quite a big gap. A whopping 3,7 billion sticks have gone missing somewhere – 185 million packs that have simply not been accounted for, and R4,625 billion lost (around $320 million).

If the data in *Tobacco Wars* is correct – and I believe it most likely is – there are only four possible explanations: either TISA made a mistake (but having seen some of the other analysis that TISA has been doing over the years, this seems unlikely); or TISA deliberately gave a wrong number (but why would they?); or TISA's members are not declaring all of the packs they produce to the taxman; or perhaps they are deliberately inflating their production volumes to demonstrate to shareholders that their operations are on the increase, when in fact they are not (and there seems to be some whispers in the industry of this indeed happening).

I asked TISA for comment. They initially asked whether I was writing this book in my personal capacity or on behalf of another organisation. They then replied as follows: 'We will not be responding to any of your questions. Most of your questions are loaded and with a clear agenda in mind. TISA represents the legal industry and to this extent we have made many public statements about illicit trade etc. You are welcome to use information on our website.'

(In a surprise twist, on 22 January 2020, a source suggested I have a look at the TISA website again. The entire TISA website had been replaced with a single page, 'TISA to be wound up,' it said. TISA was no more. The source also suggested that this was because – in his words – 'the other members no longer wanted to be associated with BAT South Africa.' Read the rest of this book, and make up your own mind on the likely reasons behind TISA's unexpected implosion.[11])

Whichever one of the above explanations sits most comfortably with you, there seems to be a snake in the grass in the big boys' club.

We also know that SARS – before it had its wings clipped – had reportedly been set to take away 15 tobacco manufacturing licences. There are fewer than 15 smaller, independent manufacturers, so perhaps one can conclude that one or more of the multinational tobacco companies also would have faced the threat of having their licence revoked.[12]

Aside from these clues hinting at something untoward, I really don't have a smoking gun, perhaps just a really warm barrel (for South Africa anyway).

What I *can* do, aside from that, is tell you how companies like BAT, PMI, JTI and Imperial developed a global business model that allowed their cigarettes to be smuggled in other countries around the world.

4. Dead easy to cheat

To understand the basics of how a smuggling empire operates, we need at least a rudimentary understanding of how the illicit trade in products like cigarettes works.

The term 'smuggling' encompasses a whole plethora of different behaviours, just as the trade in illicit cigarettes is not one homogenous concept.

Smuggling, of course, is an age-old phenomenon. As far back as the 1700s, pirates were dropping off illicit cigarettes in ports not controlled by colonial authorities, in what was a booming smuggling industry. Filling tubs of tobacco with sawdust and powdered brick in the 1800s saw the start of a counterfeiting industry, padding the tubs to falsely inflate the total amount of tobacco that could be sold, much like with modern drug dealers 'cutting' substances. (Addendum 5 has more details on the history of tobacco smuggling.)

Modern smuggling is very different and involves a variety of practices, as I have already explained. These days, excise duty is payable on every pack of cigarettes that is sold for use inside a country. It's deceptively simple – but within that simplicity lies a multitude of ways to cheat.

At its heart, the scheme is to convince the taxman that you are selling fewer packs in the country than you really are. And it's dead easy to cheat the system.

(For a far more detailed overview, have a look at addendum 1, the

4. Dead easy to cheat

SARS letter to tobacco manufacturers, in which they explain the different schemes in some detail.)

Many countries – including South Africa – have virtually no insight into production volumes, and effectively have to take cigarette manufacturers at their word. It's easy simply not to declare a batch; or to set up a covert factory the taxman knows nothing about; or to run entire unmapped contraband towns (as BAT has allegedly been doing in the Democratic Republic of Congo).

Many countries – including South Africa – do not in any notable way monitor the tobacco supply chain. They do not as a matter of course compare how many filters or cigarette papers a company buys against the number of cigarettes declared; there is no way to track where the packs go once they are sold, or to trace packs found on the market back to where they came from. Manufacturers are under no obligation to use 'know-your-customer' policies or to apply due diligence checks to the people they do business with, which means they can effectively sell willy-nilly to whoever comes to their gates.

And many countries – including South Africa – are plagued with archaic excise administration systems that cannot adequately compensate for the integrity risks that are inherent in any highly manual system that only checks a small percentage of consignments, for a commodity that poses a very high risk.

And indeed, many countries – again like South Africa – do not really regulate the purchase or importation of tobacco manufacturing equipment. In many parts of the world you can buy state-of-the-art cigarette machines online from sites like Alibaba.com for $1,5 million to $3 million, which is easily recouped when you are making over $100 million in annual sales.

In addition, big tobacco companies shift significant volumes of their products across national borders. (Consider the fact that BAT South Africa alone ships its packs to at least 22 other countries.[1]) In light of the extremely porous nature of South Africa's borders, the theoretical permutations and opportunities for under-declaration, ghost exports, round-tripping, diversion, over-supplying and otherwise playing with packs ostensibly destined for duty-free sales would be exponential, for whoever it is that ends up doing the actual smuggling.

Of course, for any company that wants to run a smuggling empire, hiding all of this entails an entirely different sub-set of criminal activities, including evading related income taxes; corruption and bribery; forgery; money laundering and sometimes fictitious transactions.

Some illicit packs are not attributable to big tobacco – so we see counterfeits emerging from places like China (addendum 3), and illicit whites (sometimes called cheap whites) rolling off manufacturing lines in free trade zones in places like the United Arab Emirates (addendum 4). And we see small consignments being dropped by drone or hang gliders; or sent by post; or carried across borders one box at a time.

If you wanted to supply the illicit market, where would you get your hands on contraband packs? Either you would have to make the packs locally and just not declare all of the packs to the taxman; or smuggle them in; or hijack a competitor's trucks.

The first source – under-declaration – is simple enough: the undeclared surplus packs are sold, tax-free, on the black market. Factories may run double shifts or run their machines at night when they know nosy customs officers are unlikely to pay them a visit, or pay a customs officer to look the other way. They may re-use a single invoice for '100 cases of cigarettes' for multiple deliveries of a hundred cases of cigarettes. Or they may claim that stock has been exported – which means that no tax is payable on it – when in fact it has been sold in the domestic market (called round-tripping or ghost exports). Commonly, they tend to have at least some kind of legitimate manufacturing and sales, with the illicit packs simply constituting a percentage of their overall sales, making it more difficult to distinguish between licit and illicit packs found on the market. This borrows from an art that big tobacco seems to have perfected decades ago: 'umbrella operations', where legitimate packs are deliberately sold to provide cover for their illegal cousins and explain their presence on the market.

The second source – smuggling the packs in from somewhere – is simple enough. In South Africa, much of this comes from neighbouring Zimbabwe, with large volumes of packs literally being smuggled in on a daily basis. At some point this heavily involved using fuel tankers and trucks which would deliver an unrelated consignment to Zimbabwe, and ostensibly return to South Africa empty, instead being stuffed with cigarettes (many trucking companies actively defray their costs by filling what would otherwise be empty vehicles with illicit loads on their way back, from cigarettes and cocaine to rhino horn and ivory.)[2] When Zimbabwe introduced vehicle scanners at Beitbridge border post, using trucks became more dangerous, so they are now mostly used by those with political protection or enough money to grease a customs palm.

Why single out Zimbabwe? Because the illicit trade in South Africa is very closely tied to its neighbour, for two simple reasons: Zimbabwe is the biggest tobacco producer on the continent, producing what is widely regarded as some of the best tobacco in the world; and South Africa is the largest, most profitable consumer market and production hub.

Not all of Zimbabwe's cigarettes that head down south were necessarily always destined for the South African market: in my conversations, a few sources have noted how South Africa was historically also used as a sanctions-busting transit space for its neighbour. When sanctions were imposed on what was then Rhodesia (today's Zimbabwe), it became exponentially more difficult to sell what was considered to be some of the best quality tobacco leaves in the world. The solution was simple, as explained by an acquaintance whose father ran a tobacco factory in the country at the time: Zimbabwean cigarettes were produced as they always had been but were fraudulently marked as having being produced in South Africa – apparently this part of the factory was blocked off, with only a few people having access to the space where the packs were marked, and with the packs subsequently being smuggled into South Africa and exported from there.

Of course, not all of the illicit packs on the South African market come from Zimbabwe: packs are to a lesser or greater degree also smuggled into South Africa from places like China, often via Singapore, or from free trade zones in the United Arab Emirates. Almost all of it is 'genuine' contraband – since around the 2000s, counterfeit cigarettes have actually made up a very small percentage of the South African market, as is true for most of the world.

The third source – hijacking a competitor's trucks – is perhaps a more uniquely South African phenomenon: BAT at one point reported that 1 412 of its transport vehicles are hijacked annually – at least four hijackings a day, and accounting for 20% of all vehicle hijackings in South Africa's Gauteng province.[3] That's a lot of cigarettes going missing – and, depending on how the taxman dealt with this, potentially a lot of cigarettes not being taxed.

So, in its simplest form, when we talk about illicit cigarettes and smuggling, what we're dealing with is the art of giving cigarettes an invisibility cloak, because the taxman can't tax what he can't see.

As you read through the next few chapters on smuggling, it may be useful to remember the anodyne synonyms the industry developed when talking about its smuggling activities (because even the most emboldened of businesses would probably not refer to its 'smuggling' business as 'smuggling' on paper.) And, so, the industry has developed a set of rather less offensive, somewhat more neutral terms to describe the illicit parts of its strategy.

Smuggling and illicit channels are implied any time you read the following words or acronyms: 'duty not paid' (DNP for short);[4] 'transit'; 'general trade' (GT for short); 'border trade', 'free markets' or 'value for money' (VFM).[5] A few of BAT's older documents quite neatly explain the terms:

4. Dead easy to cheat

- 'With regard to the definition of transit it is essentially the illegal import of brands upon which duty has not been paid.'[6]
- 'The DNP market is the volume of cigarettes produced in Venezuela, exported (mainly to Aruba), and re-entering Venezuela as transit.'[7]
- 'The imported sector in Taiwan has increased each year. This figure includes legal imports plus GT [general trade/smuggled] imports estimated at 7.6 bns.'[8]

Against that short introduction to smuggling, next we'll explore how BAT may have made as much as 25% of its profit from smuggling into China and how big tobacco ended up paying more than $1 billion in penalties for the smuggling of its packs.

5. Smuggling: A rogue's gallery

Some of the examples and case studies included in this book go back some years. It was important to include them, because they highlight a consistent pattern of behaviour spanning both decades and continents, and because it is only by understanding the industry's consistent history of obfuscation and filibustering and legally dubious behaviour that we can begin to pre-empt the future.

The examples are not meant to be an exhaustive catalogue of smuggling and tax evasion, and of course include only those cases already in the public domain, because most tax and customs agencies are sworn to secrecy. Once you start delving into the industry it becomes something of a rabbit hole. For every example quoted in this book, you can likely find ten others. And while the examples are illustrative only, they do make the point that the illicit trade in tobacco products is not limited to backyard taverns, bootleggers and mobsters, but has very much been the playground of big tobacco.

BAT kindly documented for us in detail some of its forays into China in the 1980s:[1] BAT documents note how official imports offered 'relative poor corporate profitability'[2] because of the highly restrictive import quotas and tariffs, leading to large-scale smuggling to access the world's largest market of smokers, activities foreign tobacco companies were aware of.

BAT's own records detail how they did it: by setting up BAT Distribution Ltd to manage illicit trade in Asia, which they were advised

5. Smuggling: A rogue's gallery

'should be incorporated in a tax haven of choice'[3] to ensure that the contraband trade could be carried out 'on an arms-length basis'.[4] It needed to be 'little more than a brass plate company with very low overheads and the flexibility to establish branch offices wherever the transit traders move'.[5] Its activities remained fully controlled by the BAT China Group, and the structure was approved by BAT's Chairman, to 'ensure the efficient distribution within the China markets of duty free [illicit] BAT products'.[6]

BAT invested heavily in its illicit trade stream in China, with one of their vice presidents saying: 'The best prospects for growth in the Chinese market continues [sic] to be the unofficial channels for the foreseeable future.'[7]

BAT's Head of Corporate Planning at the time recognised the contraband trade's vulnerability given the 'danger of serious action by the authorities'.[8] But that concern was not enough to stop the company from aggressively pursuing a black market for its products: 'As long as free market sales remain dominant, alternative routes of distribution of unofficial imports [i.e. contraband] need to be examined and maximised. It is recognised that distribution of our product in China is key to BAT's long-term success.'[9]

Against this background, BAT's own records seem to suggest it was physically exporting 53 times more cigarettes to China than it was officially declaring for import.[10] So, for every container it declared, 53 others appear not to have been declared to the authorities and were instead smuggled into the country. Little wonder, then, that BAT viewed China as 'one of the larger profit centres',[11] with an apparent 25% of BAT's profits coming 'from transit trade to China'[12] (and remember, 'transit trade' is an industry euphemism for smuggling).

It seems it wasn't just BAT plying the black trade – PMI apparently was too, as BAT itself claimed: '. . . the PMI model places an intermediary between PMI Asia and the transit traders. We have two objections. First the transit trade [contraband] still originated with Philip

Morris Asia and is controlled by that company. That is similar to the present situation with BAT Hong Kong. The second objection is that the intermediary adds another level of profit absorption and is harder to control. The apparent distancing has little effect since the business is transit [contraband] trade. BAT group can pretend ignorance that its cigarettes are being distributed through the transit trade as much and as justifiably as Philip Morris can.'[13]

This example from the late eighties may admittedly be relatively old. But it does raise this question: If indeed BAT had managed to secure 25% of its profits 'from transit [contraband] trade to China',[14] and if one were to give it the benefit of the doubt and assume for a moment it no longer runs a contraband supply chain in China, how has it compensated for the loss of this quite significant chunk of its profits? And if it could do this with some impunity in China, what has it managed to pull off in other countries?

It didn't end there. Smuggling has proliferated in the industry, decade after decade, country after country.

In the nineties, evidence suggests that BAT and PMI ran smuggling rings in Colombia,[15] and paid $1,7 billion in criminal fines and civil restitution for their role in smuggling schemes in Canada;[16] 11 PMI executives were charged with tax fraud in Italy to the tune of $400 million;[17] PMI was accused of smuggling cigarettes into South Africa;[18] and a BAT manager was convicted of taking bribes from smugglers in Hong Kong.[19]

In an interview, Les Thompson, a sales executive who worked for RJ Reynolds, recalled the situation in Canada after the government raised the tax on cigarettes sharply: 'Really the options were limited. The no-brainer in the equation becomes: We have to enter the black market. We have to enter the black market. We've got to pursue this tax-free environment through the illegal smuggling efforts back into Canada.'[20]

In the 2000s, *The Guardian* newspaper exposed how BAT benefitted from smuggling practices in both the UK and beyond;[21] racketeering

5. Smuggling: A rogue's gallery 51

charges were filed against BAT in Colombia;[22] *The Guardian* newspaper reported that court documents show that as much as $200 million in smuggling profits allegedly made its way to Geneva in one year alone;[23] Imperial was accused of smuggling as much as 65% of their packs onto the UK market;[24] Imperial and Rothmans were fined $1,15 billion for smuggling in Canada;[25] a BBC documentary exposed how BAT was seemingly breaking the rules in Nigeria, Malawi and Mauritius;[26] more than 20 000 internal documents highlighted how PMI's Gallaher set up a trading 'environment' conducive to illegal activity;[27] a media report based on internal industry documents attributed extensive smuggling to BAT in West Africa[28] and to smuggling in Sudan, Birao, Nigeria,[29] as well as under-invoicing in Nigeria.[30]

According to a BAT Nigeria document: 'General trade [illicit] movements to this end market will remain a priority throughout the period. Both legal and transit importing [smuggling] would be required to properly – and profitably – develop the brand. Legal imports would be loss making and significantly under invoiced because of Nigeria's high duty rates.'[31]

In 2000 the European Commission launched an investigation into contraband American cigarettes on the European market, and filed a lawsuit against big tobacco.[32] The charge sheet filed is simply astonishing: '. . . Controlling entire smuggling operations – an ongoing global scheme to smuggle cigarettes, launder the proceeds of narcotics trafficking, obstruct government oversight of the tobacco industry, fix prices, bribe foreign public officials, conduct illegal trade with terrorist groups and state sponsors of terrorism, engaging in organised crime, money laundering . . .'[33]

Around the same time *The Guardian* tells us that BAT issued a profit warning to its shareholders that profits were expected to plummet by £500 million as it was being forced to clamp down on illegal trafficking.[34] (That sounds remarkably like an admission in and of itself.)

Big tobacco settled the case on terms that are simply staggering, which included having to compensate the EU for the tax revenues lost as a result of the smuggling of its packs. PMI's liability under the settlement? $1,250 billion. Read that again: PMI had to pay $1,250 billion in compensation for the tax losses caused by the smuggling of its packs. JTI had to pay the EU $400 million (paid off over a period of 15 years), Imperial $300 million (paid over 20 years), and BAT $200 million (to be paid over 20 years, with the last payment due in 2030).[35] That's a lot of smuggled packs.

Rather tellingly, almost immediately after the settlement agreement was signed, the volume of cigarettes shipped through Antwerp, the hub from where investigators believed the contraband cigarettes were being shipped, decreased from 72 billion cigarettes to 2 billion.[36]

Just as an aside, this is on top of an earlier settlement agreement with a number of US states to compensate for the healthcare crisis tobacco had caused, where big tobacco was also forced to pay $206 billion in financial compensation.[37]

Did it stop there? No. Big tobacco seems to have been acting with impunity even more recently.

In the decade since 2010, a smuggling hub allegedly run by JTI in Russia and the Middle East was exposed;[38] BAT reportedly took over from its transiteers in Djibouti and Guinea to start smuggling itself;[39] Spain launched a lawsuit against PMI for involvement in organised crime in pursuit of a 'massive, ongoing smuggling scheme';[40] Canada filed a smuggling and racketeering lawsuit against RJ Reynolds, to the tune of $1 billion (the case was dismissed only on a technicality);[41] PMI was sued for $3 billion in damages for smuggling, money-laundering, conspiracy and racketeering in Colombia (claims it denied);[42] the EU launched a probe into JTI for a cigarette deal that is believed to have aided Syria;[43] Ecuador filed a racketeering charge against PMI, BAT and RJ Reynolds;[44] BAT was fined £650 000 for oversupplying tobacco in the EU by as much as 240%;[45] BAT was accused of having bribed a politician to ensure that a cigarette track and trace tender was

5. Smuggling: A rogue's gallery

not awarded in Kenya;[46] PMI was fined $3,15 billion for tax evasion in Thailand;[47] PMI and BAT were fined $260 million for illegal cigarette hoarding in Korea;[48] PMI was slapped with a lawsuit accusing it of fraud and corruption in relation to the implementation of its traceability solution Codentify in Buenos Aires;[49] PMI was charged with tax evasion in Thailand and the Philippines, facing 272 counts of fraud and a potential penalty of $2,29 billion;[50] and by 2017 BAT was being investigated by the UK Serious Fraud Office for corruption and bribery in (amongst others) Kenya, Burundi, Rwanda and Comoros Islands[51] (that investigation had, at the time of writing, not yet been concluded). Oh, and BAT subsidiaries have also been fined or investigated for tax evasion or fraud charges in Australia, Korea, Vietnam, Bangladesh, and Russia.[52]

In 2018, we know that South Africa's taxman reportedly found that BAT had made 'misrepresentations' and 'false declarations' relating to the use of rebates and purported exports, and the non-disclosure of material facts, and slapped them with a R214 million ($15 million) assessment for duty evasion.[53]

Then in 2019, the BBC exposed evidence of BAT's illegal operations in the Democratic Republic of Congo, in particular on the back of information provided by whistle-blower Paul Hopkins.[54] Hopkins – a former soldier in the Irish Army's special forces – worked for BAT for 13 years in Africa, where he says he ran security and anti-smuggling operations, and claimed he arranged for the payment of BAT's bribes. He fell out with the company and turned whistle-blower. In an interview with *The Guardian*, Hopkins explains why he believes fragile states in Africa and elsewhere are of particular interest to big tobacco: 'If you have no government, you have nobody annoying you about health warnings and nicotine content. No customs. You basically pay your tax to the local militias on the airfield where you are landing.'[55] (BAT has gone on record simply calling Hopkins a disgruntled ex-employee.)

Hopkins further tells how he was, on several occasions, required to take millions of dollars into the DRC, destined for what is apparently the unmapped town of Auzi, built by BAT in the 1950s with a church and a school. He has photos of himself with $2,5 million in cash which he says is from one of the drops he did for BAT. *En route* there he'd protect himself in rebel-run Congo by renting an AK47, and hiding the dollars either in BAT-branded promotional items like hats and pens, or on occasion under a priest's cassock.

'These drops had to be illegal, that amount across an international border without any government being aware of it. It had been going on before I joined,' Hopkins claimed.[56]

(See addendum 6 for selected extracts transcribed from the BBC's interview with Hopkins, and addendum 7 for more details on the various other smuggling and tax evasion cases.)[57]

The BBC documentary quoted BAT as saying that its 'accusers in [the] programme left us in acrimonious circumstances, clearly demonstrated by the false picture they present of how we do business'. The company was also quoted as saying it was committed to operating to the very, very highest standards of corporate conduct.

I asked the respective big tobacco companies for comment on the various allegations this book explores. Reynolds replied within a day that they had 'no comment'. BAT, PMI and Imperial never replied.

TISA, the now-defunct industry body that represents big tobacco in South Africa, has previously denied that their members are involved in illegal activities and have pledged to take action against any of their members found to be contravening the tax, customs or excise laws of the country.

JTI replied that the allegations were 'outdated', relying in part on a 2013 report from OLAF (the EU Anti-Fraud Office) to the effect that 'cheap whites and counterfeits (including the counterfeiting of cheap whites) dominate in large-scale seizures, and in particular in seizures related to containerised transport,'[58] but this relates only to smuggling

5. Smuggling: A rogue's gallery

in containers (which the same report says is on the decrease), and very pertinently only relates to the EU.

Big tobacco has had more than its share of felonies, fines and infringements — and increasingly so over the last 20 years. It has been faced with unprecedented monetary penalties that would have crippled most other industries. On top of that, add advertising restrictions and all-out bans, and damning evidence and criminal prosecutions in relation to covering up scientific evidence on the dangers of smoking, and the fact that it kills more than half of its customers. And yet this industry not only survives, it thrives.

Make no mistake — the industry *knows* its hands are dirty.

As Prof. Anna Gilmore, Director of the Tobacco Control Research Group at the University of Bath, puts it: 'Diverse and growing evidence shows that tobacco industry illicit (product) outstrips the problems of cheap whites and counterfeits and remains the single largest problem in illicit tobacco; that incentives for industry involvement have barely changed since their well-documented involvement in the 1990s; that tobacco companies likely continue to be involved in and benefit from tobacco smuggling.'[59]

6. Jam on their face and still they do nothing

'It is the unspoken ethic of all magicians
to not reveal the secrets.'
— David Copperfield

In fairness to the tobacco industry, it is conceivable that some of the examples I've assembled could perhaps be attributable to vindictive whistle-blowers or to rogue employees. But it is entirely inconceivable that all of them are.

The industry — even licensed, bigger players — has a long and consistent history of fines, felonies and infringements, spanning decades, across the globe.

There is ample proof that the tobacco industry incorporated smuggling and other tax and duty evasion measures as an explicit part of its business strategy.[1]

BAT's internal documents suggest that smuggling operations were almost certainly conducted with the knowledge and often the direct involvement of senior executives within the company, including regional directors, a former head of BAT's marketing department, senior marketing managers, and BAT area managers. BAT executives appear to have expressly been put in charge of various smuggling and contraband operations.[2]

And indeed, despite being publicly called out, BAT declared that it would not sue over allegations that its senior staff had been involved in smuggling, with David Hinchcliffe, the Chairman of Britain's House of Commons Select Committee on Health noting: 'I personally pressed BAT whether they intended to take legal action and they said they did not. You will draw your own conclusions from that, as I did mine.'[3]

6. Jam on their face and still they do nothing

BAT's apparent one-time plans to manufacture cigarettes in Andorra for smuggling to Spain in 1992 were not a secret – a document detailing the strategy was sent from a BAT marketing executive to the head of BAT's marketing department and copied to a BAT lawyer.[4]

In Brazil the then-Chairman of BAT Industries is directly implicated in planned smuggling operations in a memo sent from the Territorial Director for Latin America to the Managing Director of BAT Industries, the CEO of BAT's Brazilian subsidiary, the Chairman of BAT and others: 'I am advised that the BAT Industries Chairman has endorsed the approach that the Brazilian Operating Group increase its share of the Argentinean market via DNP [duty not paid, i.e. contraband].'[5]

As a lawsuit against PMI noted: 'Defendants created a circuitous and clandestine distribution chain for the sale of cigarettes in order to facilitate smuggling. The decision to establish and maintain this distribution chain was made at the highest executive level of PMI. Defendants have collaborated with smugglers, encouraged smugglers, and sold cigarettes to smugglers, either directly or through intermediaries, while at the same time supporting the smugglers' sales through the establishment and maintenance of so-called umbrella [cover] operations.'[6]

And, so, it is hardly surprising that a Reynolds sales executive, interviewed on a CBS documentary, would note that, '. . . We were considered the most – single-most – profitable business unit in the RJR Nabisco family of companies. They knew exactly where the money was coming from. On an average of approximately every other Monday, an in-house lawyer from upstairs would come down and talk to us, "Yeah, it's sensitive, but we're here. We're all in this together. And it's – it's a loophole. It's grey. It's legal, OK?" The company knows where they made the $100 million. They know the customers that produced the $100 million.'[7]

The same Reynolds executive goes on to explain how: 'We were told to keep no paperwork in this business [by vice president of sales at RJ Reynolds]. He insisted . . . "You're not keeping any documents, are you?" He reminded me on many occasions not to keep any hard copy on any correspondence with their offices.'[8]

In a statement, a spokesman told CBS that neither RJ Reynolds Tobacco nor the parent company have been implicated in any criminal investigation.

At least some had the sense to ask how ethical this was, with one fax query from BAT's headquarters to its branch office in Venezuela asking '. . . whether the company could continue with duty paid and duty not paid [contraband] in parallel and be seen as a clean and ethical company at the same time'.[9]

At a meeting at BAT's UK headquarters, a memorandum records executives discussing smuggling into Nigeria: 'Discussion was held concerning direct imports to Nigeria through Mr. Adji who would disguise the cigarette importation by calling the shipment something else, e.g. matches.'[10]

And although I haven't seen the accounts for myself, numerous sources have alleged that this part of their trade was accounted for against separate cost centres, in dedicated bank accounts, typically in offshore tax havens like Switzerland[11] – a fully entrenched, formal part of big tobacco's business practices.

My concession aside that some of the examples may perhaps be attributable to rogue employees, there are many examples of big tobacco very well knowing about their employees being involved in illicit trade and doing nothing about it.[12]

Big tobacco was articulately called out on their behaviour during the UK's Parliamentary Committee hearings on tobacco smuggling: 'When my four-year-old is standing in the kitchen with jam all over his face and I go in and say, "Have you been at the jam?" And he tells me, "No, daddy, I haven't," that is what you three have been doing here. It is unbelievable. It is called circumstantial evidence and you are simply sitting there saying, "No, no, it wasn't us. We didn't know the market. We had no idea this was going on." I believe you have lied to this committee. I believe you are the least credible witnesses that I have ever seen come before the committee of public accounts. You have lied unashamedly. If you did not know all I can say is that you must have been totally incompetent. If I were one of your shareholders I would say, "these guys are incompetent".'[13] (While we have the comments from this committee on record, unfortunately their ultimate findings were never publicly released.)

This reticence is just as apparent with BAT in South Africa: in 2016 they told us that they had requested a law firm to investigate allegations of criminality by the staff of a security firm employed by BAT. Since then? Nothing. It's been years. We don't know what that investigation found, or what corrective steps have been taken to ensure that similar improprieties would not be repeated in the future.[14]

Of course, they do nothing. As a Rothmans manager so articulately explains, 'It would be stupid to ignore a growing market. I can't answer the moral dilemma. We are in the business of pleasing our shareholders.'[15]

Big tobacco washes its hands. They sell cigarettes ex-factory, and once the truck leaves their premises, argue that ownership is transferred to the buyer and the tobacco company has no legal liability for where the cigarettes go next. At best, they may explain, 'In our work, you can't ask what they do with the cigarettes'.[16]

They are really simply rational actors, acting rationally in pursuit of profit.

It's this same reticence to confront criminality that arguably, at least in part, explains big tobacco's consistent history of unlawful behaviour. As an Imperial spokesman, Michel Descoteaux, himself has noted: 'The industry absolutely knew that most of the exports were being smuggled back. Imperial was simply shipping cigarettes in response to orders by American dealers. What would you have us do?'[17]

(I will get back to what we would have you do, Mr Descoteaux, in a bit.)

First, let me pause to say that there *are* some individuals in the industry who have tried to clean it up.

For instance, the IT consultant who had been contracted by JTI, and somehow got information on related individuals that were being investigated by European agencies for smuggling. The list included 13 JTI employees and distributors. (So we have reason to believe, for instance, that mobsters had financial stakes in some of JTI's largest Russian distributorships,[18] and in Montenegro, a JTI distributor was apparently retained despite being a convicted cigarette smuggler.[19]) The consultant passed the information on to JTI for them to investigate the allegations against their employees and contractors. The VP heading Global Brand Integrity Operations, David Reynolds, apparently wanted to take action against the individuals on the list; but instead says he was told in no uncertain terms to return the information to the consultant, to delete all copies of the data from JTI's servers, and to refrain from using similar information in the future.[20]

Mr Reynolds went on to pen an extraordinary note explaining his concerns in some detail, including noting, 'Shipments to unauthorized buyers have reached a massive scale exposing the company to fines potentially of around €30 million. We have repeatedly reported our findings to JTI management . . . but have yet to elicit any concerted effort to halt these diversions. In recent months members of my team have been directed not to investigate several instances of smuggling related to specific JTI distributors . . . and the possible involvement of JTI employees with known smugglers.'[21] (The full text of his email is included in addendum 8 – it's really worth a read.) Not surprisingly, he was fired days after sending the email, along with his assistant. JTI says he is an ex-employee spreading false information. You make up your own mind.

Another colleague in JTI subsequently commented: 'You have to ask yourself how serious they are when they bring in people from Gallaher to take over. The culture in Gallaher was very much, "Let's not get caught, but if we do get caught, be prepared to defend ourselves." They didn't take steps to stop smuggling, just to insulate themselves when it came out.'[22] (Gallaher had been bought by JTI after having been implicated repeatedly in smuggling operations, and with court papers detailing how they helped smugglers evade more than $1,5 billion in customs duties in the UK.)[23]

Two things stand out for me: the first is that big tobacco must have known and did nothing. But the second is that there are a few good souls in the industry who are willing to take a stand. We need more of those.

Even in more recent Project Sun reports – published by KPMG, and dealing with the state of illicit tobacco, commissioned by the tobacco industry – it is noted how '. . . varying sanctions across member states currently influence decisions by big tobacco about where to conduct operations or which routes to take when transporting goods across the EU.'[24] Where I come from, 'sanctions' generally tend only to worry those who have something to hide.

The question, of course, is what big tobacco's position is on this today, and how their local in-country corporate strategy and profit considerations and risk appetite differ from their global counterparts.

What we've seen with big tobacco's heavy involvement in supplying the contraband market is attributable to a permutation of only one of three possible explanations:

Firstly, perhaps it's in their DNA and it simply forms part of their business strategy (and there certainly seems to be at least some evidence of this being the case).

Secondly, maybe they just turn a blind eye. Perhaps the existence of illicit activities within the company is known, albeit perhaps not explicitly endorsed, and are allowed to perpetuate, as the bottom-line benefits from it.

Or, thirdly, perhaps they simply employ countless rogue employees across the globe who perpetually perpetrate illicit activities without their knowledge or endorsement, and with the companies unable to establish internal controls and processes to offer any level of protection against such employees.

I can't think of any other scenarios that explain the industry's persistent history of and association with criminality. Whichever one of the three it is, it means that our governments can have no confidence – at the very least – in industry's tax and duty declarations. In all three cases the solution is simple: the industry cannot be trusted to regulate itself and requires stronger regulatory oversight and more robust supply chain security measures across the tobacco value chain.

'At best, tobacco companies are failing to control their supply chain, overproducing in some markets and oversupplying to others in the knowledge their products will end up on the illicit market,' writes Prof. Anna Gilmore, Director of the Tobacco Control Research Group at the University of Bath. 'At worst, ex-employees insist JTI remained actively involved, describing "rampant smuggling". BAT staff suspected JTI was facilitating smuggling into the DRC but BAT also clandestinely moved millions of dollars in cash from Uganda to the DRC to buy tobacco leaf which was presumably then illegally exported. BAT cigarettes being distributed by a company implicated in tobacco smuggling were ending up in the illicit market with BAT staff agreeing not to discuss the problem by email.'[25]

Many other industries, with commodities that are far less hazardous, and that are far less vulnerable to criminal enterprise, and that are far less susceptible to tax evasion, have implemented far more robust supply chain security solutions than the tobacco industry has.

The number of examples where big tobacco is charged with some kind of fine, felony or infringement is staggering – not just in smaller, less-advanced economies, but in leading economies; not just in isolated instances, but globally over an extended period of time. Big tobacco is

6. Jam on their face and still they do nothing

a serial repeat offender, and is repeatedly being sanctioned, and agreeing to pay massive fines (in the billions), with very little real, substantive change being evident in their behaviour over time.

What would the industry have us believe? What are they actually doing to fix the systemic issues that recur year after year? We simply don't know. We certainly aren't seeing any real change in either their behaviour or in the risks they pose.

At the very best, giving industry every conceivable benefit of the doubt, it is clearly highly vulnerable to criminality (even if you buy its occasional plea that this is not of its own making but the doings of countless rogue employees), making the case for far stronger regulation of the industry.

As Gilles Pargneaux, Member of European Parliament, puts it: 'What are we witnessing when it comes to our dealings with the tobacco industry? It is illegal activities flirting with criminal organisations, duplicity in the fight against illicit trade of tobacco products and strategies of fiscal evasion which were unveiled by the special committee of the European Parliament on Tax Evasion. This is the worrying assessment we have to make in order to stop these practices and rein in the influence of the tobacco industry.'[26]

Why have they managed to get away with this on such a grand scale? Because our law enforcement agencies and policy makers have failed to put up a meaningful fight.

7. They play a weak defense

Despite having had centuries to refine their regulatory efforts and tactics, governments are failing dismally in their efforts to curtail the illicit trade in cigarettes.

An internal PMI corporate affairs document perhaps says it best: '[They] play weak defense.'[1] As a result, cigarette smuggling is now one of the fastest growing forms of organised crime.[2]

Cigarettes are the world's most widely smuggled legal substance.[3]

Dealing in illicit cigarettes is a lucrative, relatively low-risk activity, netting around $2 million profit on a black-market container. As one enforcement officer notes, cigarettes are easy to smuggle, easy to buy, drug dogs can't sniff out the difference between a licit or illicit pack, and you don't go to jail for 50 years if you get caught.

They differ from other illicit commodities like methamphetamines or cocaine in that they are not inherently illegal, but the business is no less dirty for it.

Against that global perspective, just how big of a problem has this been in South Africa? Some years ago, back in 2012, I was asked to coordinate the crafting of a compliance programme for SARS. At the time, our analysis suggested that the tobacco industry in South Africa was disproportionately risky, resulting in it being listed as one of the key focus areas for the agency over a coming number of years.[4]

I'd like to think that, for a small amount of time, before the walls came tumbling down, it made a difference: By 2014, SARS' focus on

7. They play a weak defense

criminality in the tobacco industry had resulted in a 25% increase in excise and VAT payments. In 2012, SARS had seized 54 million illicit cigarettes – by 2014 this had increased to 270 million cigarettes. And all of it attributable to a single project: Honey Badger.

But in real terms, this was a veritable drop in an ocean of contraband. The successes were real – but they were not and are not nearly enough. Globally, governments are finding and seizing an estimated 0,7% of all illicit cigarettes believed to be on the market.[5] In South Africa, it's almost certainly even less than that.

Are the seizures making a difference? I'd like to think so. Is it enough? No.

Even if nine containers were seized in ten, smugglers still would not be losing money, one expert in the field has suggested.[6]

Illicit tobacco consumption in the EU alone is the equivalent of more than 5 860 twenty-foot containers a year.[7]

Best estimates suggest the annual illicit trade in cigarettes is worth more than the nominal GDP of almost one quarter of the world's countries. If all the different organisations involved in the illegal tobacco trade were combined into a single company, it would be the third largest international tobacco company by revenue.[8]

An average, legitimate business may make around 25% in profit. Shoe companies tend to fare a little better, with profit margins averaging around 42%. Making counterfeit products, like handbags? You're looking at 330% profit. But, as a law enforcement officer at the DEA notes, for real money? Heroin (1 886% profit) and untaxed contraband tobacco (4 200% profit)[9] are where the stakes get really high.

Illegally trafficked cigarettes now have a higher profit margin than cocaine, heroin, marijuana or guns. A fine, or even a conviction, becomes a simple calculated cost of doing business that is easily discounted against the profits being made on other consignments.

In Australia, if you were to buy $150 000 worth of cocaine or heroin, you'd make around $2,3 million selling the consignment. If caught, you go to prison. The same $150 000 spent on smuggled tobacco would earn you $10 million. If caught, you'd get a small fine. How would you spend your $150 000?[10]

And so, globally, it is estimated that illicit cigarettes account for around one in every 13 cigarettes.[11] But the global average is not the problem: local and regional variances are. In countries with poor regulatory frameworks, and even poorer compliance cultures, the prevalence of illicit tobacco is far higher. As much as 80% of the cigarettes in some West and North African countries are illicit[12] – meaning that the vast majority of the cigarettes sold in these countries profit criminals.

Even in better-regulated Europe, the number of known illegal factories is increasing: in 2010 five illegal factories were closed down – by 2016 this figure had jumped to 55. Some of the bigger illegal factories have a production capacity of around 1 million cigarettes *per day*.[13]

An estimated one third of cigarettes that are declared for export are believed to end up in the illicit cigarette supply chain.[14] Even the simplest of analyses shows how billions of cigarettes go missing. If you were to compare the volume of cigarettes declared for export in one country, they should match the volumes of cigarettes declared for import in the destination country. Very often, they do not.

So, for example, let's have a look at cigarettes that are exported from South Africa to Botswana. The packs are shipped in a container, with two key pieces of paper: an export declaration that is submitted to authorities in South Africa, and an import declaration for authorities in Botswana. In theory, what's physically in the container should match both the export and import declarations, and what is exported from South Africa, should match what is imported into Botswana, right?

Instead, comparing publicly available data from South Africa and Botswana, it would appear that five times more cigarettes are declared for export from South Africa, than are declared for import into Botswana. The stuff in the container should match, and the data should match – they don't. Literally billions of cigarettes simply seem to be

7. They play a weak defense

going missing somewhere between this side of the border and that side of the border. But the mismatch makes sense – because you don't pay export duties on cigarettes that *leave* a country, but you do pay import duties on cigarettes coming *into* a country. There is little incentive to cheat on an export declaration, and every incentive to cheat on an import declaration.

In 2010, records would suggest that tobacco companies declared that they were exporting $219 million worth of cigarettes to Botswana – and yet Botswana records seem to suggest that country received only $28 million worth of cigarettes; in 2012 exports were pegged at $232 million – but only $38 million of this was declared on Botswana's side. At least by 2016 the numbers looked marginally better: $129 million worth of cigarettes were declared for export to Botswana, and a moderately more respectable $75 million were declared for import into Botswana.[15] If not smuggled, then where did these cigarettes go?

And as much as governments may say they take the challenges around the illicit trade in tobacco seriously, this is often not reflected in the way in which perpetrators are treated. So, for instance, in Australia, which is very publicly battling illicit cigarettes, tobacco smugglers are reportedly being fined on average $17 000 – far below the maximum $210 000 penalty allowed, while being allowed to keep the proceeds of crime, and without any profits from illicit tobacco reportedly having been seized. There have only been 24 fines imposed in five years. That is less than five fines a year – in a year when 226 contraventions were detected.[16]

What is more, most governments are simply too timid to take on the power of big tobacco, and it's easy to see why – that old quote from the Russell Crowe/Al Pacino movie *The Insider* holds true: 'The unlimited check book. That's how big tobacco wins every time on everything, they spend you to death. They'll issue gag orders, sue for breach, anticipatory breach, enjoin him, you, us, his pet dog, the dog's veterinarian, tie 'em up in litigation for 10 or 15 years.'[17]

These are companies that are willing to spend as much as $940 000 per hour[18] marketing and promoting their products in the US alone. Imagine what they'd be willing to spend on lawyers?

In truth, governments around the world have consistently failed to stem the tide of illicit cigarettes, despite the earlier introduction of some positively draconian measures. As cigarette smuggling grew in the 1700s, so did efforts to curtail it. As many as 60 000 men were sent to the galleys for tobacco smuggling; infamous French cigarette smuggler Louis Mandrin was sentenced to be broken alive on the wheel; and a French official was hanged for admitting foreign tobacco into the country. Things aren't getting better – they're arguably getting worse.

You press down in one place, it simply pops up somewhere else. You send in criminal investigators, they literally dig entire villages into mountainsides and mask the smell of tobacco with pig sties.

And, to this day, tubes of toothpaste, or punnets of tomatoes, which both most likely pose less of a health risk than cigarettes do and are less susceptible to tax evasion and criminality than cigarettes are, are better controlled and tracked as they travel through the supply chain, than a pack of cigarettes is.

Want to reduce illicit trade in tobacco? Secure the supply chain. Are we doing that? No, we're not.

8. Toothpaste, fish and fig leaves

Investigations, allegations and revelations like those in this book are typically met with a standard industry response: The industry generally denies all allegations of smuggling or criminality and pins them on rogue employees or their downstream supply chain partners (indeed, the industry has an astonishing proclivity for hiring 'rogue employees'. I'd fire my entire HR department if they landed me with so many 'rogue employees'.)

It is a tall ask of the tobacco industry to expect us to ignore the body of evidence as a whole. It is a tall ask of the industry to expect us to trust them to regulate themselves. It is a tall ask of the industry to expect us to trust them given their abysmal track record to develop internal systems that safeguard their supply chains sufficiently, so that cigarettes end up where they are meant to be. Because, I believe, they have proven themselves incapable of putting forth a serious and credible effort to implement the controls and checks needed to safeguard their supply chains. The very economics of doing so works against their overarching objective to sell as many cigarettes as they can to their addicted customer base. The industry is driven by pure profit at any cost.

Many governments and international bodies have become far more sophisticated in terms of how they regulate the industry from a health perspective. While these regulations are beginning to have an impact, relatively little has been done in terms of effectively managing the supply chains along which cigarettes travel.

The concept of trying to regulate the tobacco supply chain is nothing new. As far back as 1606 Spain's King Philip III decreed that tobacco may only be grown in Cuba, Santo Domingo, Venezuela and Puerto Rico, and – taking securing the supply chain to its logical if somewhat grisly conclusion – made the sale of tobacco to foreigners punishable by death.

But while everyone seems to agree that better securing the tobacco supply chain is critical, very little is actually being done about it. In fact, in many respects we haven't moved on much since governments first started looking at better regulating the tobacco supply chain in Maryland USA, as far back as 1666.

Maryland banned the production of all tobacco for a year in 1666, facing an oversupply; and in 1730 outlawed the bulk export of tobacco. Facing challenges with tobacco being adulterated with fillers (like dust and wood shavings) and with poor quality tobacco being exported, it also introduced rules to inspect tobacco before it was shipped. The Inspection Acts revolutionised tobacco regulation: Inspectors were empowered to break open every barrel of tobacco, remove and burn any trash inside it, and issue a certificate specifying the weight and kind of tobacco inside, making it both more difficult to ship adulterated tobacco, and easier to collect taxes. That's 400 years ago.[1]

Since then? Many countries are arguably doing less now than Maryland was doing centuries ago.

Why is this important? Because, as industry expert Luk Joossens has been arguing for more than a decade now, 'the evidence strongly suggests that the key to controlling smuggling is controlling the supply chain, and the supply chain is controlled to a great extent by the tobacco industry'.[2]

Instruments like the global Illicit Trade Protocol begin to set the scene for better regulating the industry's supply chain, but very little substantive progress has been made in terms of implementing the recommendations; there are virtually no consequences for countries who fail to implement them; and many countries have no obligations as yet under any regulatory regime.

8. Toothpaste, fish and fig leaves 71

It is common practice for tobacco companies to sell huge quantities to traders and dealers who are little more than pipelines to smugglers, and who are simply used to blur the line between the tobacco companies and smugglers – something many dealers acknowledge.³

Sales are often so indiscriminate that many dealers openly admit that both they and the tobacco companies know the cigarettes are headed for the black market.

Little wonder then that the UK's Parliamentary Committee hearing on tobacco smuggling called them out on sales that nowhere near matched the legitimate demand in the countries they pretended to export to: 'You wanted 5% of 5 million. That, to my mind, makes something like 250 000 people approximately, is that correct? We agree roughly a quarter of a million people. Yet, you imported 338 million cigarettes for 250 000 people. It does not make sense, does it?'⁴

Technically, in law, of course they are perhaps correct (in many countries). There often technically *is* no obligation on tobacco companies to secure their supply chains, to ensure that they only sell their products into legal supply chains, to legitimate customers who have a legitimate demand in a legitimate market. Technically there is often no legal liability on them once they have sold bulk consignments to middle-men who on-sell to smugglers. In most countries, technically there is no prohibition on ex-factory sales. In most countries, technically there are no 'know your customer' requirements.

For purposes of this conversation it almost does not matter whether the tobacco companies knowingly sell to traders who on-sell to smugglers, or even directly to smugglers themselves (although often they seem to know very well as we've seen in for instance Colombia where government charged that 'since at least 1991, PMI were selling cigarettes to individuals whom they knew were reputed drug smugglers'.⁵) What matters is that the way the tobacco supply chain is regulated now, in most countries, is inefficient and vulnerable.

It's a weakness that is exploited. And it's a weakness that very much sits behind perhaps most of the cases we know of where big tobacco's impunity leads to criminality.

It's also a weakness that at least some players in the industry are beginning to acknowledge: Philip Morris will tell you that they have the ability to track 100% of master cases throughout the supply chain.[6] But that doesn't help all that much, because in another publication they themselves note how tracking at a master case level isn't really enough because in, for instance, Algeria 'evidence show[s] that there was high level smuggling of cartons. The situation called for more granular controls.' And in Senegal investigations 'showed that smugglers were diverting the products in cartons and not in master cases'.[7]

Philip Morris will also tell you how in 2017, 'The outflow of PMI products from Algeria remains a top priority for PMI. Products tend to be diverted to France, Morocco and Tunisia' and how in 2014, 'we discovered that over 50% of the available supply of Marlboro in Australia was actually intended for the South Korean market'. They note that in 2015 'the UK tax authority HMRC asked PMI to review its supply chain controls in Belgium'.

They will tell you that, 'Until 2015, large volumes of PMI brands destined for the Senegalese market were seized at national airports in Europe' and in Serbia that, 'The outflow of goods intended for the Serbian market remains a major problem.'

They admit to an 'increased number of seizures and size of tobacco products originating from Ukraine' in 2017; and in 2016 that, 'Marlboro products represented a particular issue for PMI with approximately one in five consumed in Ecuador being duty-not-paid.' They note how 'Indonesia was identified as a high-risk market for diversion' and that the 'distribution model in Iraq is complex. This creates a heightened risk of product outflow.'[8]

I find this level of frank disclosure on PMI's part moderately encouraging – but I'd really still like to know what exactly they are *doing* about it. There is a plethora of relatively simple solutions that could help secure

8. Toothpaste, fish and fig leaves

the tobacco supply chain, and yet big tobacco fights tooth and nail against any suggestion of introducing them. (I'd also like to know why they only published this report once, and then never again.)

Just to be clear – industry *does* secure some of its supply chain quite rigorously, with upstream tobacco leaf traceability being possible down to the farm level.

In fact, a company like BAT has a fairly complex supplier network – its website shows that it has 350 000 farms, 1 500 direct materials suppliers and 30 000 indirect suppliers, all of whom it says are subject to rigorous independent audits and supply chain due diligence checks, and all of whom are assessed against risk scoring criterion.[9]

So, BAT would have us believe, in their own words, that, 'All suppliers undergo an independent on-site audit, conducted by the global audit firm, Intertek, in order to be appointed as a supplier and then are re-audited every three years. The Intertek audit includes criteria covering forced labour, child labour, wages and hours, health and safety, environment and management systems. We also use our integrated supply chain due diligence programme to assess supplier's inherent risks, using a series of independent indices. We prioritise those suppliers identified as being exposed to the highest risks for either a self-assessment or an on-site audit.'[10]

But this same company seemingly then tells us that it has no control over where its cigarettes end up; that it simply ships cigarettes in response to orders.

It is something of a mystery why the company would so intently secure its upstream supply chain for inputs into its manufacturing process, but do very little to secure its downstream supply chain for its outputs, in fact going so far as to very clearly state that it has no control over where its cigarettes end up or who they are sold to.

On Philip Morris' own website, the company says that it only marks and tracks a percentage of its own cigarettes[11] (in 2017, the last year for which I could find data, they say they were only marking 75% of their packs) and we don't know to what extent the other big tobacco companies are using it.

In the JTI reply to my request for comment, they noted, 'We have implemented far reaching anti-illicit trade measures, aiming at securing our supply chain. The tracking and tracing of our products are also part of supply chain control: at this date, 75% of our global production is tracked and traced.'

But why only track 75% of your packs?[12]

Every expert and his dog has recommended that all tobacco packs should be securely marked, so that packs can be traced through the supply chain, and so that we can see where a pack came from. Big tobacco has been telling the world that it has its own track and trace solution that can do just that: Codentify.

Codentify's genesis is important: it was developed as part of the obligations imposed on PMI under its agreement to settle smuggling related charges in the EU (that would be the same agreement that saw PMI having to pay compensation to the EU to the tune of $1,25 billion for the smuggling of its packs). They subsequently licensed it for use by all of the big tobacco companies. It creates a code (really just an alpha-numeric number) that is printed directly onto packs during manufacturing, so – if you know how to read it – it could in theory tell you who made the pack.[13]

Like many others, I am sceptical of Codentify-type digital tax verification solutions (in other words, one that simply uses an alphanumeric code to mark cigarette packs, without another visual security feature like a physical tax stamp), simply because they are easy to copy or clone, with the same code being reprinted on multiple packs. You would only know that a pack had a fake code on it if you scanned a second item with the same code. It is a highly inefficient enforcement tool from a customs agency perspective – the cost of detection, in terms of the sheer number of checks an enforcement officer would have to do to detect duplicate codes far exceeds the potential revenue loss.[14] In a peer-

8. Toothpaste, fish and fig leaves

reviewed paper, tobacco control economist Hana Ross – along with my colleague Michael Eads – estimated that in a relatively small market, a law enforcement authority would have to inspect almost 31 000 packs per week to have a 95% certainty that it did not miss a fraudulent pack under Codentify-type systems. A material-based track and trace solution – so, using a physical tax stamp – would require only 59 pack inspections a week to have the same level of confidence.[15] (Inexto, which bought Codentify, claims Professor Ross is not a track and trace expert. I'm not sure that is true, but she is a world-renowned expert specialising in the economics of tobacco, and her team's math adds up. Read the paper, make up your own mind.)

In Europe alone where 30 billion-plus fast-moving consumable items move through the market every year I am happy to argue that the statistical probability of finding a twin code is next to nil.

The digital tax verification-type solutions being advocated for by the tobacco industry are hardly more than a fig leaf for a morally bankrupt industry.

Not too long ago – in 2013 – BAT was accused of bribing a politician in Kenya to make sure that a cigarette track and trace tender was not awarded to an independent service provider.[16] In Uzbekistan they tried to convince government to introduce a tax stamp traceability system for *smaller* manufacturers, but from which it wanted to be exempted itself.[17]

After SARS announced a tender for a traceability solution to mark cigarette packs – after 12 years of promising to do so – in the space of less than six months, around 22 directly-related articles appeared in the media. Of those, only 3-13% argued in favour of a secure marking solution (one of them by Eads, one by the tax stamp association ITSA, and one by South Africa's Council Against Smoking). The rest all advanced an industry line that sought to delay, derail or dilute SARS' efforts to better secure the tobacco supply chain. The media onslaught was relentless: the new system had been 'rushed', 'would capture only the legal market', would 'drive illicit trade up further', accused SARS of 'wasting billions of rands', and the industry raised concerns about rolling out such a 'sophisticated system'. And yet every single expert agrees that traceability is the one key solution to curbing illicit tobacco. But it works to big tobacco's advantage if the supply chain stays opaque. Because they need our governments to believe that big tobacco has it all under control, and that additional checks and balances on big tobacco's supply chain are not necessary.

Between industry rhetoric and administrative capture, governments around the world are simply not adopting good practice measures that could easily regulate the tobacco supply chain. One would also have imagined that the tobacco industry could easily have taken a leaf from what other industries are doing to better secure their own supply chains.

The ability to know where your products are, or to trace a product back to where it came from, is not something that is unique to the tobacco industry. It is something that other companies with commodities that are far less susceptible to criminality have faced and quite successfully manage.

For many consumer products, traceability is an issue mostly because of the genuine desire to protect their brands and their reputation, and so they can coordinate product recalls if necessary.

We generally don't associate cigarettes with product recalls because there are not that many recorded instances, but it *does* happen: PMI had to recall 8 billion cigarettes (worth $100 million) because the filters used had been sprayed with a plasticiser containing half a dozen chemical contaminants, which together formed methyl isothiocyanate, a commercial pesticide used as a soil fumigant. PMI explained that, given the 'complexities' of the tobacco distribution system, it could not track where the 8 billion cigarettes had been shipped to.[18]

Eight billion cigarettes, and nobody knew where on earth they were.

Many other industries, with commodities that are far less hazardous, and that are far less vulnerable to criminal enterprise, and that are far

8. Toothpaste, fish and fig leaves

less susceptible to tax evasion, have implemented far more robust supply chain security solutions than the tobacco industry has.

Something as obscure and innocuous as a simple tube of toothpaste travels along a far more secure supply chain than tobacco does, despite the fact that tobacco kills far more people, loses governments far more in unpaid taxes, is far more susceptible to smuggling, and is far more intrinsically linked to organised crime.

When one begins to unpack the reasons other products are regulated, a curious question emerges: Why on earth are the supply chains around cigarettes not being regulated more and better?

How is it possible that tubes of toothpaste, or tins of infant formula, which both most likely pose less of a health risk than cigarettes do, are better controlled and tracked as they travel through the supply chain, than a pack of cigarettes is? How can Toyota track the more than 30 000 individual parts in one of their showroom vehicles back to its original supplier,[19] but big tobacco does not know where its cigarettes go?

A quick look at some other fast-moving consumable goods put big tobacco's supposed inability to track its products through the supply chain in perspective:

ThisFish[20] lets you trace your fish fillet back to the particular fisherman who caught it on the other side of the world, giving consumers a fish-to-fork view of their purchases.

How is it that a fisherman out at sea somewhere off the coast of Java, armed only with a smartphone, can set in motion the ability to trace a single fish fillet from a London supermarket all the way back to his boat – but the tobacco industry says it has no control over where its packs of cigarettes end up?

Harvest Mark[21] lets you trace your punnet of tomatoes back to one of its 3 000 farms.

How is it that Indonesian teak farmers on a remote family-owned plantation can achieve traceability down to the individual tree stump, across a complex supply chain that includes mills and kilns and furniture factories, all the way to a salesroom in Europe[22] – but the tobacco industry cannot track where its cigarettes end up?

It is nothing short of preposterous. Fish only rarely kill people; tobacco does so routinely.

Having a better chain of custody, with better traceability, for a salmon fillet or a bag of grapes than we do for tobacco is nothing less than astonishing.

But there is more to it than fish fillets or bags of grapes. There are arguably very few companies in the world that are quite as vilified as big tobacco. Monsanto – which has many characteristics in common with big tobacco from a supply chain perspective – is perhaps one of them.

Monsanto is interesting because it has adopted a very progressive supply chain security framework, fully digitising their entire supply chain from product development in the laboratory, to a farmer on a combine harvester, to its customers.[23]

But most importantly, for our purposes, they simply do not do business with anybody who does not secure their own supply chains.

If Monsanto can enforce supply chain security protocols on the people it does business with, surely it is possible for the tobacco industry to do the same?

An even more complex example lies in Procter & Gamble's supply chain and distribution network[24] (the company manufactures some of the world's leading consumer brands including Tide, Crest, Pringles, Pampers, Clairol and 300 or so other products). It somewhat echoes the tobacco industry's distribution network, selling to 5 billion consumers in 140 countries the world over.

P&G cut out the middle-man and now directly distribute their products to major accounts themselves; they ended their direct relationships with smaller accounts; and they focus on the use of a real-time instrumented supply chain, making it possible for them to literally track a bottle of shampoo anywhere around the world.

8. Toothpaste, fish and fig leaves

If it is possible for a company with multiple different product categories, diverse supply chains and a complex global distribution network to connect actual sales with their supply chain management process, and to cut out sales to middle-men, for a tube of toothpaste, it is entirely possible for the tobacco industry – with what is a largely homogenous product – to do the same.

Of course, it's not just private companies that have sought to benefit from more robust supply chain security practices. A number of government agencies and international instruments (like the ones for authorised economic operators and the customs trade partnership against terrorism),[25] are increasingly developing good practice principles that are as applicable to cigarettes as they are to other commodities: requiring traders to know and screen the customers they do business with; including supply chain management as a strategic objective at a corporate level; integrating risk analysis of the supply chain into business practices; screening and monitoring customers; and the use of traceability solutions. Big tobacco does not and should not qualify as a 'trusted trader' under these programmes because its supply chain inherently lacks integrity – and yet it does.

Other industries adopt these recommended practices – most often voluntarily – because they view supply chain management as a strategic asset, that is used to increase their profit margins (like Procter & Gamble) and reduce their reputational risk (as De Beers does to guard against conflict diamonds).[26]

The tobacco industry has simply not adopted these practices. Why? Most likely because it chooses not to.

This is not an industry fighting for its life. It's a thriving industry simply not being held to account for its products and its supply chains, unlike other industries that are held to account for their products and supply chains.

Want to significantly curtail the illicit trade in cigarettes? Manage the cigarette supply chain better, by stopping indiscriminate sales of cigarettes, and by creating the ability to track and trace cigarettes through the supply chain, back to their point of manufacture. Mark cigarette packs with secure, unique identifiers, so that they can be traced back to their point of manufacture. Introduce know-your-customer requirements, only allowing sales to customers who have their own strict chain of custody and supply chain management protocols; and introduce legitimate demand conditions on all sales. Stop *ex-factory* sales, only allowing for sales to larger retailers directly.

Philip Morris itself said it best in one of its vintage ads (at the time promoting their cigarettes as a healthier option): an ounce of prevention is worth a pound of cure.[27]

Secure the supply chain and watch contraband dry up. The reason it's not happening? Because the tobacco industry has developed a playbook for profit that has left it virtually untouchable, and that allows it to operate with impunity, everywhere.

Vintage big tobacco ad from the Stanford University catalogue

Date: 1943
Brand: Philip Morris
Manufacturer: Philip Morris
Campaign: Johnny Calls for Philip Morris
Theme: For your Throat
Quote: An ounce of prevention is worth a pound of cure!
Comment: Johnny Roventini (1910–1998), the famous Philip Morris spokesperson, is shown calling 'An ounce of prevention is worth a pound of cure', presenting the brand as the healthiest cigarette option. The ad capitalises on public fears over smoking-related health conditions.[28]

9. A playbook for profit

With the rise of competitors, and more stringent regulation about what it can sell to whom, where and how, big tobacco has had to change its tactics. And as big tobacco has faced more pressure, both from regulators and other competitors, so too, in my view, would the nature and sophistication of its evasion and illegal activities probably have had to change.

What may have once been pure smuggling has become increasingly complex aggressive tax avoidance with mounting evidence pointing to the use of convoluted constructs like thin capitalisation, transfer pricing, money laundering and fictitious revenue schemes.[1]

It's the very story that sits at the heart of this book: The industry may have once focused simply on getting its own products out the door, but it has increasingly become about undermining smaller competitors to maintain market share and employing corporate espionage and sabotage tactics in order to position their brands and squeeze out the competition. In many countries – probably most – big tobacco continues to dominate the landscape.

Big tobacco may, indeed, be increasingly toeing the line in markets where it is being closely watched by governments and the many anti-tobacco organisations, and where it has paid massive fines, simply because it has to. As regulatory efforts step up – at least in more advanced, better-regulated economies – its room to manoeuvre is increasingly limited.

The tobacco industry has had five centuries to refine its strategy and business model and rhetoric, and it has done so with remarkable agility.

With that as background, how successful is big tobacco really?

The Economist notes how the world's most profitable non-durable consumer good is a cigarette brand – Marlboro.[2]

Citi Research will tell you, 'We are now in the surprising position where U.S. cigarette sales are growing faster than the sales of food.'[3] US tobacco sales show a 3,6% increase, compared to for instance packaged food that only grew by 0,2%.[4]

If you had invested $1 in PMI/Altria in 1968, it would be worth $6 638 today. That same dollar invested in the S&P 500 – which measures the stock performance of the 500 largest companies listed on the stock exchange in the US[5] – over the same period would be worth $87 today. That's 98% less.[6]

Credit Suisse published a report on the performance of every major American industry from 1900 to 2010: If you'd invested one dollar in tobacco stocks in 1900, that one dollar today would be worth $6,3 million – compared to $700 000 if you'd invested that dollar in chemicals and food; or $38 000 if you'd invested your dollar in any other American industry. That makes an investment in tobacco worth 165 times more than an investment in most any other industry.[7]

Their revenues are bigger than the gross national income of many African countries.

And despite stagnating sales in many markets, profits continue to rise.

The Tobacco Atlas notes that smoking rates in Europe have decreased by 26% over the past ten years – but it's grown by 57% across Africa. And, indeed, the industry may have seen limited growth in *volumes*, but the *value* of global cigarette sales has risen by 84% in the last decade.[8]

Altria notes that it has an 'outstanding track record of creating value for shareholders, having increased its dividend 52 times in the last 49 years'.[9]

This trend of unwavering profitability continues today. By mid-2018, for example, BAT had again noted extremely impressive performance: revenues had increased by 56,9%; the volume of sales had grown by 11%; and operational profit was up by 72,4%.[10] BAT has been the best performer on the UK stock market of the past 35 years.[11]

Perhaps the key question is this: How does an industry under this much sustained pressure in terms of what it may sell, where and to whom, still manage to perform so well?

At least some of it is arguably attributable to efficiency gains in the industry itself. But that cannot possibly account for all of its success.

With volumes of legal cigarettes down, but with profits up, it begs the question: how likely is it that big tobacco continues to profit from illicit trade today? With all of the fiscal pressures on big tobacco, how does it maintain the astonishing growth rates any other industry would be lucky to see?

In fact, big tobacco actually relies on a rather predictable set of strategies and patterns of behaviour.

The tobacco industry has developed a playbook. It's a playbook that explains why it has got away with its historical complicity in smuggling and other unlawful activities for so many decades, and why it continues to be so profitable. Its playbook is structured around what I've come to refer to as the four key pillars of power that in large part explain industry's considerable influence and success.

First, it controls what we think, by controlling what we read through an ongoing and well-funded global media campaign.

Second, it controls what our politicians do, through regulatory capture – which ranges from using golden chains to convince them to adopt industry-friendly policies, to cases of outright corruption in what is nothing less than a silent coup.

Third, it controls what our law enforcement agencies focus on, by promoting itself as both victim and saviour when it comes to illicit trade, getting our enforcement agencies to focus on the competition, and aggressively infiltrating any organisation that stands in its way.

9. A playbook for profit

And finally – as we've already seen – it intentionally keeps its downstream supply chains opaque, blithely ignoring proven and tested supply chain controls.

Let's start with the first pillar of power: controlling what we think, by controlling what we read.

PART 2

Controlling what we think

10. Merchants of disinformation

'The expert magician seeks to deceive the mind, rather than the eye.'
— *Sol Stein (who authored several books on magic)*

I'm embarrassed to say it, but they had me fooled. And it's okay if they've fooled you too. We're all really just big tobacco groupies. Until we choose to stop drinking the industry Kool-Aid.

There are several reasons why big tobacco manages to remain so successful in the face of both increasing competition and more efforts to regulate it. One of those reasons is that it very much controls the rhetoric around the tobacco industry in general, and in respect of illicit tobacco in particular — the first of those 'pillars of power' I referred to earlier. To borrow a phrase, big tobacco companies have become merchants of disinformation.

To do so, they need to control what we think, by controlling what we read. An internal PMI corporate affairs presentation explains their objectives: 'Playing the political game — what are we aiming for: shaping public opinion. Ability to find the right spin. Established relationships with key reporters. Alliance of credible messengers. Third party coalition building. Think tanks and policy groups.'[1]

It's an old tactic that the industry has honed over decades. In 1953, Dr Alton Ochsner gave a speech in New York City, saying, 'The male population of the United States would be decimated if cigarette smoking increases as it has.' Tobacco stocks dropped 4 points the next day, acting as a catalyst for tobacco executives to join forces. They met in New York for the first time since an earlier price-fixing scandal (where they were fined $1 billion), and together with a public relations firm developed a counterattack on smoking studies and anti-tobacco activists.[2]

In 1998, industry worried that a study by an affiliate of the WHO would lead to increased restrictions in Europe, so they spearheaded a $2 million strategy to subvert the research agency's work, undercutting its research, and developing industry-directed research to counter its findings; shaping opinion by manipulating the media; and actively targeting government officials to prevent smoking restrictions.[3]

In 2017, the big tobacco companies were spending $940 000 per hour – per *hour* – marketing and promoting their products in the US alone,[4] buying them a significant amount of editorial clout.

It buys them the ability to sell an agenda and control the rhetoric around a number of key battlefields: the drivers of illicit trade; the size and prevalence of illicit trade in a market; who sits behind illicit trade; the impact of increased regulation, and higher taxes; and how big tobacco – as the 'victims' of illicit trade – could help government better curb illicit trade.

And so, if you trawl through enough tobacco-related media coverage, a few recurring themes emerge that drive industry rhetoric and that are used to shape public perceptions around the industry.

It's easy to understand why, as RJ Reynolds itself noted that, 'Unless countervailing steps are taken (such as lobbying), public decision-making will march with public opinion.'[5]

Let's start with the first one: the drivers of illicit trade.

The tobacco industry has a number of arguments it consistently advances. One of them is that high tax rates drive the illicit trade in tobacco products – that without high tax rates, there would be no incentive to smuggle or sell products on the black market.

Governments tax cigarettes because they want fewer people to smoke them. It is sound public policy. Selling fewer cigarettes is exactly what the industry does not want. Already facing restrictions on how it can advertise, it cannot afford to lose more consumers. Seeking to pin the rise of illicit trade on high tax rates is a genius tactic.

10. Merchants of disinformation

And as government agencies buy the rhetoric that tax rates drive illicit trade, they don't introduce planned tax increases, and hold back on regulation.

Instead of taxes making up the recommended 80% of the retail price of a pack of cigarettes, the vast majority of countries have tax rates far below that, and many countries have seen no increases in excise rates in decades. In fact, just 18% of countries have a tobacco tax policy that meets the WHO best practice recommendations – and this number has *dropped* since 2014.[6]

Lower tax rates kill: a simple 3% increase in tax rates would translate into 164 000 fewer premature deaths a year globally. And as PMI executive Jon Zoler quipped so drolly some years ago, '. . . Jeffrey Harris of MIT calculated that the price increases caused two million adults to quit smoking and prevented 600 000 teenagers from starting to smoke. We don't need to have that happen again.'[7]

So why does industry have an interest in inflating the size and prevalence of illicit tobacco in a country? Because it likes to argue that illicit trade is simply a function of high tax rates.[8]

Big tobacco's position is simple: they argue that illicit trade exists because of regulation. They argue that the main reason there is a black market for illicit packs is because government taxes are too high. If, they argue, government were to reduce tax rates – or at the very least not increase them – the incentive to sell cigarettes on the black market would disappear. But if, by contrast, government were to increase tax rates, it would simply further incentivise black market sales.

In 2016, in the USA alone, tobacco companies spent more than $71 million to fund the battle against tobacco tax increases, fuelling industry's bullying tactic – if you increase taxes, illicit trade will increase, reducing our market share, which means we will have to lay people off and move production elsewhere.[9] (More job losses in the industry are probably attributable to industry automation. In one annual report, PMI notes that it managed to achieve 'major cost efficiencies' as a result of 'factory headcount reductions through manning and shift-pattern changes'.)[10]

The industry argues heavily against increasing taxes on tobacco, but their efforts are not always successful. Once tax rate increases become inevitable, the tobacco industry has simply learnt to sneak its own price increases in under cover of tax rate increases, pinning high prices on the tax man when much of the higher price really just goes into their own pockets. In reality, most price increases are attributable to industry pricing strategies and not to an increase in taxes.

In the United Kingdom, where almost 90% of the retail price of cigarettes is tax, half of price increases are directly attributable to industry itself.[11] Between 2015 and 2018, Canada's federal tobacco taxes have only gone up by 53 cents, but the cost of a carton of cigarettes has increased by $7. Between the 1990s and 2000s in South Africa for every 10 cents government increased the tax on a pack of cigarettes by, the retail price per pack increased by 18 cents. The extra 8 cents? Pure profit going back to tobacco companies. They were making almost as much money off the tax rate increases as government was.[12]

And while I would be the first one to acknowledge that their argument intuitively seems to make sense, data shows that it does not necessarily hold water.[13] In fact, many countries have high prices and taxes but relatively low illicit trade rates (e.g. Sweden, Denmark, Norway, Finland, Ireland); and conversely many countries have low prices and tax rates, but relatively high illicit trade rates (e.g. Spain, Italy, Pakistan, Nigeria, Yugoslavia, Ukraine, Moldova, Colombia, Iran, Austria and Cambodia.[14]) Instead, most independent (objective) research seems to suggest that contraband flourishes where enforcement is poor and corruption is high – virtually independent of tax rates.

The industry's argument is patently self-serving. Higher prices mean fewer people buying cigarettes – which is exactly what excise duties on cigarettes are meant to achieve, and which is exactly what the tobacco industry does not need.

10. Merchants of disinformation

Once you understand the industry narrative around the drivers of illicit trade, their position on the size and prevalence of illicit trade begins to make more sense – the bigger the illicit trade problem appears to be, the more pressure they can apply on government to not further increase tax rates.

How big of a problem, then, is illicit trade really?

A while ago, I happened to be doing some research on illicit cigarettes in South Africa. A quick Google search and you'd know it's 'in the top 5' countries in the world with the biggest share of illicit cigarettes[15] – a number you'll find quoted in numerous publications, and that has made its way into many subsequent reports and studies and government documents. In fact, it's a number I've been guilty of quoting myself. Until I realised that it's not true. It's become a classic case of 'repeat something often enough and it becomes true.'

By all accounts illicit cigarettes *are* a scourge in South Africa – but it is *not* one of the biggest markets globally. There are actually many countries that have a far higher prevalence, like Albania, Bolivia, Bosnia, Brazil, Brunei, Ethiopia, Georgia, Hong Kong, Iraq, Iran, Laos, Macedonia, Malaysia and Uzbekistan (to name but a few.)

So, where did the 'in the top 5 countries' reference come from? As best I can tell, it seems to have come from a statement by the Tobacco Institute of Southern Africa, the big tobacco proxy. I have no idea where they got the number from. It is a statement that remained unchallenged and unchecked, and that became part of the South African lexicon, and that continues to be used in the public discourse around illicit trade in the country. (I asked TISA about this – they said they 'will not be responding'.)

Why? Because it serves industry well to inflate the number and turn illicit cigarettes into something of a bogeyman. It takes the pressure off big tobacco.

It should come as no surprise that in Australia, KPMG's assessment of the size of illicit trade was rejected, with a panel finding that '...

tobacco manufacturers cite the industry funded KPMG report on illicit tobacco in Australia, which purports to show that there has been a large increase in illicit trade. I have considered both this report and a critique. My team have also met with KPMG in order to understand their methods. I do not have confidence in KPMG's assessment of the size of – or changes in – the illicit market in Australia.'[16]

There are a number of research studies that highlight by just how much big tobacco exaggerates the threat of illicit tobacco, detailing instances where it dramatically chose to inflate the size and prevalence of illicit trade,[17] and articulating very clearly how industry-funded estimates should not be trusted. It's perhaps worthwhile running through at least a few of them, because it makes the point that inflating illicit trade figures is not something that happens in isolated cases – it happens with alarming regularity:

A UK study found that big tobacco companies were exaggerating the threat of illicit tobacco by commissioning surveys whose methodology and validity remain uncertain, planting misleading stories and misquoting government data;[18] a Hong Kong study found an industry-funded estimate to have been inflated by as much as 337% of the probable true value;[19] a Polish study found industry estimates were higher by half than they should have been;[20] and an Australian study shot down an industry-funded survey that led to claims that almost 16% of tobacco products were illicit, contradicting a far larger government survey which had found a much lower 1,5% illicit penetration rate.[21]

Some newspapers have had a field day claiming that more than one thousand illicit packs of cigarettes are being sold in Malaysia a minute – yes, one thousand a minute – on the back of research they say was conducted by Oxford Economics.[22] Despite some digging, I cannot find a report on their website, and the media coverage offers no insight on how the Oxford study was done, making it virtually impossible to engage with the substance of the claims. (The Southeast Asia Tobacco Control Alliance did later call them out for not revealing that the

10. Merchants of disinformation

study had in fact been funded by the tobacco industry, and exposing that articles in support of the research had been written by a public relations pro who has big tobacco as one of his key clients.)[23]

In South Africa, studies show how industry had adjusted earlier estimates downward to create the impression that illicit trade had suddenly dramatically increased;[24] a second South African study found that estimates of the illicit cigarette trade levels presented in industry-commissioned reports are often inflated, calling them a 'misleading math trick'.[25] In fact, the South African example on big tobacco's flexible poetic licence with data is so egregious that it has been pertinently quoted in the World Health Organization's Tobacco Atlas.[26] Since around 2014, TISA consistently (publicly) estimated the size of illicit trade in South Africa at roughly 24% – while at the same time continuing to argue that illicit trade has 'increased significantly'.[27]

The TISA figures fascinate me. I've already mentioned that thumb drive that was handed to me in Rosebank, Johannesburg? Well, a number of the documents on it both provide some insights into the TISA estimates on the prevalence of illicit trade in South Africa, and at the same time make them even more mysterious.

Based on some of the documents on that thumb drive – which largely relate to security company Forensic Security Services (FSS) that BAT had contracted to do some work for it – it seems that TISA may have been tracking the prevalence of contraband on the local market literally on a monthly basis. Over the course of 2013 their monthly estimates seem to have ranged between 25-36%; for 2014 they reported a range of between 20-26%; and in 2015 their monthly estimates sat at somewhere between 20-25%. And they don't seem to have been just tracking prevalence in general – they appear to have been tracking what percentage of the illicit market was attributable to specific manufacturers and individual brands, and the source country. They were also tracking why they believed the packs were illicit – either because they were being sold at a low price (I think this accounted for around 45% of the packs on their lists) or were otherwise non-compliant with tobacco products control legislation (mostly around the use of cigarette paper that did not comply with the reduced ignition propensity regulations).

What remains something of a mystery is just how TISA would have arrived at these figures. Evidence suggests that BAT's security company FSS was conducting purchases at retailers and corner shops, and I assume this was probably where the data came from. There are a few small problems with this approach: there may have been something of a selection bias if they focused their visits on shops where they knew they could expect to find contraband packs; illicit was simply defined as anything selling below the tax rate (which might be true, but not necessarily so); an estimation of illicit is typically better done using methods other than these 'control purchases'; and a proper academic study of the size and prevalence of illicit packs on a market takes several months, if not years. Just how TISA managed to churn out the numbers month after month is a veritable miracle.

Of course, all of this is purely speculative, because we really don't know just how TISA did it or where they got the numbers from. We don't know who did the research, or what methodology was used – and with TISA's sudden winding up early in 2020, we will perhaps never know.

If big tobacco were confident in their methodologies, one would have thought that they would have had no qualms in sharing where the numbers come from. Instead – as is so often the case – we are simply met with silence. Which brings us right back to the myth that South Africa is 'in the top five countries' with the biggest illicit cigarette problem: because big tobacco tells us so.

Seemingly, big tobacco not only inflates the size and prevalence of illicit products, it also deploys some other math tricks. So for instance, in Ireland it quoted illicit market share, to hide the fact that in absolute terms the illicit cigarette consumption was in decline.[28] Or it may construct a narrative that makes it seem as if much of the illicit cigarettes are attributable to counterfeiters when in fact counterfeits only account

10. Merchants of disinformation

for around 2% of illicit cigarettes globally (addendum 3 has more details).[29] So we see how 'a quarter of illicit cigarettes in Europe were PMI's own brands, compared to just 5% being counterfeited PMI brands and 10% comprising leading illicit white brands'.[30] Despite this, PMI emphasises the problems of counterfeits and illicit whites, because it deflects attention away from them.

Even a respectable company like Euromonitor — which routinely conducts illicit trade analyses — has not escaped scrutiny, and a number of studies have found what they term 'striking inconsistencies'[31] between country-specific estimates done by Euromonitor for the same years. The criticism will hardly abate now that Euromonitor has openly acknowledged that it receives funding from the tobacco industry.

It should come as no surprise, then, that big tobacco also uses the illicit trade studies it commissions to finger its competitors as the main perpetrators.

And in fingering smaller local competitors we are seeing the same laxity with data as we saw with how big tobacco inflates the size of illicit trade: In 2012, SARS estimated that cigarettes smuggled from Zimbabwe accounted for 70% of the illicit market.[32] In 2013, TISA is quoted as saying that 50-55% of illicit cigarettes in South Africa came from Zimbabwe[33] (with the rest coming from a mixed bag of countries like China, the UAE, Dubai, Botswana, Swaziland and Lesotho). In 2014, we were told it was 40%.[34] In 2015, TISA said 30% of illicit cigarettes came from Zimbabwe,[35] and in 2016, 40%. Then, in 2018, in a dramatic turnaround, TISA suddenly suggested that 75% of illicit packs on the South African market came from a single local producer in South Africa — an astonishing about-turn, and a veritable market share miracle for that one single manufacturer in the space of only two years. What had happened to the Zimbabwe line?

Because we have no idea where TISA gets its numbers from, or how they were calculated, we simply cannot engage with the substance of what they are saying.

Remember, big tobacco's biggest enemy is arguably not anti-smoking taxes or legislation but competition, and black-market sales is one of several ways for a competitor to enter the market.

An anti-smuggling campaign is often simply a defensive strategy by a monopoly.

Because of this, I've become increasingly ambivalent about much of what we read and think we know about these smaller low-cost manufacturers. Are they controversial simply by way of the company they keep? To what extent is our perception of somebody like controversial businessman Adriano Mazzotti based simply on his alliance with firebrand politician Julius Malema? In believing that he and people like him are responsible for the illicit packs on the South African market, are we simply buying a line from the big tobacco playbook, or is there *real* evidence that supports this? Are we vilifying the right people? How much of what we think we know is simply big tobacco propaganda?

The UK's Parliamentary enquiry into tobacco smuggling saw right through the spin: 'You were asked how your profits would be hit if smuggling was cut and you said you expected your profits to increase. Your profits have increased. How do you explain that? We have heard a lot from you about your "triple whammy" and our hearts bleed for you. It does not show in your profit figures though. Your profit figures over the last five years have varied very little at all, they are relatively constant. The idea that you have not somehow been benefiting in terms of your total profitability as a result of illicit activities does bear examination does it not?'[36]

But there is even more to it than that. You see, big tobacco almost has us feeling sorry for it. It has us feeling empathy for the employees they have to lay off because of illicit trade eating into their margins. It's a line we are seeing more and more often in countries like South Africa – the line that big tobacco will cease to exist as illicit trade eats into its profits. And you could almost believe them.

Except, well, there is this one other little fact they forget to mention:

there are a few countries where big tobacco itself tells us it is exceptionally profitable. Countries like Brazil, Turkey, Mexico, Egypt, Nigeria, Bulgaria and Poland.[37] And, curiously, these countries all have high rates of illicit trade, too (ranging from 27% in Brazil and Bulgaria, to a moderately lower – but still concerning – 17% in Egypt). So how does big tobacco manage to be so profitable in these countries with their high illicit rates, but supposedly not in South Africa? Why is illicit trade seemingly not a problem for big tobacco in these other countries, with a comparable illicit market, but in South Africa they argue it will spell the near-certain death of the industry?

I actually don't know the answer to this little conundrum. But I suspect it has much to do with keeping regulation at bay, which is perhaps not as big a threat in these other countries.

What I do know is that, as with much of the industry-driven rhetoric, whether it relates to the size of illicit trade, or the extent to which it is attributable to smaller low-cost competitors, or how big tobacco is the victim, it all plays on creating doubt.

It's what the industry was advised to do decades ago by iconic public relations firm Hill and Knowlton: 'The most important type of story is that which casts doubt. Eye-grabbing headlines are needed and should strongly call – Controversy! Contradiction! Other factors! Unknowns!'[38]

It's what the industry seems to continue doing today.

It creates controversy around almost every aspect of tobacco and its control – not just on the harm caused by their products, but on everything from the size of the trade in illicit cigarettes to the implementation of supply chain controls.

An old PMI document says it best: 'Doubt is our product since it is the best means of competing with the "body of fact" that exists. It is also the means of establishing a controversy. Spread doubt over strong scientific evidence and the public won't know what to believe.'[39]

They tried convincing the world that smoking did not cause cancer – setting up their Project Whitecoat to make us believe that lung cancer was caused by coffee or poor ventilation designs in buildings.⁴⁰ Just like they are trying to convince the world today that big tobacco is a victim of illicit trade, and not complicit.

This won't be the last time you see these tactics being deployed. Big tobacco may have perfected them, but they are increasingly being adopted by other big corporates: A Harvard Law School paper lays out how food companies are using tobacco industry tactics to deny the existence of an obesity epidemic. A *New York Times* article notes how coal companies are taking a page from the tobacco playbook. Forbes writes about soda companies doing the same.⁴¹

It's a message that is being echoed around the world, including by bloggers like Doug Porter, who wrote: '[Tobacco companies] know arguing in favour of tobacco use won't work, so they've unleashed a blizzard of bullcrap advertising seeking to confuse and obfuscate the matter. Their experience at "marketing" is being used by dirty energy, drug pushers and the poison food industry to encourage a host of bad behaviours.'⁴²

Ultimately, big tobacco's rhetoric has a simple objective: delay, dilute, derail or disrupt anything that has the potential to interfere with its profit margins. Big tobacco does not need to win the debates it manufactures — it simply needs to foster and perpetuate the illusion of controversy enough to muddy the waters around issues threatening the industry, blurring policy options, and buying it time and space to lobby. And it's working brilliantly.

Because while we doubt — whether tax rate increases could perhaps drive an increase in illicit trade; which of the smaller independent manufacturers to investigate first; whether traceability systems actually work — we suspend action. And while we suspend action, we leave voids that big tobacco is more than happy to fill.

11. Astroturf, ghost writers and bots

Have you ever watched a magic show?

The art, of course, lies in smoke to obscure what lies behind, mirrors to reflect false truths, and misdirection to make you take your eyes off the spot where the real action is.

It's no coincidence that there are so many articles referencing 'smoke and mirrors' in relation to the tobacco industry. Big tobacco companies are masterful magicians. They're the David Copperfields of commerce. Entire consignments disappear while we're looking the other way.

Sometimes, you can spot the tobacco industry a mile off. It's brazen, but effective. A bottle-blonde girl from Eastern Europe sidles up to suited men at conferences, purring seductively. She actively targets whose backs to rest her hand on: she knows which companies they work for; she knows what papers they have written; she knows the arguments they make for tobacco control. But rather worryingly, she also knows what arguments they raised in confidential meetings, and what advice they gave in restricted-access documents.

And, so, it's understandable that there is almost a sense of paranoia that pervades the circles in which tobacco control activists move. You'll notice their PowerPoint slides start with a big note: 'I have never received any funding from the tobacco industry.' And before they will engage meaningfully with you, they want assurances that you haven't either.

'While the industry is infrequently cited directly in articles (9%), frame sponsors with links to the industry, who articulate arguments favourable to the industry, are frequently quoted (in 70% of the articles),' writes Simon Fraser University research fellow Julia Smith in her piece *Death and taxes: Causes and policy responses to illicit tobacco*. 'These include consultancy firms commissioned by the industry, think tanks, etc. – all of which receive industry funding. Connections to the tobacco industry are rarely mentioned; these sources are presented as independent experts. Tobacco companies then cite these sources, fomenting the impression of consensus.'[1]

Perhaps nobody knows that big tobacco suffers from a trust deficit better than the industry itself. And so big tobacco itself notes in one of its internal corporate affairs presentations how it was advised by public relations firm Porter/Novelli to, 'Put your words in someone else's mouth . . . There will be times when the position you advocate, no matter how well framed and supported, will not be accepted by the public simply because you are who you are.'[2]

As a result, industry often uses fronts, proxies and (more recently) bots on social media to speak on its behalf.

Some older PMI documents call it the battle for a 'share of mind'. They are clear on what they call the success factors in corporate affairs: 'Have the best expertise on our side; effective use of consultants: lobbyists, door-openers, strategists, spin doctors.'[3]

Take Argentina as an example: the tobacco industry was faced with legislation aimed at banning tobacco advertising and restricting smoking in public places. They developed a strategy with media and advertising executives that would make it politically palatable for the President to veto the legislation. A whopping 129 articles appeared in newspapers and magazines – 105 of them favourable to the industry's arguments. The President vetoed the bill.[4]

Remember the earlier analysis I did on the media coverage after SARS had announced a tender for a traceability solution to mark cigarette packs? Only 13% argued in favour of a secure marking solution. The rest all advanced an industry line that sought to delay, derail or dilute SARS' efforts to better secure the tobacco supply chain. And yet every single expert agrees that traceability is the one key solution to curbing illicit tobacco – but you wouldn't know that, because that is not a message you would have read in the media.

Piling on the pressure in the media works. But it works even better if the arguments appear to come from seemingly independent voices and proxies.

Big tobacco frequently uses think-tanks as key proxies, which position themselves as independent thought leaders, but which typically do little more than regurgitate industry rhetoric.

There are multiple examples of this: BAT has been bankrolling the Institute of Economic Affairs,[5] a think-tank that has been lobbying heavily against measures designed to crack down on smoking – and which is ranked as one of the three least transparent organisations in the UK. Although not necessarily directly related to big tobacco, the institute has reportedly donated at least £166 000 to 30 members of Parliament, possibly securing a chance to speak directly to politicians.[6] Institute staff appear frequently in the media to criticise tobacco control legislation.[7] But perhaps more importantly, as one of their own staff members commented, 'When [Council for Tobacco Research] researchers found out that cigarettes were bad and it was better not to smoke, we didn't publicise that.'[8]

PMI agreed to produce an annual report about illicit tobacco (Project Star, and then Project Sun) as part of a $1,25 billion smuggling-related settlement with the EU. An evaluation of Project Star by the Tobacco Control Research Group found that the report was subjective, 'served the interests of PMI over those of the EU and its member states' and relied too heavily on their own surveys that were not independently verified.[9]

PMI also funded a series of reports by the Università Cattolica del Sacro Cuore in Milan, in an attempt to lend academic capital to the industry's efforts to represent regulation as the main driver of illicit tobacco. They failed to mention where their funding came from, creating the impression of broad independent support of the industry's arguments against something like plain packaging – when in fact it has been criticised as being neither independent nor objective.[10] (For what it's worth, these Transcrime reports, spanning everything from tobacco to money laundering and firearms trafficking, to gambling and theft of medicines from hospitals, are actually very comprehensive and detail-rich – I am not suggesting they lack value, just that the source of their funding should be kept in the back of your mind when you read them.)

The problem with this type of funding – from an agency and regulatory perspective – is that it works to spread (flawed) industry rhetoric.

The International Tax and Investment Centre – a non-profit research and educational organisation – was publicly rebuked by the WHO after having been sponsored by BAT and PMI, and subsequently promoting false information on behalf of the tobacco industry, and attempting to derail a WHO summit aimed at increasing taxes on cigarettes.[11] An ITIC report funded by PMI significantly overestimated illicit cigarette consumption in Hong Kong at 36% (more objectively assessed at between 8% and 15%.)[12] ITIC had to ask tobacco representatives to resign from its board, and now no longer accepts sponsorship contributions from tobacco companies.

In 1998 a New York Judge went so far as to place the Tobacco Institute and the Council for Tobacco Research under receivership,[13] following a government lawsuit accusing them of abusing their tax-exempt status by acting as tobacco-funded fronts that serve 'as propaganda arms of the industry'.

PR firm Burson-Marsteller's advice to the tobacco industry was clear: 'For the media and the public, the corporation will be one of the least credible sources of information. Both these audiences will turn to other experts to get an objective viewpoint. Developing third party support and validation for the basic messages of the corporation is essential. This support should ideally come from medical authorities, political leaders, union officials, relevant academics, fire and police officials, environmentalists, regulators.'[14]

It is simple, really. As the industry's other long-time public relations firm Hill & Knowlton observed, 'There is only one problem – confidence, and how to establish it; public assurance, and how to create it.'[15]

A growing number of academic institutions have now introduced policies not to accept tobacco industry funding (or funding from foundations primarily funded by the industry). This makes the tobacco industry somewhat unique among legal industries (except maybe for the arms industry) in being subject to formal policies of exclusion from research.[16]

A number of reports that are frequently quoted in the media when it comes to tobacco control arguably suffer from a credibility gap simply because they are funded by the industry, raising questions about their objectivity – including Project Star, Project Sun and various publications by KPMG (BAT is a key long-time client).[17] This does not mean these reports necessarily inherently lack value – simply that they are likely to take lines and advance arguments in line with industry views, and should be read in that context.

I am both guilty of quoting from industry-backed documents, and ambivalent about it. Sometimes, the only source of data for a country or on a specific issue is an industry-funded report, and many of the industry-backed reports are undeniably beautifully crafted. Our colleagues in tobacco control urge us not to quote them, not to give them credibility. They urge us, instead, to only use academic estimates that may well be more accurate and based on objective transparent methodologies – but that are often as much as a decade old, and are frequently unavailable for the countries we are researching. The simple fact is that oftentimes the only sources we have are the ones put out by industry. It remains something of a conundrum for me, and one that I can only solve with an element of pragmatism that tries to weave together a story that accommodates both industry and academic versions, triangulating what industry tells us with a heavy dose of scepticism and whatever other data may be available.

It's not just industry-backed research that should have us worried, though. Even seemingly independent op-eds and other editorial pieces become problematic with the wide-spread use of ghost writers.

According to the Tobacco Control Research Group at the University of Bath, Reynolds ran a ghost writing programme which let it review scientific research before being submitted for publication; in Washington tobacco lobbyists were ghost writing letters for governors to send to the Food and Drug Administration; the USA's Tobacco Institute recommended using ghost writers for newspaper articles; consultants recommended ghost writing to BAT to portray the company as 'responsible'; and Philip Morris used ghost writers as part of its Chesterfield advertising campaign.[18]

The Center for Tobacco Control's Dr Stella Bialous explains that: 'By attempting to control information and surround itself with allegedly 'independent' expertise (and exploiting the fact that many parties are still building capacity to address implementation), the industry is attempting to dominate the agenda and distract from the steps required for implementation of the (Illicit Trade) Protocol.'[19]

More work is needed to create awareness of industry tactics, and the risk of NGOs, research bodies and other agencies giving legitimacy to an otherwise tainted industry. And far more work is needed to encourage journalists and policy makers to be more critical of research and studies funded by the tobacco industry or its proxies.

By accepting donations or sponsorships from the industry, they contribute to crafting a veneer of legitimacy for an industry that has repeatedly been linked to dirty tricks and illicit trade.

(The TobaccoTactics website maintains an updated list of organisations acting as proxies for the tobacco industry.[20] It's well worth a visit.)

Of course, proxies are not limited just to think-tanks. Increasingly, as the Tobacco Research Control Group reports, we are seeing big tobacco turn to 'astroturfing'.[21]

'Astroturfing' is the creation of a fake grassroots movement, where the agenda and strategy is controlled by a hidden company or organisation behind the scenes. ('Astroturfing' being a play on the fake Astro-Turf grass that is simply rolled out for instant effect.) It is a typical third-party technique: the use of front groups pretending to be voicing their own opinions, while acting at somebody else's behest.

Think about something like the Alliance of Australian Retailers. The alliance purports to represent 'the owners of your local corner stores, milk bars, newsagents and service stations' and wants to 'make the voices of small retailers heard'. It only very recently disclosed its tobacco industry connections, and originally simply presented itself as a grassroots, small business campaign – which it wasn't. Internal tobacco industry documents revealed that the alliance was in fact set up and run by the tobacco industry to lobby against plain packaging, with the director of PMI's corporate affairs office being instrumental in its establishment and day-to-day running, and with PMI, BAT and Imperial reportedly contributing more than $5 million between them to fund the campaign. The campaign objective was to 'seek a change in policy such that there is no introduction of "generic packaging" into the Australian market'. A former press secretary of a leading Australian member of Parliament appears to have been working for the alliance, lobbying MPs against the tobacco reforms, earning more than $20 000 a month.

The Australian campaign was ruthlessly targeted: TCG, the PR firm behind it, said the campaign needed to 'Build concern among the decision makers that the campaign will not cease, is likely to increase and will extract a political cost . . . the campaign will keep damaging their political standing unless they change their position . . . the campaign needs to repeatedly take [then-PM] Rudd off message and reinforce prejudices about him being superficial, making policy-on-the-go . . . the campaign needs to be edgier and stronger than any considered by tobacco companies in recent times.'[22]

We see a similar pattern repeated in the USA, where extracts from an internal tobacco industry memorandum documents how and why it set up the Consumer Tax Forum in the US: 'The experience of the last few years has shown that the excise tax problem needs to be approached using more inter-industry organization. The Forum's prime task is to create an atmosphere which will make it difficult to enact new excise taxes. This can only come about if lawmakers understand they will have to pay a political price for these actions. As a complement to direct lobbying activities, the Forum can also provide the tobacco industry with a most effective means of persuasion with those policy makers who seem to believe there is no end to the amount of excise taxes which can be imposed.'[23]

In South Africa big tobacco's now-defunct body TISA quietly funded a #takebackthetax campaign aimed at raising public support for the fight against illicit tobacco ostensibly being made by their smaller competitors;[24] BAT launched its #keepit100 campaign which sought to gain public support against illicit tobacco,[25] and JTI their #handsoffmychoices[26] campaign which argued that smoking was a personal choice, all nicely rounded off with a #notjustajob campaign which sought to protect employees in the tobacco sector. All of these tobacco industry-generated campaigns were launched within the space of a few weeks, and – curiously – just as government signalled its intention to regulate the industry more tightly, through tighter supply chain controls. But perhaps most importantly, not one of them explicitly noted that they had been set up and were being funded by big tobacco, instead creating the impression that they were independent grassroots campaigns. Astroturfing at its finest.

'The workers union urged them to act against illicit cigarettes, which they claimed would cost 11 000 jobs. They also ran a huge social media campaign #notjustajob, profiling tobacco workers. The campaigns were carefully crafted to conceal that they were funded by a big industry player. JTI's #handsoffmychoices is so sophisticated that it would be difficult for an ordinary citizen to tell that it was funded by the company. JTI's campaign is strikingly similar to TISA's #takebackthetax,' wrote journalists Masutane Modjadji and Kerry Cullinan on the website Daily Maverick.[27]

For the first time in our professional lives, we saw actual protest action outside the taxman's head office in Brooklyn, Pretoria. The protestors demanded that SARS act against illicit trade.[28] It was the perfect smokescreen, making it seem as if, somehow, the illicit trade in tobacco would cost thousands of jobs.

As an aside: you may have noticed how media coverage at the time suggested that 72 000 people in the South African tobacco industry stood to lose their jobs because of the escalation of illicit trade. Well, curiously, it turns out BAT only employs around 2 187 people in the country. The rest of the 70 000 includes what BAT itself calls 'indirect and induced' numbers,[29] which essentially includes the cashier at the fuel station who rings up your pack of cigarettes – making their numbers a bit of a stretch.

It was rather opportune timing from an industry perspective, because the protest action outside SARS coincided with the world's largest tobacco harm reduction conference being held in Cape Town at the same time. The media focused on what many suspect was simply a staged protest, drowning out nearly all of the other media coverage around an event that filled Cape Town's convention centre (and that was in fact far more deserving of media coverage).

Perhaps the most concerning example of these fronting practices, however, is the widespread concern around the independence of a secure marking system originally created by big tobacco. Codentify was developed as part of the obligations imposed on PMI under its agreement to settle smuggling related charges in the EU (that would be the same agreement that saw PMI having to pay compensation to the EU to the tune of $1,25 billion for the smuggling of its packs). It creates a code (really just an alpha-numeric number) that is printed directly onto packs during manufacturing, so – if you know how to read it – it could in theory tell you who made the pack.[30] PMI subsequently licensed it for use by all of the big tobacco companies.

But Codentify had a small problem. Under the new global Illicit Trade Protocol, countries are required to introduce a traceability solution for tobacco products. And – importantly – that traceability solution has to be *independent* from the tobacco industry. Codentify was clearly not independent from the industry – it was developed *by* tobacco companies, *for* tobacco companies. So, once the Illicit Trade Protocol comes into operation, tobacco packs would need to be marked with *another* traceability solution that did not have its genesis in the tobacco industry itself.

Around this time, Codentify was sold to Impala, who effectively rebranded it as an offering under a new company, Inexto, also owned by Impala (albeit, they told me, in the process adding some bells and whistles). Inexto was founded in 2016 – just before Codentify was acquired. At the time when Impala bought Codentify, it seems to have already owned its own company specialising in authentication and traceability solutions (which, their website says, included traceability solutions for tobacco products). Codentify as a solution was however not simply absorbed into the existing entity. An entirely new legal entity was created to house the product, one that could, on the face of it, compete for business with Impala's existing holdings.

Impala now owns two 'identity and security' companies: Inexto, and Arjo Solutions. The CEO of Arjo is also the Chairman of Inexto.

Some media reports have suggested that Codentify may have been sold for 1 Swiss Franc, despite a claimed development cost of €400 million.[31] This remains an unverified claim and, when asked for comment, Inexto vehemently denied it, saying that the purchase of the technology by Impala was a multi-million Euro transaction, and that these reports are false allegations propagated as part of a concerted attempt by some of their competitors to discredit them and their technology.

But why was Codentify sold in the first place? Well, that depends on who you ask. Industry critics claim the sale was simply a tactical move, so that the tobacco companies could continue to use their own traceability solution. By selling it, and rebranding it, one could argue the tobacco industry was simply trying to ensure that its own traceability solution could be touted as being 'independent' enough, effectively still leaving the foxes guarding the hen house.

The inventors of Codentify have all moved from PMI to Inexto as part of the sale. The key staff at Inexto are apparently all ex-tobacco industry employees and their new office is right down the street from its progenitor, PMI.[32] Inexto confirms as much, saying that the purchase of the Codentify assets was conditional upon the transfer of competent personnel familiar with the technology.

A Twitter account was opened in Inexto's name in January 2017. Twice the account tweeted a link to a Wikipedia page titled 'Codentify" that is candid about Codentify's links to big tobacco. What does that say about just how 'independent' Codentify really is?[33]

I find it difficult to see the Inexto solution for tobacco as anything other than a transmogrified version of Codentify, which was developed by the tobacco industry, for the tobacco industry. (Inexto disagrees, saying, 'The tobacco industry has no equity interest in, governance, or control of Inexto. The commercial interests of Inexto in relation to the tobacco industry are arms-length and of a supplier-customer relationship in both form and substance.')

To what extent does the Inexto solution technically differ from its progenitor Codentify? We really don't know. Is the new Inexto solution robust enough to reassure us that it is truly independent from the tobacco industry? Inexto says it is. I'm not so sure.

I'll pause here to make a quick point about Inexto as a company:

I am not suggesting that the Inexto solutions inherently lack value – by all accounts they run a slick show with their other traceability solutions for commodities like watches, pharma, spare parts and beverages. I am simply arguing that other traceability solutions – that do not come with the same challenges from an independence perspective, and that have a proven track record of curbing illicit trade – may be more suitable for cigarettes in particular; and that governments need to be extremely careful in assessing whether Inexto's solutions are, in fact, sufficiently independent considering the solution's genesis.

Perhaps industry expert Michael Eads explains it best: 'The problem with the industry digital codes is that they generate it, have access to it and we have no way of knowing how they are securing them from a storage perspective – and the codes could simply be loaded in bulk to a flash drive straight from a production line, making them easy to copy and clone.'[34]

Ultimately, then, the Inexto cigarette marking and traceability solution – whether offered by Inexto itself, or by one of its licensees, suffers from at least two challenges: Proving that its tobacco marking and traceability solution is technically superior to that offered under Codentify, and has remedied the various constraints noted in respect of Codentify; and establishing itself as sufficiently independent from the tobacco industry to assure the watching public that we have not made the fox watch the hen house. How it goes about doing just this remains to be seen.

It's not just Inexto we should be keeping an eye on, though – evidence suggests that companies like BAT have other ways of getting their 'digital verification solutions' through the door (but still using the same underlying Codentify / Inexto solution). BAT's International Solutions Engagement Manager for Global Supply Chain Tracking and Verification, noted in a leaked email to BAT Kenya: 'Following the launch by the Kenya Revenue Authority of the tender that clearly favoured SICPA [a system BAT was opposed to], we agreed the use of

FractureCode (FCC) to support you in fighting/amending/cancelling this tender. It is worth noting that not using a third party such as FCC to respond to the tender is likely to severely reduce our ability to shape events and prevent SICPA from winning.' Documents suggest that BAT had 'purchased' the tender on FractureCode's behalf, had commissioned FractureCode as a consultant to represent them at a KRA question and answer session, and had drafted a letter on behalf of FractureCode to be sent to the Commissioner General of the KRA.[35]

It's hard for any government to compete against the sheer deluge of pro-industry propaganda, fuelled by their considerable public relations spending[36] across the spectrum of tobacco control, and makes for a fundamentally unfair playing field.

And the disparity is only growing: we know that, aside from using traditional proxies like think-tanks and academic institutions, tobacco companies have also started going a bit more high-tech in their onslaught, with the use of online bots on social media.[37]

A study by researchers at San Diego State University into tobacco-related tweets found that 70% of the 200 000 tweets analysed was produced by bots. And despite the fact that these accounts were not being run by actual people, 59% were tweets about personally using electronic cigarettes.[38] The robots, it seems, really are taking over.

12. Hashtags, headlines and Ipsos

The hashtags and headlines war played out perfectly in South Africa. To recap, the very short version:[1] Big tobacco's industry body in South Africa, the Tobacco Institute of Southern Africa, commissioned market research company Ipsos to conduct research into illicit trade in the country.

(I'll add a big disclaimer here: Ipsos is a well-respected and well-known name in market research. But – just based on the other research they've published on their website – I suspect that they may not be illicit trade specialists, which might unwittingly expose them to the mercy of their briefing client for context. We don't know what brief they were given, but the outcome of their research on this particular issue is contentious, if nothing else.)

TISA only published minor excerpts of the research – they showed the world some PowerPoint slides, very explicitly fingering their smaller competitors, but without publishing the report itself, or explaining in any detail how the findings were come by.[2] We still haven't seen the actual study. TISA hasn't released it, and it is nowhere to be found on the Ipsos website. What was the brief TISA gave Ipsos? We don't know. What methodology did Ipsos use? We don't really know. What did the Ipsos report actually conclude? We're not really sure.

In subsequent court papers, one of the smaller producers claimed that Ipsos sub-contracted the research to another company. This company in turn retained several individuals, who were paid R100

12. Hashtags, headlines and Ipsos

(around $6) per interview. It was further claimed that these individuals then sub-contracted the interviews – and based on an affidavit I saw, allegedly with an instruction to 'only sample shops selling cheap cigarettes'. They ended up covering around 2% of shops in South Africa (which strikes me as perhaps not being a sufficiently representative sample). The woman conducting the research later said in court papers that her research was 'skewed and not a fair representation of what is happening in the cigarette market.'[3]

The report seems to have simplistically defined an illicit cigarette as anything that is sold at a price lower than the tax rate, which poses a few problems: this is not how illicit cigarettes are defined internationally; it ignores an entire body of research on how best to actually calculate the prevalence of illicit packs on a market; selling cigarettes below the tax rate is not illegal in South Africa; and – far more interestingly – according to Ipsos itself some big tobacco packs are also being sold below the tax rate, including BAT's Peter Stuyvesant, Rothmans and Dunhill. If indeed sales below the tax rate are indicative of a pack of cigarettes being illicit, then what on earth are BAT's packs doing on the list?

TISA is quoted as saying that the research was peer reviewed by experts and academics. Maybe so, but I haven't been able to track those experts down. When the Bhekisisa Centre for Health Journalism asked them for the data they said they'd be happy to disclose it to organisations 'who are qualified to analyse it and who will guarantee its confidentiality', but then reportedly refused to hand the data over to what has to be one of the leading experts anywhere in the world, Professor Corné van Walbeek.[4]

(I asked TISA about this. They said they had no comment.)

Anyway, on the back of that Ipsos report – which I'd read with a heavy dose of scepticism – there was a sudden flurry of activity in the South African media. And on the back of it, big tobacco insisted SARS take action against their competitors; and used it to convince supermarket chains not to stock their competitors' products.

Why were our newsfeeds being inundated with stories about illicit cigarettes? Why that sudden deluge of headlines and hashtags and billboards next to the highway about tax money going up in smoke?[5] Hardly a day goes by in South Africa now without some mention of the scourge of illicit tobacco which has suddenly emerged as a big bogeyman facing the South African economy.

In the wake of that report we have also been told that South Africa is now unique in the world in having an illicit brand as its best-selling cigarette – 'R10 illegal cigarette pack becomes SA's top seller', the headline shouts.[6] We're told that steps really should be taken urgently to curtail the success of the black market brand in question. Except, when powerhouse analytics firm Nielsen went in to assess the situation, guess who they say actually held the best-selling cigarettes – in both volume and value? BAT. And in the same period where they claimed to be suffering heavy losses, their sales actually increased by more than 41%.[7] Sounds like little less than alarmist scaremongering to me – a tactic to shut out the competition.

Why this sudden flood of stories in the media about illicit cigarettes?

The answer is timing.

That Ipsos report, and the #takebackthetax and #notjustajob and #keepit100 and #handsoffmychoices campaigns, the call to act against the smaller guys – all seem to be part of a broader industry tactic aimed at preserving the market dominance and continued existence of big tobacco – and they're but the tip of an iceberg of manipulation.

Because 'the art of a magician is not found in the simple deception, but in what surrounds it, the construction of a reality which supports the illusion', according to Jim Steinmeyer (an American designer of illusions).

Yussuf Saloojee of South Africa's National Council Against Smoking has warned: 'The days when they can march in with their colonial arrogance and treat Africa like some lawless frontier are over. Africa has enough problems without multinational corporations undermining the stability of our governments and national policies.'[8]

Beyond hashtags and headlines, there is also the story of how big tobacco puts lipstick on that pig of theirs (which is not illegal, of course, but it's still a pig).

13. Lipstick on a pig

Big tobacco has mastered the art of greenwashing,[1] allowing it to use its corporate social responsibility activities to portray it as a responsible, responsive industry.

With stricter regulation of tobacco advertising, promotion and sponsorship, tobacco companies have simply increased their corporate social responsibility spending (like the controversial £3,8 million BAT gave to Nottingham University to set up the International Centre for Corporate Social Responsibility).[2]

At one point, Philip Morris was spending $115 million a year on charity – and $150 million on an advertising campaign to tell us about it.[3]

And even though the numbers may sound impressive in nominal terms, it generally amounts to only around 0,3% of their profits (and quite logically tend to support projects that are in the best interest of tobacco companies, like entrepreneurship programmes for young tobacco growers).[4]

As PMI noted in one of its internal corporate affairs documents, 'We need to get ahead of the curve on public expectations of a corporation. That will reduce the risks of lawsuits and improve our standing, when we are sued, as a "responsible corporation".'[5]

PMI reportedly spends the lion's share of its corporate social responsibility handouts in Indonesia (around $6 million a year) and the Philippines ($1,8 million a year), which are also its largest cigarette markets in south-east Asian countries. All governments in the ASEAN region, except Brunei and Thailand, reportedly receive contributions (monetary or otherwise) from the tobacco industry.[6]

I'd happily argue that industry-sponsored CSR activities do little real good, with little apparent sense of the realities of the countries they operate in.

They'll make loans available to farmers to buy oxen to better cultivate tobacco farm-land – but the oxen cost $320 each, in a country where the average tobacco farmer earns $200 a year. They'll punt the development of new barns that could reduce the wood used for curing of tobacco by 50% in Malawi, but because they cost $700 each in a country where 65% of the population lives on less than $2 a day, they end up being installed in only 1 000 of the 400 000 tobacco farms in Malawi.[7]

In the Philippines many government departments have drawn up Codes of Conduct banning government officials from receiving or supporting industry-related CSR activities, but industry still contributes to local government through foundations and the American Chamber of Commerce.[8]

Many other initiatives simply do not adequately compensate for the damage caused by the industry: More than 600 million trees are cut down every year to cure tobacco leaves, and another 9 million trees to make matches. BAT has been accused of being responsible for 30% of total annual deforestation in Bangladesh, allegedly cutting down 200 000 hectares a year. The industry's reforestation programmes are said to be having little discernible impact on deforestation: the trees planted are often not indigenous (the eucalyptus trees used by industry are thirsty, absorbing significantly more water than indigenous trees, and drastically reducing water tables). The reforestation is arguably not intended to replenish the forests destroyed by the industry – they are planted because industry needs them for tobacco curing. JTI's tree planting project is said to only compensate for around 6% of the annual cost of tobacco-related deforestation in Malawi and Tanzania, costing the two countries an estimated $8,1 million a year. The estimated benefit believed to accrue to tobacco companies from child labour and deforestation in general reportedly jointly comes to more than 50 times the amount they spend on their CSR activities in these two countries.[9]

And their CSR efforts do nothing to curb the scourge of litter – the industry's cigarette butts leave 175 tons of waste behind every year and are responsible for 38% of all beach waste. Cigarette packaging waste weighs 2 tons a year (more than plastic bottles, at 1,8 tons.) The manufacturing process leaves behind 6 million tons of non-recyclable nicotine-containing waste, and another 45 million tons of solid waste. And the tobacco industry is responsible for 5% of all global greenhouse gas emissions – the equivalent of 1,5 million cars.[10]

And as with most other industry tactics, big tobacco's greenwashing works. As one commentator notes, 'Tobacco industry association with social and environmental responsibility may weaken opposition by making it politically more difficult to criticize tobacco companies.'[11]

Of course, it doesn't always work, leaving the industry to turn to another diversionary tactic: creating an even bigger bogeyman, arguing that regulatory and enforcement efforts would be better spent on something else rather than on the tobacco industry.

So, for instance, the tobacco industry embraced an unlikely ally: the anti-AIDS cause, with an elaborate campaign to use concern for HIV to distract from concerns around tobacco-related illness and tobacco regulation.

Indeed, for a time, big tobacco argued that HIV/AIDS posed a far bigger risk to our communities than smoking does.

That the industry got around to this startling point of view is perhaps unsurprising. As we see in a report prepared for BAT by public relations firm Campbell Johnson a few years earlier, the PR firm was actually arguing that cancer was 'an essential ingredient of life'. The document noted that '. . . with a general lengthening of the expectation of life we really need something for people to die of. The argument is obviously not one that the tobacco industry could use publicly. But its weight in perpetuating people's taste for smoking as an enjoyable if risky habit, should not be under-estimated . . .'[12]

As the international community began working on the Framework Convention on Tobacco Control the industry sought to divert attention and question the World Health Organization's priorities. PMI launched its Fair Play programme, urging AIDS organisations to demand more government support, suggesting that too much energy was being funnelled into the anti-tobacco drive which it argued should more appropriately be directed towards anti-HIV campaigns. PMI also sponsored a tennis tour to support HIV groups. A representative of a BAT subsidiary, eager to discredit a major anti-smoking conference in Argentina, proposed the following strategy: 'Being the disease of the century and a preventable disease, AIDS should be "public enemy no. 1" because of its terminal consequences at every age.'[13] He argued that AIDS was the sole matter capable of eclipsing the conference.[14]

Julia Smith from the Global Tobacco Control Program commented how 'HIV was legitimately so terrifying that it was also a good health issue to put up and say, "Wait, this has to be the urgent priority, as opposed to looking at tobacco control".'[15]

Not too bad a thing then that we are already seeing many HIV groups now disavowing tobacco funding as what they call a 'pact with the devil'.

Instead of condemning the tobacco industry, our governments are glossing over their appalling behaviour with awards as 'employers of choice', or other frivolous awards like 'Dream Company', 'Highest Income Taxpayer' and 'Export Champion'.[16]

When all is said and done, CSR activities by tobacco companies amount to little more than putting lipstick on a pig. That may not be illegal, but the way they have captured our policy makers should be.

Vintage big tobacco ad from the Stanford University catalogue

Date: 1953
Brand: Chesterfield
Manufacturer: Liggett & Myers Tobacco Company
Campaign: Pseudoscience
Quote: No adverse effects on the nose, throat and sinuses of the group from smoking Chesterfield.
Comment: The industry-sponsored research institutes and scientific symposia developed favourable propaganda and dubious methodologies. Health claims were made on the basis of these so-called studies, as in this Chesterfield ad that suggested that nose, throat, and accessory organs were not adversely affected after a six-month period of medical observation (including X-rays) by ear, nose, and throat specialists.[17]

PART 3

Spies, hitmen and a silent coup

14. Captured

'We're starting to realise that magicians have a lot of implicit knowledge about how we perceive the world around us because they have to deceive us in terms of controlling attention, exploiting the assumptions we make when we do and don't notice a change in our environment.'
  – *Psychology professor and magician Richard Wiseman*

Beyond proxies and bots and lipstick on pigs, perhaps the single biggest asset the tobacco industry has is the power it has over government agencies – its ability to administratively capture agencies. In an internal corporate affairs presentation, the industry itself notes that 'all politics are local'.[1]

In South Africa, the term 'state capture' has come to mean a particular thing, the apparent takeover of some of the highest offices of government to serve the direct interests of outsiders. But as I outline below, the way I use capture in this book is a bit different.

While some types of manipulation are directed toward changing how existing laws, rules, or regulations are implemented, capture, as defined within the context of this book, refers to efforts to influence *how* – and oftentimes *if* – those laws, rules, and regulations are formed and implemented.

It is engineered to foster a relationship of trust and to position big tobacco as a trusted partner. It sees the industry exploiting the limited capacity at customs and law enforcement agencies and stepping in to fill the void with offers of assistance that are often nothing more than self-serving. It sees government agencies identifying with the interests of the very industry they are supposed to regulate, becoming tied to the tobacco industry with golden chains.

As with many things in life, it's a matter of degrees: at what point does somebody go from being independent, to engaging at an arm's length, to becoming unduly influenced, to being captured and becoming virtually indistinct from the very person they are meant to be regulating?

Harvard's Professor Malcolm Sparrow summarises the dilemma as follows: 'Regulators, under unprecedented pressure, face a range of demands, often contradictory in nature: be less intrusive – but be more effective; be kinder and gentler – but don't let the bastards get away with anything; focus your efforts – but be consistent; process things quicker – and be more careful next time; deal with important issues – but do not stray outside your statutory authority; be more responsive to the regulated community – but do not get captured by industry.'[2]

It is a potentially slippery slope in the best of cases, but when faced with an industry that has a veritable playbook on how to influence and capture agencies, it becomes even more so.

Capture is nothing new: In 1624, the Catholic Church banned the use of tobacco in holy places, considering sneezing from using snuff too close to sexual pleasures. In 1692 five Spanish friars were found smoking during a church service and were sentenced to death – they remain entombed today behind the walls of the Santiago de Compostela in Spain. All of this changed in 1724 when Pope Benedict XIII learned to smoke and repealed all rules against smoking. Suddenly, an entirely new Catholic market had opened up. Target the right decision-maker, and Bob's your uncle.

Capture ultimately results in governments losing the requisite professional scepticism they need to remain objective in applying their minds to regulation and policy formulation, instead defaulting to rhetoric that is unduly favourable to industry.

The tobacco industry has been relentless and effective at penetrating government and anti-tobacco structures over the years. You need look no further than the European Tobacco Products Directive, which was heavily influenced in the end by industry lobbyists, who were effective in watering down many key provisions.[3]

In an investigative piece, the news agency Reuters found that PMI was running a secretive campaign to block or weaken the global anti-smoking Directive. 'Confidential company documents and interviews with PMI employees reveal an offensive that stretches from the Americas to Africa to Asia, from hardscrabble tobacco fields to the halls of political power, in what may be one of the broadest corporate lobbying efforts in existence.'

The Guardian has written extensively about how PMI seems to have picked up key government delegates from a tobacco control conference in a white minivan, for meetings at the hotel where PMI executives were staying.[4] Little surprise, then, that the tobacco industry managed to exert a significant amount of influence over the policies that ended up being adopted in the EU.

Initial policy proposals referred to the industry abusing international trade and investment rules and made a call to exclude tobacco from international trade agreements. The industry succeeded in having all references to the industry's 'abuse of rules' deleted, and to exclude any provisions aimed at treating the tobacco industry differently. Initial policy proposals referenced 'tobacco industry interference'. The industry succeeded in having all references to 'industry interference' removed. Initial policy proposals included a binding dispute resolution mechanism. The industry succeeded in international trade being excluded from the dispute mechanism. Initial policy proposals stated that the right to health takes precedence over any laws related to tobacco use, and that there is no fundamental right to tobacco use. Industry succeeded in having this watered down, so the policy now simply acknowledges that the implementation of the convention on tobacco control contributes to the achievement of health. PMI described the last day of the conference as a 'tremendous outcome'.

The industry's aggressive tactics have ensured that seven of the eight traceability solution providers in Europe have question marks hanging over their independence;[5] and governments are not a party to the traceability contracts, leaving the solution providers with no legal duty of care towards government.

Customs and excise agencies almost invariably have limited capacity. Because they generally contribute relatively little to a tax agency's overall revenue collections (sometimes as little as 2%) they are often last in line when it comes to modernisation initiatives or budget allocations, and there are simply far fewer excise experts than there are, for instance, VAT experts (VAT law gets taught at law school – customs and excise not).

An agency like SARS is no different: it has a handful of excise officers scattered around the country, and even fewer policy specialists at head office. They are – for the most part – generally competent, good people. But they simply do not have the capacity they need to look beyond the superficial. SARS has never made excise a priority. It has traditionally been understaffed, misunderstood by executives and generally left to its own devices. They essentially operate the same way they did 20 years ago, whilst the rest of SARS has moved into and embraced the digital age. They have historically struggled to develop tobacco-specific risk profiles that would allow them to accurately direct their enforcement officers to find non-compliance, and have generally had access to little real data – that doesn't come from industry – on the size and prevalence of illicit trade. They have no means to distinguish between licit and illicit packs found on the market. And so it comes as little surprise that they might turn to the company that is ostensibly responsible for as much as 27% of all of its excise revenues for help.[6] A company that is known to have operated with impunity elsewhere.

And companies like BAT know only too well how to play to our decision makers, explicitly noting in one of their internal documents: 'Government officials responsible for tobacco excise and VAT planning and control . . . should be identified and sufficient regular contact maintained while Ministerial (Government and Opposition) contacts should also be maintained to ensure that the Company is well placed to have its views taken into consideration. . . . Such relations should establish BAT as the Company to which Government will turn when they need advice and assistance upon any aspect of excise taxation . . .'[7]

I recently came across this statement: 'Allegations that the tobacco industry cannot be trusted are absurd, given that we collect more than $32 billion in excise tax for governments across the world.'[8] It came from the Vice President of Fiscal Affairs of one of the big tobacco companies. I'd argue that the distrust is well-earned.

An appreciation of the economic power of tobacco is nothing new: Napoleon III, when asked to ban smoking replied: 'This vice brings in one hundred million francs in taxes every year. I will certainly forbid it at once – as soon as you can name a virtue that brings in as much revenue.'

What this has done is to make our customs and law enforcement agencies highly susceptible to administrative capture. Its main source of information on illicit trade – what it looks like and where to find it – is big tobacco. It's easy to understand why: it's a most convenient source, offered by somebody they have traditionally developed a close relationship with.

What we're seeing in South Africa is a pattern we've seen the world over, where capture includes the shaping of an environment where government is set up to view big tobacco as a partner in the fight against illicit trade; where effort goes into convincing the agency that it shares a common enemy with big tobacco ('illicit trade'); where the agency is convinced to implicitly trust big tobacco rhetoric; and where the agency perhaps loses its professional scepticism and stops critically assessing the arguments and evidence put before it by big tobacco.

The risk of capture in relation to the tobacco industry cannot be over-stated. It's about substituting government's objectivity and duty of care with pre-packaged industry rhetoric – where the industry manages to use its power and relationships to bend and sway government's position to more closely resemble that of industry. It is happening all over the world and is one of the key reasons that governments the world over are failing in their efforts to curb contraband.

'State capture is more systematic than plain vanilla (banknote-stuffed envelope) corruption, which seeks to exploit existing opportunities. State capture goes one better by changing regulations and laws to work in one's favour,' writes David Pilling in the Financial Times.[9]

When capture works, it results in virtually incestuous partnerships between tax agencies and big tobacco, in giving industry access to law enforcement structures and intelligence on competitors, in trusting the industry to secure its own supply chains, in relying solely on industry-sponsored research, and in the formulation of policy positions that favour big tobacco.

When governments no longer write their own legislation, relying instead on the very industry being regulated, the capture is complete: When the Director of the US Joint Committee on Taxation was asked how a $50 billion tax break for tobacco companies was written into a US tax bill, he answered simply, 'The industry wrote it and submitted it, and we just used their language.'[10] In Kenya BAT issued a press release noting how 'The law was actually drafted by us but the government is to be congratulated on its wise actions.'[11]

In Uzbekistan, their influence was even more astonishing, after BAT's Chairman promised the Uzbek President 'a team of excise experts to advise and assist the Uzbek authorities'. As a result, research published in the American Journal of Public Health shows how: 'BAT thoroughly redesigned the tobacco taxation system in Uzbekistan. It secured (1) a reduction of approximately 50% in the excise tax on cigarettes, (2) an excise system to benefit its brands and disadvantage those of its competitors (particularly Philip Morris), and (3) a tax stamp system from which it hoped to be exempted, because this would likely facilitate its established practice of cigarette smuggling and further its competitive advantage.'[12]

In South Africa, big tobacco's close relationship with law enforcement agencies secured it many favours – documents at my disposal show how they got police support to have their own radio frequency allocated;

paying police sources for intelligence on competitors and their finances; providing police with the list of questions to be asked of suspects; etc. The cosy relationship also meant that BAT's trucks were given a police escort to safeguard them against hijackings,[13] a concession not extended to other manufacturers. Who was paying for those escorts? That's right, you and I were. (I'm assuming you pay your taxes.)

Even prosecutors – who are meant to be independent and impartial – had fallen prey to the TISA magic in South Africa. One of the documents I received from a source notes how a senior prosecutor instructed other prosecutors that 'Only senior prosecutors and control prosecutors who have attended the TISA presentation on illicit cigarettes be permitted to authorise withdrawal of cases.'[14] As a one-time prosecutor, I fully appreciate the need for prosecutors to receive subject-matter training, but TISA does not represent the tobacco industry in South Africa – it represents big tobacco. And given what we now know about TISA I am not convinced that it would necessarily have been the most objective of briefings. (To make matters worse, the person tasked to give the presentations did not even work for TISA; he worked for FSS, BAT's security company.)

One TISA-hosted illicit trade conference apparently saw more than 100 delegates from 23 African countries being hosted in South Africa's swanky Bantry Bay. Many of them were from law enforcement agencies. When somebody asked why the local manufacturers weren't present, he was asked to leave the conference. The problem with these big tobacco-funded conferences is that they seem to be focused on crafting alarmist rhetoric that further propagates big tobacco interests, making unfounded, exaggerated claims – like apparently accusing the independent manufacturers of child labour (with no evidence of that happening in South Africa, although ironically loads of evidence of it applying to big tobacco in places like Italy),[15] or claiming that South Africa had lost R14 billion in one year to illicit cigarettes (false), and completely ignoring big tobacco's own dirty hands.

Our agencies and policy makers are influenced by alarmist rhetoric that actively and aggressively suggests that smuggled cigarettes make their way into the country in containers mixed with guns and weapons, or drugs, and that the profits from cheapies are being used to fund organised crime, prostitution, human trafficking and terrorism.[16] I had actually assumed this to be true. Turns out, this narrative is not necessarily borne out by the facts – at least not in South Africa. As best I can tell, not a single person convicted of smuggling cigarettes into the country has actually been found with guns, weapons or human trafficking victims in their consignments, or is in any way associated with terrorism. Not one.

Oftentimes the effects of administrative capture are so subtle you might miss it: A tender process simply does not get off the ground; the project manager gets distracted with red herrings; the agency is subtly nudged to walk away because it cannot afford to offend one of the country's biggest employers and taxpayers; and doubt is created about whether the agency can really expect to see the benefits it hopes to achieve from the introduction of a proposed policy. The silent coup has been completed. Why? Because these are good guys we trust.

We see it when industry drafts legislation on behalf of government (as happened in Kenya); when industry drives government policy to the extent that government actively encourages the tobacco industry to grow (in places like Indonesia and Zambia); when industry begins to dictate law enforcement activities (Australia); when industry holds the power to walk into a Customs Commissioner's office and successfully demand the cancellation of a traceability programme because it would inconvenience big tobacco (in one African example); and when industry gets virtually unfettered access to law enforcement resources that allows it to direct who is targeted (as it did in South Africa).

Tih Ntiabang, Regional Coordinator for Africa of the Framework Convention Alliance, says: 'In the past it used to be invisible interference, but today it is so shameful that it is so visible. They know they have this economic power. The budget of tobacco companies like BAT could be as much as the whole budget of the Africa region.'[17]

We see the silent coup in action when the industry secures the confidence of mid-level government employees responsible for audit or implementing new controls on tobacco products or a new traceability programme, resulting in delay after delay; when industry convinces governments to let it use its own questionable traceability system instead of an independent one; and when the larger industry players try to convince government to engage only with them, and not with smaller lower-cost producers.

The industry's activities are highly structured and targeted. Nothing the industry does is by chance. Their messaging, positioning and engagements are all calculated and strategic. They pre-empt agency positions and influence their thinking long before policy decisions even come up for discussion. They use media and personal relationships so subtly that agencies do not even realise they have been captured by industry rhetoric.

Where does this leave an agency like SARS?

As far back as 2007, SARS had signalled that it intended to introduce more appropriate measures to securely mark and track tobacco products. It publicly undertook to do so again in 2010, 2013, 2016, 2017 and 2018. It tried to launch a secure marking programme in 2019. Guess what? It's been delayed. Three times.

Have individuals at SARS been administratively captured by big tobacco? I'd be willing to bet on it. Not because its staff are corrupt or incompetent – they've simply been outplayed by a machinery that over time managed to effectively insinuate itself into the SARS excise management paradigm.

And it's not just SARS – it's the other law enforcement agencies, too.

The tobacco industry told us they had scientific evidence that smoking Chesterfields for ten years didn't cause any adverse effects. And most of the world believed them, because we'd become a captive audience. Their ads captured the world's attention, just like their targeted rhetoric continues to influence our agencies today.

Understanding capture is critical, because it explains why our customs agencies are seemingly being used as economic hitmen to take out smaller competitors, and why law enforcement agencies turn a blind eye to big tobacco's corporate espionage, and perhaps why our tax agencies often apply a light touch to auditing big tobacco. It very much explains why big tobacco's links to smuggling remain unbroken. And it explains why, for the most part, the tobacco supply chain remains almost entirely opaque, and – in many countries – with virtually no way to make sure that cigarettes end up where they are supposed to.

As Daily Maverick columnist Ivo Vegter aptly puts it: 'Despite the appearance of a hostile relationship, the tobacco industry and the government are partners in an unholy alliance. The industry is a massive cash cow for the government, and in return, it gets protection against upstart competition . . . if you think "illicit tobacco trade is a major problem", you've swallowed the spin of a monopoly industry that uses its cosy relationship with government to keep competition at bay.'[18]

15. Political patronage

'It is an unpalatable fact that growth in this industry will take place where governments are least hostile.'
  – South Africa's Medical Research Council[1]

At least part of the reason why big tobacco has managed to get away with some of its shenanigans is because it has pulled off something of a silent coup.

Any South African can tell you the value of political patronage. They'll tell you that it comes at some cost – buying power is not cheap, but once bought, you become virtual Teflon.

Much of big tobacco's success is attributable to the fact that it knows how to build a strong network of political patronage. The tobacco industry neatly explains their approach by way of a JTI corporate affairs presentation: 'Building allies across several ministries; developing the ability to influence the influencers; targeting their activities based on political power maps; finding the "right spin" in relationships with key reporters; making effective use of door openers and spin doctors; and developing one-liners that resonate with the public.'[2]

At the heart of the tobacco industry's success in thwarting regulation lies a simple truth: they are masters at playing politics. And how you play politics often lies in a selection or sometimes combination of four tactics: lobbying; making donations; making corrupt payments; or blackmailing politicians. One or more of these appear to be evident in the tobacco industry.

Lobbying is essentially about meeting the right person at the right time with the right arguments. Industry seems to be good at it: the EU's transparency register suggests that industry lobbyists get almost a hundred times more meetings with top EU Commission officials than trade unions do – 16 540, compared to 168.³

That kind of access – and buying patronage in general – comes at a cost: John Boehner – who went on to become the Speaker of the House of Representatives in the US – reportedly handed out tobacco industry cheques to other members in the house just before they were due to vote on a bill to abolish a $48 million subsidy for the tobacco sector. The subsidy stayed.⁴

NPR wrote an exposé on US politician Mitch McConnell, who they say has received more donations from tobacco companies than any other member of congress. McConnell is quoted as explaining his support of the tobacco industry in simple terms: 'Farming tobacco put shoes on kids' feet, it put dinner on the table.' But I'd be willing to bet his support perhaps has more to do with how the industry seems to have lined his pockets. He is reported to have received at least $650 000 in campaign contributions from tobacco, on top of $889 000 that was donated to his McConnell Center at the University of Louisville. And it wasn't just money – he apparently got tickets to NFL and NBA games and a Ringo Starr concert, 'top-quality brandy', and a 'beautiful ham'. Little wonder then that a Reynolds lobbyist calls him a 'special friend' of the industry.

McConnell wrote a letter to the White House chief of staff, saying, 'Many choose to attack the tobacco industry however, I have chosed [sic] to defend the people of this industry.' He reportedly stood up at a closed-door meeting of Republican senators and promised tobacco-backed TV ad campaigns for whoever vetoed an upcoming tobacco control bill; he opposed banning in-flight smoking; and opposed banning smoking in federal buildings on the basis that it singled out tobacco smoke over other carcinogens like aerosol cleaners (a statement that was reportedly crafted for him by the Tobacco Institute). When the Department of Justice accused tobacco companies of fraud and racketeering, McConnell introduced the Litigation Fairness Act to protect companies

15. Political patronage

from government lawsuits – legislation that was drafted with the help of tobacco company attorneys as part of a PMI lobbying plan. He has been criticised for moving beyond trying to brazenly influence the process, to being 'as close to an outright bribe as you could find' – as simple as politics for sale.

McConnell ended his thank you notes to tobacco lobbyists with, 'Please feel free to call on me whenever I may be of assistance to you.'[5]

An internal PMI memo makes big tobacco's thinking clear: 'In the end, candidates act in their own self-interest, so few who have taken our money in the past will stop taking it.'[6]

The tobacco industry spends $72 million a year just on lobbying against tax rate increases in the USA alone.[7] In 2017, Altria and Reynolds paid lobbyists $26 million to stop a tobacco tax bill in Montana – it worked. In the 2018 (non-presidential) US election cycle, the tobacco industry contributed more than $5,4 million in campaign donations alone.[8] And in the USA, 23 tobacco companies officially employ 174 lobbyists, who in any year make more than 185 representations to government agencies. PMI spends more than $5 million a year on lobbyists in the EU alone (more than any other corporation), including David Cameron's election strategist. In the space of six months their lobbyists claimed almost £1,25 million in expenses for their meetings with parliamentarians (making for some pretty expensive lunches).[9] Across Europe, 35 tobacco companies have an in-house lobbying capacity.

American comedian Jackie Mason had a point when he said, 'It is more profitable for your congressman to support the tobacco industry than your life.'[10]

The industry undoubtedly knows the power of lobbying and making political donations because this allows it to – in BAT's own words – 'continue to put forward its views to wider business and government bodies.'[11] This reasoning, as journalist Rob Rose notes, exposed it: the implication is that without 'donations', it wouldn't have the ear of government officials.

But it's not all lobbying and F1 tickets – there also appears to be some evidence of cases where power was bought corruptly. It has been reported that Reynolds paid bribes to politicians,[12] and PMI has admitted to making corrupt payments 'for the purpose of expediting administrative action,' including payments for tax rulings and to secure pro-industry legislation.[13]

PMI's then-Senior VP of Worldwide Regulatory Affairs said to its Board of Directors: 'Our goal is to help shape regulatory environments that enable our businesses to achieve their objectives. Our overall approach is to fight aggressively with all available resources, against any attempt, from any quarter, to diminish our ability to manufacture our products efficiently, and market them effectively. In short, we are very clear about our objective – an unyielding and aggressive defence of our rights to make and sell our products.'[14]

For the most part however, big tobacco has a myriad of legal ways that it exerts influence on politics, which do not involve outright corruption.

It's effective. As a *New York Times* editorial noted, 'With the tobacco industry under siege in recent years, New York State has offered cigarette manufacturers a legislative safety zone. Such a smoke-friendly atmosphere does not appear by accident. In fact, the tobacco industry, particularly Philip Morris, has been plying the state's lawmakers with gifts and goodies.'[15] It got so bad in New York that the Lobbying Commission hit PMI with the largest fine in commission history and forbade PMI's CEO from lobbying for three years.

In 1980, the Japanese tobacco market was controlled by a government owned monopoly. A 90% import tariff meant that international tobacco companies controlled less than 1,5% of the market. A PMI plan noted how it would use the US Special Trade Representative to place pressure on the Japanese government to increase market access – which included threatening Japan with sanctions if it did not accede to the US demands. They successfully convinced the Japanese government to lower the tariff on imported cigarettes from 90% to 20%. In the space of one year, the US government had achieved what the industry had not been able to do by itself in ten years. In the space of little over ten years, PMI cigarette sales in Japan increased from 4 billion to 44 billion. Within a month of Japan's decision South Korea and Thailand had both similarly opened their markets to US tobacco.[16]

Margaret Thatcher, then the UK's Prime Minister, reportedly visited Turkey to help PMI launch on the Turkish market.[17]

Reynolds and Altria donated $1,5 million to help celebrate the Trump inauguration. Which may partly explain why his vice president has been quoted as saying that 'smoking doesn't kill', notes a report in *The Guardian*.[18]

BAT reportedly acted against an MP in Uganda who sponsored a bill banning the sale of cheap single cigarettes. A letter informed him that the company would no longer be contracting with the 709 tobacco farmers in his region, rendering his support of the bill political suicide.[19]

In Kenya, BAT developed close ties with political leaders. When a tobacco competitor emerged, BAT itself drafted legislation that was passed by the Kenyan government, which encouraged farmers to sell tobacco leaf to BAT rather than competitors.[20]

We have seen how the British High Commissioner in Bangladesh helped BAT to fight a demand for £170 million in unpaid VAT; how the British ambassador in Panama intervened with authorities on BAT's behalf; and in Pakistan how the British High Commission lobbied the Minister of Finance on behalf of BAT to drop the government's plan to apply 85% pictorial health warnings on cigarette packs[21] – forcing the Foreign Office to issue guidelines to its staff that they may not engage with foreign governments on behalf of the tobacco industry, and forbidding officials from encouraging investment in the tobacco industry or providing any assistance in influencing local business policies on behalf of the tobacco industry.[22]

'This is a company currently under investigation by the UK's Serious Fraud Office over allegations of bribery in East Africa, so what on earth is a senior diplomat doing acting as its lobbyist?' asked Deborah Arnott, Chief Executive of health NGO Ash.[23] (At the time of writing this investigation was still ongoing.)

In Indonesia, VAT for all consumer products is charged at 10% – cigarettes are taxed at 8,7%; and a trade agreement with Pakistan secured duty free imports of tobacco. In the Philippines, PMI reportedly received a tax holiday for up to eight years, leaving it paying only 5% tax on gross income; it also received an exemption from duties and taxes on imported capital equipment and spare parts, material and supplies. Thailand has awarded tax exemption for native tobacco leaves; in Cambodia registered farmers producing more than 3 000 tons of tobacco leaf are exempt from export tax. Zambia actively encourages tobacco manufacturing, because of its economic reliance on the industry.[24] Lao's 25-year joint venture agreement with Imperial secured a preferential tax rate of 15%, foregoing government revenues to the value of $144 million, and the close relationship has meant that no action has been taken against Imperial for non-compliance with pictorial health warnings on its packs.[25]

Tobacco companies are legal businesses, plying a legitimate trade, but for governments to actually encourage their business – and give them preferential fiscal regimes to grow their business – is nothing short of staggering. Tobacco kills, and any government that actively encourages the trade is nothing less than complicit.

South Africa is no less susceptible to the pressures of political patronage: You already know that SARS, in its golden days, was making real inroads into dismantling criminal enterprise, and took out some big names. They also, of course, looked at some of the tobacco barons in the country, including Yusuf Kajee.

As Jacques Pauw explains in *The President's Keepers*, Yusuf Kajee used to run a tobacco outfit called Delta Tobacco, which was eventually liquidated by SARS after a tax investigation. Delta arose from the ashes as Amalgamated Tobacco Manufacturers, which couldn't get a manufacturing licence because of Delta's past, so, in 2008, it roped in Edward

Zuma – former President Jacob Zuma's son – as a director. And Amalgamated Tobacco Manufacturers, we know, was found to have produced four times more cigarettes than they declared. Delta and Amalgamated – along with Kajee – had some problems. Problems that the right kind of patronage may have solved.

(Kajee did publicly confirm a tax dispute with SARS at the time, but his quoted numbers and those that SARS reportedly calculated were owed, didn't quite tally.)

As Pauw further explains, Kajee was not taking the investigation lying down. Not only because it would have meant paying big penalties, but also because it seems South Africa's spooks may have wanted him to run an undercover smuggling operation for them.[26]

(It seems that elements within the South Africa's State Security Agency and police Crime Intelligence planned to set up their own front companies to infiltrate the illicit cigarette trade under various similar types of projects, one of which was named Project Robin.[27] Intelligence experts I've spoken to agree that schemes of this nature were unlikely to have been legally sanctioned; and that it was more likely simply a front for SSA agents to pocket profits for themselves. In any event, at some point, they were pinning their hopes on Kajee running such an operation for them, which he could not do if SARS took him out. Ultimately Kajee would reject these schemes, reportedly handing over the evidence of it to SARS.)

Kajee and Edward Zuma – and, it seems, some at the State Security Agency – would have wanted the SARS investigation against Kajee to disappear. So Zuma (junior) put together a dossier about how the first black-owned tobacco company in the country was being unfairly targeted by SARS.

When that and other appeals to SARS to walk away didn't work, they ramped things up a bit. Edward Zuma and his associated companies may not only have had the ear of Jacob Zuma because Edward was his son. They also had his ear, and presumably his sympathies, because through a company called Royal Sonic, they allegedly made payments that were used to upgrade Jacob Zuma's Nkandla homestead and fund Edward's and another few Zuma-pals' living expenses.[28] Every month. Where did Royal Sonic get the money from? Reportedly from smuggling tobacco.

Royal Sonic was also being investigated by SARS, for racketeering, evasion, money laundering and fraud. The cash cow was about to meet an untimely death.

In a recording Kajee says: 'I can bring SARS to its knees with all the shit that we have. I'm meeting the old man [Jacob Zuma] this weekend. I'm going to tell him this fucking Dutchman [Van Loggerenberg] is getting clever, he affects everybody ... Because if they going to fuck us up we can't do the project.'

Enter Tom Moyane, widely reported to be a Zuma ally, and the man Zuma appointed as the new Commissioner at SARS. And the cases against Amalgamated Tobacco, Royal Sonic and Kajee? Sources suggest that Kajee's matters were dealt with rather speedily once Moyane had purged SARS and shut down most investigative units. While Zuma may have had his own reasons for the appointment of Moyane, the outcomes of the cases concerning Kajee remain a mystery. (Kajee also reportedly invited Moyane's new head of SARS' anti-corruption and tobacco investigations units and some very senior police officers to his lavish birthday party.[29])

As Jacques Pauw eloquently notes: 'The South Africa that Zuma has created has rendered sleazebags blameless, guiltless and even righteous. There are no consequences for those who evade tax or launder money or do corrupt deals.'

It's a pattern of patronage that is repeated across the region: Gold Leaf Tobacco's Simon Rudland is widely reported to be a big contributor to Zimbabwe's ruling Zanu-PF party and frequently attends their rallies. Somewhere between 70 and 80% of South Africa's illicit cigarettes have been attributed to Gold Leaf.[30]

Savanna Tobacco's Adam Moloi is married to former President Robert

15. Political patronage

Mugabe's niece. Savanna makes Pacific and Gold Leaf cigarettes, which are reported to make up the majority of seized illicit cigarettes in South Africa.

And BAT? Who would BAT's political patrons be?

Whilst we seem to have some insight into the political affiliations of the independent tobacco manufacturers in South Africa, what we do not have sight of is who the big boys have donated to, how much, or why. We do know that BAT's security company's plan to derail the activities of its smaller competitors noted how 'Client has the potential to overcome political and socio-economic obstacles.'

We also know that BAT seems to have secured for itself the grand prize: the support of the State Security Agency and other key law enforcement agencies. More than one source has commented on the closeness of the relationship between the two – noting how some of their activities are often virtually indistinguishable, blurring the lines between the regulator and the regulated – an unholy alliance. And from what you'll see in later chapters, with a country's spooks and law enforcement on your side, perhaps you need very little else.

In a WhatsApp message from Johann van Loggerenberg that has since been made public he says: 'ATM/Kajee – Edward Zuma and Deputy Minister Justice John Jeffery; Phoebus Apollo / Delport – Deputy Communication Minister Stella Ndabeni; Carnilinx/Mazzotti & Wingate-Pearce – EFF and Julius Malema; BAT – SSA and Gibson Njenje/Ferdi Fryer. Can you see the trend?'[31]

As important as a network of political patronage may be, many within the industry maintain that high-level political influence isn't always necessary to conduct business. According to one former cigarette smuggler, 'You don't need high-level corruption, you just need the people looking at production sheets, and tip-offs about raids.'[32]

Which is exactly why big tobacco has perfected the art of playing both victim and saviour.

16. Victims and saviours

'Misdirection. What the eyes see and the ears hear, the mind believes.'
— *John Travolta*

Big tobacco's illicit trade advertising campaigns are important, because they help to position the multinationals both as a victim of illicit trade, and as the saviour from it. The rhetoric is simple: illicit trade is a big problem; somebody else is causing it; and we can help fight it.

I did a quick calculation: On BAT's Twitter account, over a six-week period, around 87% of its posts related to calls on government to do more to counter illicit trade. The calls serve a purpose: they create a dynamic that puts pressure on government to act, which for the most part is translated into acting against smaller competitors, against which big tobacco is more than happy to provide intelligence and evidence, much of it perhaps real, albeit of dubious legality.

Once big tobacco has convinced us that they are the *victims* of illicit trade — and of course not as often the perpetrators, despite what we saw in our earlier rogue's gallery of evidence regarding the way it behaves around the world — it is easy enough to secure an agreement to partner with the local tax or law enforcement agencies.

To paraphrase Pulitzer Prize-winning David Shipler's quote — originally intended to apply to foreign affairs — watching big tobacco at play 'is sometimes like watching a magician; the eye is drawn to the hand performing the dramatic flourishes, leaving the other hand — the one doing the important job — unnoticed'.

There is a substantial body of evidence that suggests that cooperation agreements often serve the interests of the industry and not that of government; the information sharing agreements often end up providing them with confidential information on their competitors; and their anti-illicit trade campaigns ensure that government focuses on smaller low-cost producers and never on big tobacco. They feed their 'partners' in government with intelligence and leads on the competition's illicit shipments, which translates into busts and seizures that government can take credit for, leaving big tobacco as the 'good guys' who saved the day.

Moreover, once big tobacco has established a partnership with an agency – and particularly where it has done so through a formal memorandum of understanding – it becomes relatively easy for the industry to argue against additional regulation.[1] Big tobacco, through its purported commitment to government, tells us that it is entirely capable of self-regulating; production controls and supply chain security measures are argued to simply increase the burden on legitimate producers and to have a negligible impact on illicit trade; industry's own traceability systems are punted as an easier solution to implement than those of independent third party solution providers. All of which, industry then argues, makes additional regulation entirely unnecessary.

The agreements are proliferating and mushrooming because big tobacco needs to hold governments close as pressure increases to implement the Illicit Trade Protocol, which they can hardly afford to support, and because the agreements give them an inside track, allowing them to direct where the agencies focus their efforts.

BAT has an MOU with the Mauritius Revenue Authority on the sharing of information, expertise and best practices. Imperial signed an MOU with the French customs authority to exchange information. The Iranian Tobacco Company entered into a cooperation agreement with the Ministry of Finance to inspect all stores, shops, and supermarkets to find smuggled cigarettes. BAT Nigeria donated a fleet of Ford Ranger trucks to the Nigerian Customs Service and pumped $300 million into the local economy just as central government launched a lawsuit against big tobacco to hold it accountable for mounting healthcare costs[2] (the lawsuit disappeared, although of course this could just be a coincidence).

Botswana's government was forced to cancel its MOU with TISA, and its police was slammed for accepting a vehicle from BAT, after complaints that both of these violated the Illicit Trade Protocol.[3]

In Australia big tobacco helped prop up enforcement in the fight against illicit cigarettes, providing law enforcement with high-level intelligence, identifying targets, and paying for surveillance technology. The arrangement was not publicly known (it was leaked by a whistle-blower) and operational targets and tactics were discussed over breakfast meetings at cafes, where the tobacco industry executive would hand over intelligence gathered by their 'contractor'. New South Wales Police are now explicitly banned from accepting any support from the tobacco industry.

You may, perhaps, think that these examples are simply donations or selfless assistance from a kindly company wanting to help an overburdened government agency. Keep reading.

JTI, in their reply to my request for comment, notes that, 'Customs and law enforcement authorities have recognized JTI as the Number 1 partner when it comes to providing information that regularly helps them seize illegal products and crack down on the organized crime networks involved in illegal tobacco trade.'

In South Africa, as we'll see later, many enforcement targets were explicitly selected using intelligence provided by big tobacco (some of it apparently fabricated, much of it of questionable legality) under cooperation agreements that very strongly included big tobacco but very pertinently excluded the country's smaller independent manufacturers.

Even international organisations like Interpol aren't exempt from big tobacco's charms.[4]

PMI established a very strategic relationship with Interpol, helped on by a substantial €45 million donation to Interpol between 2011 and 2013 – constituting an 8% increase in Interpol's annual budget.

So it came as no surprise when, in 2012, Interpol announced a partnership with the tobacco industry, and made the industry's contentious Codentify traceability solution available on its Global Register; and in 2015 listed big tobacco's Digital Coding and Tracking Association as a strategic partner on supply chain security.

Interpol also published *'Countering Illicit Trade in Goods: A Guide for Policy-Makers'* which suggested that only three systems fully comply with the requirements of the Illicit Trade Protocol: Codentify, ATOS and Arjo Wiggins. Arguably, in fact, none of them fully comply with the Illicit Trade Protocol, because there are concerns about their independence from the tobacco industry. ATOS developed Codentify for PMI and audits the system. Arjo Wiggins is a manufacturer of technical paper with links to BAT and with its own partnership with Interpol.

Consequently, both the guide and Interpol's position have been heavily criticised: Codentify's independence has long been challenged. Many other solutions on the market may in fact be far better aligned with the Protocol, but were omitted from the list – leaving Interpol heavily criticised for promoting tobacco industry interests without doing its own objective analysis of which systems would be best suited to curb the illicit trade in tobacco.

I approached Interpol for comment, but did not receive a reply.

The industry's deal with Interpol illustrates the ease with which it has been able to portray itself as part of the solution, and to integrate itself and its preferred solutions into law enforcement processes. (It has also resulted in the WHO refusing to let Interpol anywhere near the Illicit Trade Protocol, citing a clear conflict of interest.)

Given the limited capacity and the budgetary constraints we see at most agencies, it is easy to understand why assistance from industry is welcomed, and why so many agencies place so much reliance on intelligence provided by industry. Indeed, in my early days as an agency lawyer it is something I would have encouraged. I know better now.

We saw some hope that this capture of our law enforcement agencies was beginning to wear thin in South Africa: When SARS started insisting on BAT following formal channels to provide intelligence or information on their competitors, and refusing to select subjects for investigations based simply on big tobacco's say-so, and started excluding big tobacco from its investigations, BAT had to change tack. In an internal PowerPoint presentation they note (quite wrongly, though) how customs had 'no desire to prosecute the [competitor's] business for its wrongdoing', and subsequently in several documents discuss how to 'focus prosecution possibilities beyond customs and excise; look at Prevention of Organised Crime Act, Financial Intelligence Centre Act, exchange control, fraud'.[5] (We'll see later why SARS' investigators weren't playing ball with TISA/FSS/BAT anymore – because it had begun to see through big tobacco's smoke and mirrors.)

Even the police had become sceptical, with minutes from a BAT/FSS meeting noting one threat in particular: 'a change in government politics'. Another report explains, 'Meeting held with law enforcement agency as there appears to be a change in attitude concerning clamping down on possible illegal activities,' and laments the 'lacklustre approach by law enforcement agencies to act on suspects', and customs officers being 'hesitant to share information for fear of losing their employment'.[6] Other documents suggest how one police general apparently refused to help FSS, accusing FSS and BAT of 'price fixing, wanting the monopoly and creating hearsay evidence in order to get projects registered in an attempt to manipulate the opposition'.[7]

In one of his affidavits, BAT's project manager for their spy ring in South Africa notes, 'In the ordinary course a law enforcement agent acting within the purview of the law would not take seriously some of the frivolous complaints orchestrated by BAT. However, a cooperating law enforcement agent who is being rewarded would be glad to assist.'

Unfortunately, as we'll explore in the chapter on big tobacco's friends in high places, when SARS and some other agencies no longer wanted to do big tobacco's dirty work, it simply turned to an even bigger, more powerful ally: the State Security Agency.

Agreements, partnerships and MOUs with the tobacco industry are problematic, whether they are entered into with the taxman, bobbies on the beat, the state security, or an international organisation like Interpol:

First, because it makes enforcement efforts focus myopically on just one of the ways in which tobacco-related fraud manifests itself, at the expense of a broader more objective view of where risk lies more broadly (and which could very well include non-compliance by big tobacco itself).

Second, because there are examples of big tobacco manufacturing or otherwise illegally obtaining evidence.

Third, because aside from ultimately being prohibited under the Illicit Trade Protocol, it is simply a slippery slope, and one that almost certainly ends in capture, where the agency loses independence and fails to use the necessary professional scepticism when considering the 'evidence' provided to it, and potentially becomes subject to the whims of big tobacco.

Finally, for me, perhaps a bit more poetically, because it may very well result in our law enforcement agencies becoming little less than economic hitmen for big tobacco.

In any industry these would be substantive risks. But when it comes to tobacco, the industry suffers from what I'll politely call a 'trust deficit', making the selective choosing of bedfellows so much more important.

Remember: as much as 98% of illicit trade in tobacco comes from legal manufacturing operations,[8] many of which are owned, operated by, or contracted by big tobacco, which continues to control more than 80% of the world's tobacco market.

17. Sex, lies and videotape

The world already had some inkling of big tobacco's use of spies, informants, in-place sources and captured officials when BAT's Paul Hopkins broke rank.[1]

As the BBC explores in *The Secret Bribes of Big Tobacco*,[2] Hopkins worked for BAT for 13 years in Africa. In 2018 he gave the Serious Fraud Office in London evidence of how he not only bribed politicians and policy makers across Africa at BAT's behest, but also paid managers at one of BAT's biggest competitors for inside information. The payments totalled more than $300 000, and got him access to things like minutes of marketing meetings; early access to a parliamentarian report on a competitor and – once they increased the payment – the power to actually amend a parliamentary report to reflect a position more favourable to BAT; and an advance copy of a piece of anti-tobacco legislation that let them amend it to more appropriately reflect BAT's chosen rhetoric.

In Hopkins' own words: 'I was a commercial hit man. My job was to ensure that the competition never got a breathing space. They're quite shocking in this environment, but, as it was explained to me, in Africa that's the cost of doing business.'

Hopkins also explained how BAT allegedly paid bribes to get the inside track on one of their main competitors (from both board members at competitor Mastermind, and from the tax man) in Kenya:

17. Sex, lies and videotape

Interviewer: How much money's worth of black ops is here?

PH: To cover you, a couple of hundred thousand pounds? Minutes of the marketing meeting. This would be the most useful. I got to see it usually 12 or 14 hours after it happened.

Interviewer: But if you hadn't paid any money, how many files would we have in front of us?

PH: Oh, none. BAT is bribing people, and I'm facilitating it.

Interviewer: BAT managers knew you were bribing people?

PH: Yes.

(The BBC's documentary makes for fascinating viewing, see addendum 6 for selected transcribed extracts.)

But the Hopkins case, and the evidence he gave us, pales into comparison when you see what happened in South Africa.

One otherwise-unremarkable Friday afternoon I received a message to meet somebody in Rosebank, Johannesburg. He had something for me. A thumb drive, he said, the size of which belied its explosiveness. On it? What appeared to be meticulous details of how BAT actively spied on its competitors in South Africa. Which is quite something, considering the fact that, as Reuters reports, the local BAT office is the world's second largest tobacco company by sales.[3]

The documents on that thumb drive confirmed those touted earlier by at least three other industry players: Luis Pestana, Francois van der Westhuizen and Belinda Walter.

Luis Pestana, a small player who sold cigarette filters and cheap cigarettes, was approached by BAT's contracted security company – Forensic Security Services – to act as an informant for them. But there was a twist. The guy representing BAT – Van der Westhuizen – had a second objective: he was reportedly angry that his salary had been cut and wanted to get back at BAT and FSS. He gave Pestana access to hard drives with evidence that showed how BAT was spying on competitors and had police and SARS officials on their payroll. But not only that. They also spied on SARS officials and their families. Why on earth would they have done that? When it became apparent that it would be difficult to monetise the information, and he instead began fearing for his safety – his bodyguard was shot in what seems like a failed assassination attempt[4] – he created a Twitter profile, where he publicly posted all of the evidence (@espionageafrica).[5]

Francois van der Westhuizen – the original snitch who had passed FSS documents on to Pestana – also made several affidavits, to which he attached several records seemingly supporting his version.[6] He certainly seems like an informed source, because he had been the project manager of what appears to be BAT's spy ring.

Belinda Walter was an attorney acting for Carnilinx – Adriano Mazzotti's company, which was one of the smaller independent manufacturers in South Africa. She was also the founding chairperson of the Fair Trade Independent Tobacco Association (FITA), the industry body that had been set up to represent smaller independent manufacturers – in other words, everybody who does not belong to the big boys club. She was *also*, we know, an agent for both the State Security Agency (apparently registered as agent 5332) *and* BAT. At some later point she seems to have worked with individuals at the State Security Agency on a scheme *against* BAT. She later tried to walk away from both BAT and the State Security Agency. Somewhere in and amidst her varying alliances, she made an affidavit in which she made some startling admissions.[7]

(I tried to track down Ms Walter to ask her for comment. She seems to have disappeared off the face of the earth. After internet searches and messages to industry insiders asking for help in tracking her down proved unsuccessful, I sent a message to the last known email address for her. The mail came back as undelivered.)

Between the thumb drive that was passed on to me, Pestana's Twitter posts, affidavits from Van der Westhuizen and Walter, and interviews with some of those who were being spied on – all of which triangulate and correlate and match up – I can tell you the following story:

17. Sex, lies and videotape

It seems BAT was under some pressure from the new entrants in the South African market and wanted to claw back some of its market share.

BAT signed a contract with security firm Forensic Security Services (FSS) worth around R150 million (roughly $10 million) – explaining as follows, 'Client is losing market share. Client has seen the need to establish a project to curb the flow of this alleged illegal trade by incorporating the expertise of FSS and law enforcement.'

(I also tried to ask FSS for comment. They, too, seem to have disappeared off the face of the earth. As with Ms Walter, after internet searches and messages to industry insiders asking for help in tracking them down proved unsuccessful, I sent a message to the last known email address I could find in their various internal documents. The mail came back, noting the domain name no longer exists.)

The BAT team was a formidable one. They weren't rookies – they were outright professionals.

BAT's Ewan Duncan – who it seems provided training and acted as a handler to the FSS team – had reportedly been the Queen's most senior military intelligence officer in Iraq. He would literally have been among the most skilled and highly trained operatives in intelligence tradecraft on the planet. (He had apparently warned that Britain's 'milder interrogation' methods in places like Iraq were problematic.[8]) And then he went and joined a tobacco manufacturer – BAT Plc. This was no neophyte nerd crafting white papers in a back office somewhere – this was a war dog who had come to clean up.

He was reportedly joined by other long-time spies – ex-British intelligence officers and former espionage agents in the Irish Republican Army.

The FSS team, by contrast, were seemingly somewhat less skilled in tradecraft:

FSS initially appears to have mainly consisted of ex-policemen from Reaction Unit 9 in Durban, of which FSS' operations manager –

Mike Vosloo – had at one point been the Commanding Officer. 'Re-action Units' had been deployed to combat urban terrorism and quell local riots – their role was largely a tactical boots-on-the-ground one, and their members would not have had any specialist investigative training or experience. Van der Westhuizen himself explains that its members 'had no investigation, surveillance or other skills that relate to being able to give evidence in court, which is essential in investigating any syndicate operations / infiltrations'.[9]

To compensate for this, BAT seems to have secured training for the FSS team, which included courses such as defensive surveillance training, complete with certificates embossed with a BAT logo.[10] Van der Westhuizen explains, 'BAT SA management had me trained in industrial espionage by ex-UK military intelligence agents. We were trained in vehicle tracking systems, counter surveillance and information peddling. We were tasked to spy on local cigarette manufacturers. I ran two projects for nearly four years. The main reason was to disrupt the operations of BATs competitors.'[11]

But BAT apparently also insisted on FSS recruiting a set of new agents with investigative backgrounds and direct contact with senior law enforcement officers, so that they could secure police profiles on subjects, and access vehicle searches, bank account details, and get access to registered police sources[12] (this is not legal, by the way).

The objective of the project was explained simply as a 'reduction of low-priced products in the market' through 'ongoing disruptive activities', but on occasion being quite specific about an intent to 'bring illicit trade down by 51%'.[13] (According to Van der Westhuizen, this was an entirely arbitrary number.)

FSS greatly relied on a network of informants, longer-term in-place agents employed by the competition, 'consultants' who were paid for occasional services, law enforcement officials who were kept on monthly retainers (evidence suggests at least 171 of them), and a range of technologies. (BAT also does not appear to be the only tobacco company that's turned to a network of spies – one internal memo from JTI's security consultancy notes how, 'We are working with local Iraqi police on buying information as it relates to cigarette movements to locations. Dangerous, well, being in Baghdad is dangerous, it is what it is, a way to gain information.'[14])

The way in-place agents were apparently used are discussed in great detail across a number of documents, of which this monthly evaluation report is typical, 'SIN096 [a unique number assigned by FSS to an agent] reports all information via MMS and SMS by means of the phone that was issued to him. He would take a picture with his phone of delivery notes and invoices and passes this information to handler daily. Source provides weekly feedback on the quantities distributed, addresses of the various role players and is updating handler on a continuous basis of the latest trends and different role players. The source also supply [sic] photos of invoices to whom he deliver to [sic] every week and the amount of stock that he delivers. It is strongly recommended that he be kept on a retainer basis with a view to a possible increase to R5 000 as motivation for future successes.'[15]

Recruiting and managing agents was about more than simply using sources that were already in place – some of the documentation suggests that BAT went to some lengths to actively recruit and infiltrate its own agents into its competitors' businesses. In an affidavit Walter claims, 'I became aware that BAT UK had planted informants / spy's [sic] within Carnilinx's factories and had intended that contracted Phillipino [sic] workers would provide BAT UK with information regarding Carnilinx's production and distribution.'[16]

FSS appears to have invested heavily in high-tech spyware for what they termed 'intel ops'. (Minutes from one meeting note their strengths as 'technical skills'.[17]) They apparently managed to convince the traffic department to point their static cameras at a competitor's premises for 24 hours a day, for six weeks. While those cameras were pointed at business premises, they were probably not monitoring what they should have been. Who effectively paid for that? That's right, you and I did. There is evidence of them placing tracker beacons on competitors' vehicles, pretending to be Telkom employees, or sneaking in under cover of darkness (that's called breaking and entering). Their PowerPoint slides are emblazoned with images of 'spy gear . . . under cover spy cam'.

FSS also appears to have written up a detailed guide for BAT on how to gather evidence – not legally – using spyware on cell phones. The document notes that they could install virtually undetectable spyware, giving them access to all content on a phone, including messages, browser history, Skype calls, WhatsApp messages etc.; allowing them to track the phone's location; letting them block apps or calls; and making it possible for them to activate the microphone remotely to listen in on conversations.

An FSS Employee explained it in a funding request to BAT as follows: 'Cell phone Spyware is a versatile tool we can deploy on suspect phones. An application is installed that is completely hidden on the phone and to the owner, and within 30 sec of connection you have complete access to the phone. We would need access to the phone for at least 5 to 10min to install the software. This a huge risk exposing your intentions to a potential suspect but with great risk comes great reward. To have complete access to communications is a huge advantage, we will know when our cover has been blown or where the next drop will be. Yes to get the software installed on a phone will require more than your average operation and some clever thinking from our part, but I am confident in our ability to rise to the occasion.'

Of course, not all of it was high-tech glamour – it seems they also went through their competitors' trash on dustbin day.

They'd allegedly get law enforcement officers to open up containers and insist on 'TISA certificates' for consignments of cigarettes and then have the consignments detained when none were forthcoming. 'TISA certificates' don't exist.[18]

As for how the FSS guys explained their visits to retailers and stores?

And how they explained to their in-place agents why their services were needed? They simply said that they were 'doing market research and sustainability probing'.[19]

The evidence suggests that their extensive no-holds-barred 'intel ops' approach seems to have got them everything from the home addresses of sales representatives to the times when their competitors' manufacturing machines broke down; from what time SARS officers left a competitor's premises, to how much tobacco dust was produced. They knew what was being exported, and how competitors were disposing of their waste products. They had photos of most of their competitors' invoices and delivery notes, and of the machinery in their factories. They knew their competitor's Wi-Fi passwords, which they could use to hack into their internal security cameras. They knew at what speed their competitors' machines were running, and when the machines were cleaned. Not once, not occasionally, but in a steady stream of information that was systematically catalogued, analysed and reported on.[20]

And they don't seem to have been averse to crossing any lines:

Minutes from one meeting note a discussion: 'Can we utilise current network to "set up" any one?' and in another noting that they wanted to 'cause a substantial rift between the distributors. This can be done through means of jealousy or false reports.'[21] Another email notes, 'There is only a certain amount of law enforcement action available at our disposal and in my opinion if they want to go the harassment route they can.'[22]

Another WhatsApp exchange that has gone public notes, 'YK [Yusuf Kajee] seems to be getting away with everything. Shall I spread misinformation?' before getting to more serious discussions, 'Can he bring in a hitman? . . . It's the first person I want dead . . . I don't hurt people, but he is a cockroach . . . so we can exterminate him.'[23] (In what could be a sheer coincidence, Kajee ended up being poisoned, resulting in him losing a kidney.)

As Jacques Pauw noted, 'The tobacco industry is a cut-throat business in which participants have no qualms about scamming one another, ratting on each other and spreading vicious rumours. In short: if I can eliminate a competitor, I might just bag a chunk of his business. There is always money to make: if not as a snitch, then by way of a smear campaign, blackmail or extortion.'[24] Except that it doesn't just apply to the smaller guys – it very much applies to big tobacco too.

And BAT must have known exactly what was going on. Despite its protestations that the company does not 'tolerate corruption in our business anywhere in the world' and that its policy 'is to take all appropriate action' on any allegation,[25] they made the somewhat telling comment to the effect that BAT will no longer instruct anti-illicit trade activities of the kind that have been the subject of the allegations.[26] Why not?

FSS had not gone rogue on it. I believe the evidence shows it was acting at the behest of and with the full knowledge of BAT, not just in South Africa, but at least potentially with the knowledge of some at BAT Plc in the UK. BAT explicitly retained 'the authority to make decisions'.[27]

The evidence I have suggests that they met at least monthly for debriefing meetings, typically attended by both BAT's head of anti-illicit trade in Africa, who flew in all the way from the UK, and FSS, and with the findings being consolidated into an information package which was handed to BAT's local head of anti-illicit.[28] FSS invoices, detailing the use of 'probers', 'consultants', 'surveillance', 'intel ops', and 'technical equipment' were sent to BAT for payment.

Recommendations to pay rewards to informants – made monthly – were seemingly individually signed off by BAT's head of anti-illicit trade for Africa, and their local head of anti-illicit trade in South Africa, and BAT's country manager.[29] In several emails BAT and FSS jointly discuss targets for law enforcement interventions. A number of in-place agents are pertinently recorded as having been recruited by BAT's anti-illicit trade manager himself. BAT and FSS both consistently quoted the same details in their reports and presentations. Some BAT presentations were done on FSS-branded PowerPoint slides.

Van der Westhuizen, in an affidavit aimed at getting him indemnity from prosecution stated, 'Our primary work description from the onset was to spy on competitors and disrupt business operations on behalf of BAT South Africa. BATSA was fully aware that FSS was obtaining information illegally and these included obtaining recorded conversations.'[30]

No, FSS had not gone rogue on BAT. I believe BAT knew what they were up to.

What is more, they all seem to have had an idea that what they were up to was risky: In a PowerPoint presentation on a slide headed 'What are the risks', they discuss the issue openly: 'Investigator exposure; possible civil action; interdict or damages claims; conflict with SAPS investigators re-applied pressure to act satisfactory [sic]; antagonism.'[31]

In one email an FSS manager requests, 'that you do not send it to everyone addressed. Just myself please. Once the document is sanitised I will forward it. Is that clear?'[32] Documents that need to be 'sanitised' tend to have something you and I are not supposed to know. In another document on naming conventions they explicitly explain, 'Always refer to insource / outsource and not electronic monitoring, plugging, advanced monitoring or beacon on. Always refer to "investigation done" and not "observation", "surveillance" or "monitoring".'[33]

In another email they discuss how a tracker that had been placed on a truck was problematic, noting, 'Please retrieve unit and DO NOT report any further on this activity. I repeat do not repeat these activities, because if someone sees us working on it, we are . . .'[34] (He didn't complete the sentence, but you get the gist of it.)

In yet another email they discuss how 'Constant disruption by the same law enforcement agency might lead to allegations of harassment and subject might get a court order to stop actions. Continue to disrupt and retrieve documentation at other provinces but do not use the same law enforcement agency.'[35]

And their interactions with some police officers and prosecutors could only have confirmed their fears that what they were doing was risky. In one email an FSS handler notes, 'Captain x and I had the opportunity to discuss the case with advocate y. I explained our approach. To be honest I could sense that he was not 100% committed to the idea. Captain x is to look up the case law to study entrapment.'[36]

Walter explains how she was told not to keep any evidence of BAT's dealings with her, 'Throughout the relationship we texted, skyped, whatsaped [sic] and BBM'ed regularly. I did not retain copies of all correspondence. Initially I did so but Evans [BAT intelligence manager] was horrified when he saw it and demanded that I destroy all evidence of the relationship.'[37]

When she wanted out and ostensibly tried to make things right in South Africa, 'BAT UK's responses to my requests for clarity made it abundantly clear to me that the relationship we shared may well fall within the ambit of a corrupt or unlawful relationship. BAT UK's representatives offered and indeed paid me a reward for acting improperly.'[38]

Part of the problem with the work FSS was doing for BAT was that they operated under a somewhat perverse incentive scheme. FSS' success was measured against the 'amounts of detentions'.[39] And the size of rewards paid to their agents and other sources was calculated starting at R100 per master case, and adjusted up or down depending on a score that rated them against the relative risk they took, the effort they put in and the number of cigarette cases detained.

The problem with using detentions as a measure of success is that it is a fundamentally easy performance indicator to cheat: all that is required for a detention is a mere *suspicion* that the goods may be unlawful (to seize the goods, you need to have actual incontrovertible *proof*).

That incentive scheme very much drove the wrong behaviour, as Van der Westhuizen explains in one of his affidavits, 'If there was no reporting from the informants, they would not get "rewarded." Often this forced the informants to fabricate allegations of illicit cigarettes transport [sic] by Carnilinx just so that they could be "rewarded." BATSA must have foreseen that the informants would fabricate stories and feed it to the law enforcement agencies because they wanted to be rewarded. It was expedient for BATSA to allow that, and it did.'[40]

The FSS contract did not come cheap, and BAT understandably needed to see results for the investment it was making. At some point, BAT must have got a bit impatient with the lack of impact, with an FSS manager noting to his agents, 'As you are aware client wants to cut retainer payment unless there is proof and motivation that they need to be maintained' and an email from BAT's head of anti-illicit trading asking, 'Can I please have a [sic] evaluation on the production of the sources that are currently on retainer.'[41] (And in the background, TISA seems to have set itself a target to reduce illicit trade to 20%, and the market was sitting at 23%, putting even more pressure on FSS to deliver.)

For all of this effort, one would imagine that between BAT and FSS they would have had some astonishing successes at pinning criminal charges on their competitors. They didn't – and that was apparently not the goal anyway. The goal seems to have been simply to disrupt them, to taint them – not to actually bring them to justice and have them face their day in court.

But it is easy to understand why BAT would have started getting antsy. For instance, in the first half of 2014, it seems that between TISA and FSS they had lodged 110 criminal cases[42] against the smaller independent manufacturers. One hundred and ten. And you know what? I couldn't find one mention of a conviction. Not one. That's not to say there wasn't one, but given the level of detail that FSS was going to, to impress both BAT and TISA, with exceptionally thorough tracking and reporting of all of its activities, one would have imagined that a successful prosecution would have been shouted from the rooftops. That's a lot of harassment for relatively little to show for it. Van der Westhuizen's affidavit confirms as much: 'FSS was never able to show trading in illicit cigarettes by either a non-payment of customs and excise duty on the part of Carnilinx or dealing in counterfeit goods by Carnilinx's customers.'

How many cases do you think they formally reported to SARS, through formal channels, for further investigation? How many cases do you think they reported to the department of health on those reduced ignition propensity products they were ostensibly looking for? I don't know for sure, but I'd hazard a guess it wasn't many.

In fact, they could not even quite figure out just exactly what their competitors were doing wrong. 'What are we missing? Exact method of abuse of customs and excise legislation.' So, despite the BAT/FSS alliance's best efforts they couldn't figure out just how their competitors were supposedly cheating the system.

What is more, their agents and sources of course had to be paid. They apparently paid some of their in-place sources monthly retainers of up to R40 000 ($2 700).[43] Belinda Walter says BAT paid her – a practising attorney – to spy on her clients (around £36 000 a year).[44] The payments to the undercover agents – which could constitute significant amounts – could almost certainly not be done legally, so BAT apparently set up a system using Travelex cash cards, which could be pre-loaded with a set value, and used anonymously at any ATM around the world.

Walter explains in an affidavit: 'A Travelex card from the UK would be given to me. It would not be in my name and could not be traced to me personally. BAT UK would load funds in the UK each month. I was advised that an offshore account would be difficult to open and easy to trace. I was assured that the Travelex cards were widely used by BAT UK's intelligence network internationally. From discussions in my presence, I am aware that the system of payments through the Travelex cards by BAT UK to its intelligence network was not confined to agents in South Africa. My own further research also given [sic] rise to concerns that the use of the cards in contemplation of the concealment of BAT UK's relationship with me may possibly also amount to money laundering and form part of a scheme of racketeering.'45

This meant that BAT's agents were effectively paid in cash, which they would have had difficulty explaining in a tax return. It also meant that BAT had moved large amounts of currency across borders with the intention of avoiding detection.

In addition, big tobacco managed to weaponise something innocuous as a way to silence their competitors: For many in law enforcement, under-declaring a consignment of cigarettes may seem like little more than a parking violation. To get their attention, sometimes you may need to amp up the danger a bit, make the threat sound bigger than it really is. So at one point big tobacco crafted an extremely alarmist affidavit, stating that action should be taken against one competitor in particular because 'many of the role-players have links to foreign nationals and it is possible that money laundering benefits international terror networks. Most of the kingpins are orthodox Muslims which could indicate links to certain radical movements. Money could be remitted outside the country to fund these radical movements abroad.'46

Here is why that really sticks in my throat: I have trawled through more than 4 000 of their documents. And despite BAT and FSS' extremely thorough, comprehensive and longstanding spying on these individuals, there was never so much as a whisper or a stirring or a footnote or a shadow that they might be sending money offshore to fund radical movements, or fears of terrorist motives, or a mention of their faith. There is not a single note or comment in any of the reports or presentations that suggests any evidence, or even any suspicions, of their involvement in radical networks. What BAT/FSS appears to have done was to play to the collective fears of some. Their 'links to foreign nationals'claims were little more than smoke and mirrors.

Of course the espionage scheme also had some unintended (but perhaps easy-to-anticipate problems): some of the handlers underpaid agents and sources, keeping the money for themselves; one handler sold seized cigarette packs from her garage.[47] Turning the tables somewhat, there are also indications that one of the smaller producers may have paid FSS R100 000 to release a container of counterfeits.[48]

I'm fairly certain that most of the BAT/FSS operations could not have been legal, as are the other enforcement and intelligence experts I've spoken to.

South Africa's Criminal Procedure Act details the requirements for undercover operations when investigating criminality. As one highly-experienced criminal investigator I spoke to noted, these requirements include that the undercover agents may not themselves commit or promote crimes; may not enrich themselves; may not do anything that may provide an opportunity for somebody else to commit a crime; and may not exploit people based on the nature of their relationship. But perhaps the single biggest proviso is that undercover operations require advance approval from the National Director of Public Prosecutions.

From my time as a prosecutor, and subsequently as an investigator, I can't see any way for that approval to have been given to either BAT or its security company for what they got up to. And I definitely can't see that approval having been given to Walter, who was not only a lawyer with a professional duty of care in general, but the lawyer for the very company being spied on.

Make no mistake – companies like Carnilinx *did* try to take BAT to court. They laid corruption charges against BAT's directors, accusing them of spying, and noting how, 'Evidence has been collated of instances which point to various practices by certain role players in the tobacco industry that speak to unfair treatment of some by the state, preferential treatment in other cases, and various anti-competitive practices.' Perhaps not surprisingly, nothing came of it. (You'll understand why when we get to the next chapter on big tobacco's incestuous relationship with the spooks in South Africa.)

Carnilinx also lodged civil litigation against BAT, but their case was dismissed on a technicality (they incorrectly brought it by way of a motion, which is usually used when the facts in a case are not in dispute, instead of by way of an action, which would be used where there may be a potential dispute of facts. In dismissing their case, the judge explicitly noted, 'I should make it clear that this order should not be understood as suggesting that there is no merit in the applicant's case. The main application falls to be dismissed without dealing with its intrinsic merits.')[49]

These cases, unsurprisingly, died a quiet death, perhaps because as that earlier quote explained, the way big tobacco wins litigation is simply by 'outspending the other son of a bitch'.

Eventually, the whistle was blown on BAT's underground activities in South Africa.[50]

A money laundering and corruption investigation has since been launched by the UK's tax and customs office HMRC, and the European Commission's Anti-Fraud Office OLAF[51] (but before you rejoice, have a look at the later chapter on whether big tobacco is too big to fail).

As much of this became public knowledge and the story got legs in the media, BAT's local CEO expressed his shock at the allegations and committed to appoint a law firm to investigate. That was in 2016. In September 2016 BAT announced that it had severed ties with FSS.[52]

As for what happened next at BAT? Maybe we will never know:

Ten months after BAT appointed Linklaters to conduct an 'investigation', and just as the media storm had started dying down, the oddest thing happened: BAT announced that it had cancelled the brief for Linklaters. Why? 'For matters of efficiency.' We don't know what Linklaters did, or what they found.

Linklaters was ostensibly replaced by a small law firm, Slaughter & May. We don't know what Slaughter & May did, or what they found.

But then, when some of the independent manufacturers decided to take BAT to court, and Pestana released his trove of documents, and with media focus now again squarely on BAT, the company was again spurred into action, this time appointing Norton Rose Fulbright – the firm also used by BAT's auditors, KPMG.

The guy who had been heading BAT in South Africa until then, rode off into the sunset (his LinkedIn profile using the tagline 'Gap year . . . enjoying the good that life has to offer').

Several years and at least three legal firms later, BAT has not breathed a word publicly of what they found, or what they did to ensure criminal practices like this are not repeated either locally, or on a global scale. FITA sued to get a copy of their report – BAT refused to disclose it, with BAT's local head of external replying that the report in question 'is legally privileged and was prepared for the purpose of British American Tobacco obtaining legal advice. The contents of the report may be relevant to ongoing investigations and litigation. British American Tobacco has made disclosures to the appropriate South African and other law enforcement authorities.'[53]

Was this just an isolated incident?

We already know from Belinda Walter's affidavit that BAT Plc was apparently telling her that they were paying their agents globally the way they paid her, pointing to other agents and spy networks dotted around the globe.

Evidence also suggests that this was apparently not BAT's first foray into spying on its competitors in South Africa: as far back as 2000, two other ex-cops are alleged to have been approached to set up an investigative firm that could conduct investigations for BAT. Their role? To focus on BAT's competitors, which they say included illegally intercepting competitor's communications, and placing undercover agents in competitor's businesses. Not long after their contract with BAT was terminated – in favour of FSS – one fine day somebody came to 'fix' their computers, and in the process deleted all the evidence the duo had implicating BAT.[54]

But there is more: the Zimbabwe *Independent* broke a story about a similar network allegedly being run in Zimbabwe in 2012: 'BAT Zimbabwe is allegedly spying on its competitors and had adopted an industrial espionage strategy . . . BATZ set out to identify the company's key contacts, people who could divulge strategic information and get sound marketing intelligence . . . Local tobacco industry players say the Tobacco Institute of Southern Africa contracted a security firm, Forensic Security Services, to monitor Zimbabwean manufacturers whose brands are giving stiff competition. The security firm is said to have recruited spies within the workforce of Zimbabwean manufacturers,'[55] quoting from an internal BAT document entitled the 'Competitors Strategy Document'.

18. From taxman to hitman

When we set up SARS' Special Compliance Unit, focusing on high-risk, high-profile tax investigations, and when I later headed up SARS' Criminal Investigations nationally, efforts were well underway to change the way in which criminal investigations were done.

At the time, the criminal investigations paradigm at SARS was problematic from a number of perspectives: it was run by an empire of traditionally white male investigators who had got used to a particular way of operating. Criminal investigators could effectively choose who to investigate – and who not to – and how often to investigate them, using what can only be described as fluid processes and not really being held accountable for the outcomes.

Over time, this changed: cases were selected based on a business intelligence system that assessed the risk posed by different cases, and prioritised those where there was a bigger potential risk. Criminal investigators could no longer choose their own cases – they were automatically and randomly allocated to investigators, who were now required to use a structured investigations process, and they were increasingly being held to account for the outcomes of the cases.

But back in the day, in selecting the cases they investigated, they invariably relied on tip-offs and information and bits of evidence gathered from whoever they had personal relationships with – and in fairness, at the time, they perhaps had little else to base investigations on.

18. From taxman to hitman

Because many of the investigators had started their careers in SARS as either customs or excise officers, they had naturally developed relationships with some of the bigger clients with whom they had frequent interactions, like the bigger tobacco companies.

The close relationship was largely a product of how excise controls were designed. With no other real production controls in place to allow SARS to assess how many packs had been produced, other approaches were deployed: an officer might be permanently based at a tobacco manufacturer to keep an eye on their goings-on, or could be called out to seal a container when it was ready for export, or could be required to conduct cyclical verifications at the manufacturer's premises (they might have called them audits, but they were hardly more than simple, very rudimentary validation checks). Between the regular interaction, and the light-touch checks, it was typical to see a collegial relationship between SARS and excise manufacturers.

Given the dearth of other sources of leads and tip-offs, it was only natural, then, that there was a time when SARS officers would happily accept intelligence from the bigger tobacco manufacturers on where to go digging for smuggled or undeclared packs of cigarettes. Time and time again, their tip-offs tended to pay off, and some or other smaller player was successfully prosecuted. (This bears a bit of a resemblance to the turf wars we see with rival drug cartels getting enforcement agencies to take out their competitors.)

Working on tip-offs is pragmatic but not entirely without problems – it leads to highly selective targeting. So, perhaps, one might argue that some of the big tobacco companies aren't necessarily opposed to illicit trade in general – they are opposed to illicit trade where it threatens to eat into their share of the pie.

Corroboration comes from an unlikely source: Belinda Walter. It seems she passed on to BAT a treasure trove of information on a specific manufacturer about whom she had received substantial, reliable information, with supporting documentation. 'No action was taken against this entity, or passed to the law enforcement agencies as the manufacturer did not appear to pose a threat to BATSA's operations.'[1]

Anyway, the old paradigm worked: SARS got convictions, and it seized some illicit packs from the market. But statistically, in relation to the sheer size of illicit trade, it was and is a drop in an ocean of contraband.

But more than this: certain SARS officials also developed a close relationship with TISA – the one-time big tobacco proxy – which assisted in compensating for some of the capacity gaps at SARS, helping out with the destruction of illegal cigarettes, having regular operational meetings with SARS, and providing training to SARS and other law enforcement staff on illicit cigarettes.

It had become part of big tobacco's playbook: directing where our enforcement agencies look and effectively turning our tax agencies into economic hitmen in their turf wars against their competition. And we've had a few prime examples right on our doorstep:

Hennie Delport was my first real introduction to the intrigues that seem to live and thrive in the shadows of the tobacco business. I suspect Mr Delport has seen enough coverage of his life and his business to last him a lifetime, so I hope he'll forgive me for dissecting some of his story yet again, all these years later.

I really couldn't tell you when I first heard his name – literally decades ago now, some time in the nineties, I guess – but he is a bit like the Tigon[2] of tobacco (Tigon was the company listed on the Johannesburg Stock Exchange that collapsed in 2002, and only in 2019 went to trial with more than 3 000 charges of fraud, racketeering and tax evasion.)

Delport's is the case that just won't die: his name always popping up somewhere, from as far back as the early nineties, to the occasional mention even today. Some SARS officials will tell you his is the second biggest investigation in SARS' history (second only to that of Dave King, who got handed a whopping R3,2 billion – around $209 million – tax assessment.)

18. From taxman to hitman

While he may well have been guilty of some of the things he had been accused of, it's the process around establishing his guilt that – in hindsight – doesn't necessarily sit well with me.

So, with Mr Delport's indulgence, here is a small story that shows how big tobacco could work to secure its market share:

In the 1980s Delport flew as a pilot across Southern and Central Africa, initially mostly transporting famine relief consignments, but later branching out into foodstuffs, whiskey, and wine.

He secured a contract with South Africa's Rothmans International to distribute their cigarettes, but when Rothmans merged with BAT (in the process becoming BAT South Africa) that contract came under threat. Delport still had a distribution agreement with BAT but realised he would need to branch out yet again, and started manufacturing his own cigarettes, under a brand called Exclusive.

His early interactions with SARS were cordial: his books were regularly audited and his warehouses frequently inspected, with nary a worry in sight. Indeed, he was at one stage even appointed as an official cargo carrier for the South African government.[3]

But Mr Delport was about to become a victim of his own success. As his Exclusive brand started to gain ground, it was eating into BAT's share of the pie, ultimately resulting in BAT reportedly attributing the closure of their Malawi plant in part to him.[4]

In court papers Delport states he was later approached by two private detectives who – having seemingly been short-changed by BAT and who wanted to turn the tables on them – provided evidence that they had been hired by BAT to spy on his operations, sometimes posing as police officers, and on a number of occasions illegally tapping his phones, often for as long as two months at a time, on at least three different occasions.[5]

Much of the rest of Delport's story is not in the public domain, but what we do know is that he maintained that certain SARS officials took action against him in large part based on evidence provided by

BAT and its investigators. And more than that – a handful of SARS officials appear to have been more than just passive recipients of the information, having instead actively participated in planning meetings with BAT and the private investigators to assess how best to take Delport down.

As far as I can tell, this was the first time in history a judge had granted a search warrant for SARS offices, to secure evidence that SARS officials had colluded with BAT in targeting Delport. A judge in one of the many court cases between SARS and Delport noted, 'Some compelling examples of obstructive and one-sided behaviour by SARS officials are illustrated.' SARS was rapped over the knuckles for effectively ignoring evidence submitted to them by Delport, with the judge labelling SARS' attitude towards Delport 'uncooperative' and 'unfair', and stating that 'the conduct of SARS fell far short of the constitutional imperative of providing procedurally fair administrative action'.[6]

Which perhaps in part explains why, when Project Honey Badger came about, many at SARS were so at pains to avoid BAT, its security company FSS and their coterie of spies and a multi-agency government task team that worked very close with them, with an instruction sent out to staff prohibiting them from engaging with these parties without prior written approval. It does seem though, that three particular SARS officials ignored this and continued their interactions with BAT and FSS.

(I only very recently realised that Delport's attorney back then was somebody we've already met: none other than the ubiquitous Belinda Walter. And would you believe it, in 2017 she reportedly again offered to act for him, this time to get SARS to walk away from the now-decades-old case against him. He says he paid her R50 000 in cash (around $3 500). Which is somewhat problematic, and not just because lawyers really should know better than to receive wads of cash from clients. Delport's estate is being managed by a curator under a preservation order to ensure that he can't dissipate his assets pending the litigation with SARS, making it perhaps a little curious that he had this sort of money to throw around. Ms Walter probably should have known all this, as she was at some point retained as the lawyer on that very case by KPMG.[7] Yes, the same KPMG who also has big tobacco as a client.)

To be clear, on a balance of probability, Delport may have had a case to answer, and may have profited from contraband cigarettes that were smuggled across South Africa's porous borders. But what should have been a simple investigation, seems to have been turned into Delport being targeted again, and again, and again.

It was only much later, when I started piecing together the strands of this book, that I started wondering about some bigger questions: to what extent had the selection of Delport as the subject of a criminal investigation been driven by BAT's need to preserve its market share? If, for instance, Delport had been smuggling shoes or beer, instead of cigarettes, would he have received the same level of scrutiny from BAT's few friends over at SARS? If it weren't for him encroaching on big tobacco's turf, and for BAT's apparent desire to get rid of him, would the handful of SARS officials perhaps have simply seized his consignments and moved on?

Was SARS simply being used by BAT as a veritable economic hitman, to take out a competitor?

But there is more to it than that. In hindsight, we now know, at the very moment that BAT was busy pointing SARS officials in Hennie Delport's direction, they were busy with their own questionable activities elsewhere in the world: their Colombian executives were busy detailing how they were managing the local contraband market; their manager in Hong Kong was being convicted of corruption; they were being sued in Canada for smuggling; they were running extensive smuggling rings across much of Africa; and they were being sued by the European Union for '. . . controlling entire smuggling operations – an ongoing global scheme to smuggle cigarettes, launder the proceeds of narcotics trafficking, obstruct government oversight of the tobacco industry, fix prices, bribe foreign public officials, conduct illegal trade with terrorist groups and state sponsors of terrorism, engaging in organised crime, money laundering . . .'

At the very moment they were targeting Hennie Delport, BAT themselves were having to pay $200 million in smuggling-related damages elsewhere.

In fairness to SARS, the Delport example is an old one, and the criminal investigations paradigm has changed significantly since those days when investigators could choose their own cases. But it still paints a cautionary tale.

(It hasn't entirely stopped – until not too long ago there were still examples where FSS/BAT would apparently lead the unpacking of containers with suspected illicit loads – after having been tipped off by traffic officers – and paying bystanders to help doing so, with customs officers simply watching from the side-lines; and some law enforcement and intelligence officials seem to remain unduly close to BAT.)

Big tobacco found something of a Trojan horse in its ability to infiltrate intelligence and law enforcement structures, and policy advisory groups, and the South African example illustrates beautifully how big tobacco quite easily goes about its business – using all the tricks in its playbook.[8]

On reflection, it is easy to see what was happening: the big tobacco companies appear to have been directing where SARS was focusing their enforcement activities, and ensuring that their own activities came under less, if any, scrutiny.

The South African experience shows how our law enforcement agencies run the risk of being used as little more than big tobacco's hitmen. They cannot be allowed to do big tobacco's bidding in terms of who gets selected for audits and investigations. They cannot continue to focus only on smaller players, while ignoring big tobacco's blatant hypocrisy and its own links to criminality.

18. From taxman to hitman

Big tobacco obviously has an interest in shutting down its smaller competitors,[9] which may be par for the course in a capitalist market economy. But big tobacco does it differently. This is not a patent war between Apple and Samsung, or aggressive legal marketing and pricing. This often ranges from subtle manipulation of enforcement agencies to pure undiluted, criminality, posing as collaboration with government.

Some at SARS began to understand this, and actually appealed to manufacturers like BAT to use structured processes to provide information or intelligence, instead of passing tip-offs to contacts at SARS over a beer – a request that BAT and others seemingly ignored:

> 'SARS appeals to you to opt to use the existing channels such as the SARS Hotline or online Suspicious Activity Report. Alternatively matters should be referred to law enforcement agencies such as the SAPS. Should they wish to bring such matters to the attention of SARS directly, reports should be in writing and addressed to this office. This is because SARS's case selection process provides for an operational distinction between the areas that generate and select cases for further attention, and the teams that execute against that risk. Cases are generated in a multitude of ways, and therefore require a careful weighing up of risk across tax types and risk factors so as to ensure fair and equitable case selection criteria.'[10]

Unfortunately, when SARS started insisting on BAT and the other big tobacco companies using formal structures to rat on their competitors, and started turning its attention to suspected mischiefs by BAT itself, the entire paradigm changed.

19. Unholy alliances and friends in even higher places

We've already seen how both SARS and some policemen had cottoned on to how big tobacco was abusing its access to state structures, forcing it to simply turn to and bring in an even bigger, more powerful ally: the State Security Agency.

While other tobacco companies may have been courting politicians, in the State Security Agency BAT may have found the ultimate political patron, and it made them (at least for a while) almost invincible.

A Tobacco Task Team was established in South Africa, consisting of FSS, TISA, BAT, the State Security Agency, National Prosecuting Authority, police, Crime Intelligence and the Hawks (South Africa's investigations unit which targets serious crime). Walter explains, 'It is my understanding that BAT funds "projects," provides resources and chooses targets for the task team to focus on.'[1]

The task team excluded SARS but appears to have kept a surreptitious line open to their three pals over at SARS investigations.[2] It had to exclude SARS because they knew SARS knew just what FSS/BAT had been up to and was insisting on changing the way it engaged with them.[3]

In many respects – in part through this task team – FSS, TISA, BAT, the State Security Agency, NPA, police and the Hawks had become virtually indistinguishable: Payments to FSS sources and agents had to be counter-signed by BAT's head of anti-illicit trade; some payment invoices were allegedly signed by police colonel Hennie

19. Unholy alliances and friends in even higher places

Niemann, which was highly irregular, given that he was a cop assigned to crime intelligence gathering.[4] When Carnilinx found a tracking device on one of their trucks, it was reportedly traced back to an FSS cell phone, but using a police Crime Intelligence sim card (Carnilinx lodged a criminal complaint with the police, the police did nothing). Walter's affidavit alleges that the first meeting of the industry body representing the independent manufacturers was bugged by the SSA, but using FSS/BAT's equipment.[5]

One document suggests that when an FSS agent was fired for stealing payments meant for sources, TISA's head became the new handler for the sources in question.[6]

The main man on the Tobacco Task Team, police crime intelligence officer Hennie Niemann, had also been working closely in Mogadishu with none other than the ever-present Ms Walter.[7] When Niemann left the police, his small farewell party included some guys from FSS, and two of their contacts at SARS.

Niemann's objectivity as a policeman isn't only called into question by his personal relationships with individuals in FSS and possibly Walter – it's patently blown out of the water by the fact that he appears to have shared top secret information with them. The alliance was more than simply questionable, it was unlawful: Back in March 2014, at a café in Pretoria's Menlyn, Niemann reportedly shared with them what is described as 'stealthily intercepted communications conducted by our state intelligence agencies – for which they likely did not have authority to do so'. What he was sharing were transcripts of intercepted phone calls. As a rule, these are classified as top secret, the highest secrecy level that state documents carry. Niemann may have had such clearance on account of his work at crime intelligence – but the FSS people certainly could not have had. Niemann didn't just show the transcripts to the FSS guys; he allegedly gave them copies. That may well constitute a criminal offence.[8]

As for flipflopper Walter, it's difficult to know who she was working for – it seems sometimes for Carnilinx, sometimes for BAT, sometimes for the State Security Agency. When Walter was receiving her payments from BAT, FSS agents were apparently doing counter-surveillance to make sure she wasn't being spied on.[9] Sometimes she seems to have spied for BAT; at other times she appears to have been actively plotting against them. Sometimes she appears to have spied on individuals at SARS; other times she handed them bundles of evidence exposing the whole rotten business.

Anyway, despite all of these shenanigans, rather curiously, as more than one of my sources pointed out, I could not find proof of a single successful prosecution attributable to the Tobacco Task Team. Not one. What little success they had seems to typically have been limited to the arrests of truck drivers or factory workers and incidental busts.

It may not have had much success in court (that we know of) in terms of sinking competing businesses, but the State Security Agency was seemingly not averse to getting stuck into helping big tobacco in other ways:

According to a report in the *Mail & Guardian* newspaper, a SARS investigation into Paul de Robillard's Rollex accused the company of doing millions of rands in off-the-book transactions smuggling tobacco into South Africa. Rollex had an ace up its sleeve – it was owned by Lonrho, a hundred-year-old international conglomerate, which was understandably keen to protect its investment in what was ostensibly one of its most profitable divisions. While Lonrho is not big tobacco as defined for purposes of the rest of the book, it *is* a big multinational company with big tobacco interests, and in the context of this story, is very much big tobacco.

Lonrho called in some big guns and reportedly engaged Ferdi Fryer, then the head of commercial intelligence at South Africa's State Security Agency. Fryer, along with the director of the SSA seemingly agreed on the need to treat Lonrho – Rollex's parent company – as an innocent victim and entered into a 'cooperation agreement' with Lonrho.

19. Unholy alliances and friends in even higher places

As part of this cooperation agreement the SSA allegedly gave Lonrho access to detailed intelligence reports on its subsidiary Rollex – including confidential evidence from whistle-blowers. Lonrho was accused of having tipped De Robillard and Rollex off. By the time SARS conducted a raid on Rollex's premises, they found nothing. Agents at the SSA had probably ensured that nothing would come of SARS' investigations into Rollex and De Robillard, and Lonrho's investment was safe.[10] And wouldn't you know, at the time, a key 'legal advisor' to Lonrho was none other than Belinda Walter.

In a WhatsApp exchange that has since gone public, Van Loggerenberg says, 'Ferdi caused this country so much damage. If we were able to have bust Kajee, Ayabatwa and Lonrho when the chance was there, and then Carnilinx and Simon, imagine where we would have been now. What's going on now is the result of Gibs, Ferdi and BAT UK's shenanigans. From a casual point of view, we would have nailed all these guys including Delport long ago if they didn't interfere and play games.'[11]

20. BAT's Christmas present to the underworld?

'Magicians are manipulating your consciousness. They're getting you to construct a narrative, which simply isn't true. So that means they know how to make you aware of certain things and blind to other things.'
— Psychology professor Richard Wiseman

BAT/FSS lamented on several occasions about how there was 'no interest from Customs to capitalise; no desire to prosecute the business for its wrongdoing.'

Of course, they were quite wrong. SARS very much *was* interested in prosecuting these businesses. It just wasn't interested in sharing that information with BAT. And it had long since realised that any decent criminal investigation does not focus on single consignments or invoices for individual transactions — proper criminal investigations took their time to dismantle entire structures and schemes and the kingpins behind them. And had SARS had the time to do so, that is exactly what would have happened. Until BAT's agents quite fortuitously gave the underworld what I would argue was an unanticipated early Christmas present.

We've already seen how at some point companies like BAT indisputably had a good relationship with SARS, but then a few things changed, which put their once-cosy relationship with SARS under pressure. The dynamics started changing because for the first time SARS really started looking at BAT not as a *source* of information, but as the *subject* of an investigation.

So, what went wrong? It is a bit of a mouthful, and the details are only now slowly becoming apparent: SARS notified a number of manufacturers — including BAT — that they were under investigation for a range of offences (an extract of the letter that was sent to them is attached as addendum 1.).

20. BAT's Christmas present to the underworld?

Its investigations – under Project Honey Badger – reportedly uncovered big tobacco spy networks being run across South Africa, and in Zimbabwe, Mozambique, Swaziland, Lesotho, Botswana and all the way to Namibia.

SARS had reportedly discovered evidence of how individuals within the TISA/BAT/FSS/Tobacco Task Team alliance were allegedly engaging in racketeering, money-laundering, tax evasion, corruption and fraud. This meant a few of the police officials, SSA agents, prosecutors and crime intelligence spooks were in for trouble together with their tobacco company mates.

At the same time, SARS sought to completely change the way it engaged with BAT. It explicitly instructed SARS officials not to engage with BAT, and centralised all tobacco-related engagements under Project Honey Badger. This, you can imagine, must have been immensely frustrating for a company like BAT, which until now had enjoyed almost unfettered access to SARS information. So, they resorted to using informal contacts at SARS – three individuals in particular seem to have been very happy to pass information on to the alliance. My sources suggest that these three moles – who were not part of the Honey Badger team – could tell big tobacco that SARS had *something* on them but couldn't tell them exactly what. So now the alliance knew that something was brewing, but were getting frustrated with their SARS contacts who didn't have quite enough clout to make the SARS case go away.

The alliance began to panic slightly. They knew something was coming, but not quite what it was, or how to stop it.

So, they launched an all-out effort to understand what dirt SARS had on them. They needed to know who at SARS was involved, and how they could discredit them. They turned their espionage expertise from focusing on their competitors, to focusing on investigators at SARS (even taking pictures of the kids of the head of the SARS criminal investigations division). And by all accounts, evidence seems to suggest that they launched a secret weapon: Belinda Walter (triple spy; the Mata Hari of Hatfield). She was already spying for them on their competitors, and was easy to set up as what can only be described as a honey trap to get rid of the peskiest of those SARS investigators – Johann van Loggerenberg.

Unfortunately for them, it seems Walter was not really cut out for the job and ultimately blew the whistle on them and handed over copious amounts of data and evidence that exposed the dirty rotten spy ring BAT had been running, even though she would subsequently flip back to their side.

The data Walter had (willingly) handed over had to be discredited somehow. Evidence that has been obtained illegally, as a general rule, cannot be used in subsequent legal proceedings. If the people implicated in the evidence on the flash disk could suggest that the evidence on it had been obtained illegally – through an illegal, unauthorised interception, for instance – whatever was on that disk could not be used against them. Who was implicated in the evidence on that disk? Individuals from BAT, FSS and SSA.

Bear with me as we run through a quick timeline of some key events that are evident from documents in my possession and which – I would argue – suggest that big tobacco may well have started the narrative about a covert, unlawful unit at SARS.

We have more than enough evidence to support the contention that Walter was an agent on BAT's payroll and had been so since approximately August 2012. To do so, she had to be deregistered as an SSA agent – this was seemingly a precondition from both BAT and the SSA.

Evidence suggests that on 24 May 2013 she met with Mr Evans of BAT Plc, who was – in her words – 'horrified' when he realised that she had been keeping copies of her correspondence with them. She was instructed to delete all the copies.

We know that from around October 2013 she became involved in a relationship with Van Loggerenberg, to whom she disclosed her com-

20. BAT's Christmas present to the underworld?

promised situation, and who sought to provide her with some advice on how best to extricate herself.

As a result, by January 2014 Ms Walter recorded her willingness to testify about the unlawfulness of her relationship with BAT, and on 1 February 2014 disclosed to her erstwhile client Carnilinx that she had been spying on them, for BAT. She also sought to get her ducks in a row, so to speak, by getting copies of the electronic evidence she had on her cellphones and stored online. To do so, she needed Van Loggerenberg's assistance, and he put her in touch with a data recovery expert. Once the data had been recovered, she kept one copy herself – and gave a second copy to Van Loggerenberg. When he eventually had the opportunity to look at the information, he says that it was very clear to him that Walter, BAT SA, BAT UK, FSS, police crime intelligence informants, and former and current SSA officials were involved in a range of illegal activities which had cost the fiscus hundreds of millions of rands.

On 13 May 2014, Van Loggerenberg ended his relationship with Walter, in a break-up that has been described as 'acrimonious' in the media.

Evidence shows that on 23 May 2014, Walter sent a letter of demand to BAT UK for monies still owed to her. As far as we know, she sent the letter only to BAT UK. Five days later – out of the blue – she was approached by her handler at the State Security Agency, who told her that her breaking rank was a problem, that she had to withdraw the demand and 'get off BAT's back', and in return would be granted indemnity and assistance in taking on Van Loggerenberg.

On 27 May 2014, Walter met with law enforcement officials – including Crime Intelligence officer Lt Colonel Hennie Niemann. She explained, in an affidavit, 'I was advised that it would be difficult for them to assist me if I was simultaneously at loggerheads with BAT UK and the State Security Agency. I was made to feel that I had "broken rank" and I was on my own and nobody would assist me. I acceded to the requests of withdrawal of the demand and I was assured that I would be provided with immunity from prosecution.' (This, by the way, is a legal impossibility – the NPA cannot provide indemnity, and most certainly not for an investigation and prosecution that does not even exist.)

She was in effect told that she would not face prosecution, but only if she withdrew her legal demand against BAT UK. This was important, because – I would argue – the Serious Fraud Office in the UK would likely have been very interested in this relationship and the payments made.

But she also faced a second conundrum: the very people she met to discuss her 'indemnity' with were implicated in the documents she had handed over to Van Loggerenberg. Not only that, but they knew that Van Loggerenberg had evidence that – he says – implicated them in a host of other criminal offences.

Van Loggerenberg explains, 'There's no doubt in my mind that they knew that what I had in my possession was going to prove to be a problem if I remained within the system. There's no doubt in my mind that she needed assistance and the assistance was "look, we're all in trouble, Johann has got the data, he knows about this, he knows about the whole racket, he knows about the whole FSS network of spies, he knows everything. And it's just a matter of time when he is going to start rolling these things up. So, we're going to make a plan. JVL is a problem."'[1]

On 2 June 2014, after all of the foregoing had taken place, Walter suddenly suggested – for the very first time – that her phone calls had been intercepted by SARS.

On 23 June 2014, Walter formally withdrew her letter of demand against BAT.

Importantly, towards the end of June 2014, a panel that had been tasked with reviewing Walter's complaint against Van Loggerenberg made no mention of any allegations of an unlawful or covert unit, so this narrative had clearly not yet been advanced at the time.

20. BAT's Christmas present to the underworld?

On 20 July 2014, Walter met with Ferdi Fryer (reportedly her first handler at the SSA) and confirmed the purpose of that meeting in a follow-up email. 'Removal of the entire leadership of the South African Revenue Service,' it said.

In August 2014, in papers in a high court application brought by Carnilinx against her and BAT, she wrote that SARS ran an unlawful, covert unit that intercepted taxpayers' communications.

In the same month that Walter filed her affidavit, the *Sunday Times* ran a front-page story with a headline that shouted 'Love affair rocks SARS'. You guessed it, the story detailed Walter's love affair with Van Loggerenberg. According to Jacques Pauw, the story was leaked to the newspaper by Walter herself.

It was to be the first of a series of articles the newspaper published about a so-called 'rogue unit' at SARS. (These articles were subsequently withdrawn, with the *Sunday Times* apologising for running them and admitting that it had been played.) But, at the time, the narrative about a covert, unlawful unit was born and it gained traction. It became known as 'the rogue unit' and it still features, quite dubiously, in South African politics today.

On 19 December 2014, Walter sent an email[2] to Chris Burger (her SSA handler), copied to Herbie Heap (the Gauteng Hawks head), and blind carbon copied to Hennie Niemann (the crime intelligence representative on the now defunct anti-illicit tobacco task team), Jay Govender (from the office of the inspector general for intelligence) and Andrew Leask (a former top Scorpions investigator who, incidentally, had faced criminal charges for allegedly being involved in the bugging of offices of the National Prosecuting Authority, before turning state witness against, of all people, Van Loggerenberg).[3] In the email, Walter makes the following comments: 'In 2012 when you issued the letter and sent me whatsaps [sic] confirming the termination, deregistration etc. of me as a SSA agent/informant – I did not misunderstand. You know as well as I do that BAT would not have any relationship without that confirmation. You say that the SSA has turned its back on me and I am on my own. I gave you more than 4 years of my life. I took ridiculous risks for you and did it all because I believed in what we were doing. As long as you were getting the information and looking like a hero you simply didn't care. In that respect JVL was at least right – I was on a collision course and there was no happy ending for me.

'When I was assaulted in September 2013, you did not even pick up a telephone. That incident set the wheels in motion for JvL to enter my life. You ran around behind my back spreading rumours. You sent JvL messages defaming me. After you did that – who did I have left? Only JvL! And considering the way you had treated me and all the lies you had told me over the years (which JvL neatly unpacked for me) what did you think I would do? I am not lying or covering for any of you. I should in August have opened my mouth and I would not be in this current predicament. But instead I kept quiet to protect you. And for what? You threw me under the bus every chance you get. Why did you not disclose your cosy correspondence of November 2014 with JvL to the IG? Did you try sell me out to him again to protect yourself because you had seen what was on the memory stick I gave you? I also warned you to keep your distance because the smaller players will be watching. You did not heed my warnings and now there are evidently photographs of what the descriptions sound like you, Mads [understood to be Madelein Schlenter from SSA], Ewan [from BAT] and Alan [from BAT] at some social setting in Cape Town. Being in bed with private companies is not going to end well for government departments. You know that but yet it persists. I have had more than enough bad publicity – I am not going to be tainted by your relationship with BAT. I have already had enough answering to do about my relationship with them. I gave you the opportunity to do the honourable thing and return my memory stick to me or to provide me with a copy. You refused to do so to protect yourself at my expense.'

On 11 August 2014, one of the independent tobacco traders in South Africa sent an email to two high-profile journalists in South Africa –

20. BAT's Christmas present to the underworld?

with the subject line 'Fact not fiction' – setting out in shocking details a series of allegations against Walter, including a number of confessions he says she had made to him. The list of examples stretches over five pages, and includes that, '. . . she began to explain in detail about how she intends infiltrating Johann van Logerenberg [sic] for Bat as they [BAT] are unable to control him. Showed us her correspondence with Johann van Logerenberg [sic] on whattsapp. I believe he fell in love with her not realizing that she had ulterior motives. She Said [sic] that they wanted Van Logerenberg's [sic] hands tainted and removed from Sars as he was becoming a problem for BAT. He had caught up with their transfer pricing model, paying royalties to their offshore company at a rate of R12 per packet, R120 per carton, R6 000 per case, which equates to R1,44 billion per month of which one third should actually go to the Sars as company taxes. This is approximately R4 billion stolen from Sars annually. BAT not so clean after all. She thereafter began to leak information to Clifford Collins and Yusuf Dinat [sic] from the Sars anti corruption department in order to discredit Van Logerenberg [sic].'

In May 2019, the country's former top spy, Arthur Fraser, is reported to have confirmed in an affidavit that he had evidence that showed that SARS had been the target of coordinated intelligence operations aimed at derailing its investigation into tobacco smuggling and the local tobacco industry. Former spy boss Gibson Njenje was fired from his position as special advisor to the State Security Minister. Aside from that, little seems to have happened. As *The Citizen* newspaper notes, 'Somewhere, at either the SSA, the Directorate for Priority Crime Investigation (Hawks), the office of the inspector general for intelligence (OIGI) or the National Prosecuting Authority (NPA) apparently lie copies of a very special flash drive – and it seems no one wants anything to do with it because of its alleged association with the multibillion-rand tobacco industry.'[4]

It was the perfect storm.

The fake narrative ended up being fed to the *Sunday Times* newspaper, KPMG, Judge Frank Kroon and investigative TV programme

Carte Blanche. They even managed to rope in FITA members and Carnilinx to advance the 'rogue' story for their own benefit at the time. (All of them – every single one of them – subsequently had to issue apologies for buying into what was little more than an old apartheid-style disinformation campaign, but the damage was done.)

The 'rogue unit' narrative gave South Africa's underworld two precious gifts:

It gave everybody who had in recent years been the subject of a SARS investigation a putative, spurious defence, allowing them to (wrongly) argue that evidence gathered against them may have been similarly intercepted illegally, tainting the information SARS had based its findings on. (Of course, the only evidence I've seen of illegal interceptions relate to BAT and friends – there is to this day no evidence of SARS having done so.) Nonetheless, this resulted in SARS walking away from most of its recent investigations (helped on by then-Commissioner Tom Moyane who seemingly favoured the 'rogue' narrative, arguably because it might have come in handy for Jacob Zuma who had his own tax woes.)

And it handily gave the new Commissioner the perfect excuse to entirely dismantle SARS' investigative capacity. He dispatched the 'rogue' employees; ordered the disbandment of SARS criminal investigations; and terminated all investigations and audits into the tobacco industry. All of them. (Which may similarly have been useful for Mr Zuma, whose son, you may remember from one of our earlier stories, was also involved in the tobacco industry.) At that time, the Hawks, the prosecuting authority, the police, the State Security Agency and a host of other state departments were all being hijacked as part of what would become known later as 'state capture'. The 'rogue' story became the perfect pretext for the capturing of SARS.

While the rogue unit narrative may have served many purposes to many individuals, I believe it can all be traced back to big tobacco and its agents. They were the thin end of edge of the wedge.

20. BAT's Christmas present to the underworld?

When that thin blue line was gone, it was open season for smugglers. (Perhaps helped along by Walter and friends actively planning the demise of anybody else at SARS who made life difficult for them, asking about one pesky tax investigator in particular, 'Do we sink the bitch . . . do I carry on with matters that will hurt her career?')

It's perhaps not surprising, then, that South Africa has seen a dramatic increase in illicit cigarettes in recent years. Between 2014 and 2017, the number of cigarette packs on which tax was paid reportedly fell by 27%.[5] In 2015, SARS had seized around 204 million sticks of cigarettes. By 2016, this had dropped to 133 million, and by 2018 only 61 million sticks were seized.[6] The prevalence of illicit cigarettes had grown from a reported 10% to 33% in the space of seven years.

Van Loggerenberg – the mastermind behind Project Honey Badger – and acting Commissioner Ivan Pillay lost their jobs and faced trumped-up criminal charges for running a 'rogue unit' that supposedly spied on taxpayers. The entire SARS executive committee was disbanded – they should have known about this supposed rogue unit, no? – leaving the man Zuma appointed, Tom Moyane, to run the organisation with impunity.

The SARS we knew was dead. Its demise started with an investigation into BAT's dirty hands. The nail in its coffin was BAT having to discredit evidence about its very intimate relationship with criminality.

> 'SARS [had] provided imperfect but perceptible enforcement through its investigations and raids. When these declined, it led to unrestrained competition between tobacco smugglers, which fuelled tensions between the various players. This tension has been linked to assassinations (successful and failed) and acts of vandalism. Cigarettes have also emerged as a preferred currency in the underworld as their ease of distribution in cash-based markets makes them ideal for money laundering.'
> – *The Atlantic Council, in their paper on illicit tobacco in South Africa*[7]

Vintage big tobacco ad from the Stanford University catalogue

Brand: Chesterfield
Manufacturer: Liggett & Myers Tobacco Company
Campaign Theme: Movie Stars – Men
Publish Date: 1949
Quote: I am sending Chesterfields to all my friends. That's the merriest Christmas any smoker can have – Chesterfield mildness plus no unpleasant after-taste.
Comments: Ronald Reagan (1911–2004), 40th President of the United States features in the ad. Aside from his prolific movies career with 76 films to his credit, he served as President of the Screen Actors Guild. Reagan quit smoking after his brother developed cancer of the larynx. Famous, healthy voices had a particular appeal for cigarette advertisers: If a famous actor entrusted his voice and throat to a cigarette brand, then it can't be so bad.[8]

PART 4

Quo Vadis?

21. Avoidance, evasion and glass houses

Illicit tobacco *is* a problem deserving of our attention. But we tend to think of it as an excise duty problem – it is not. It is but one small part of the tax gap attributable to the tobacco industry more broadly – a small part of the money we are defrauded of by the tobacco industry.

We are so busy focusing on the product – cigarettes – that we lose sight of the entity that makes them. If we truly want to have an impact on the illicit trade in cigarettes, we need to spend more time focusing on the *entities* that manufacture them – which includes large tobacco companies.

One of big tobacco's biggest successes lies in its ability to make us believe in the bogeyman of illicit trade – we are so intent on chasing it and fixing it that we have lost sight of the big picture: the big tobacco magic show of misdirection and illusion.

We are so busy focusing on the smaller players that we lose sight of the fact that big tobacco's own hands may be dirty. And that, in part, explains why our law enforcement agencies have relatively little real impact on the illicit trade in cigarettes.

I had initially consciously stayed away from the more sophisticated tax avoidance and evasion schemes that multinationals dabble in (and as early drafts of this book proved, who'd want to read a book about tax avoidance, profit shifting and base erosion, right?)

But of course, while there is evidence of big tobacco probably still profiting from the black market, increasingly much of their profits must be coming from more sophisticated tax avoidance and evasion schemes.

The difference between tax avoidance (which is legally playing with the interpretation of legislation so you pay less tax) and tax evasion (which is not paying tax and which is *not* legal), has famously been described as the breadth of a prison wall. The way big tobacco structures its affairs leaves it playing to that thin line and while they indisputably often end up on the right side of the wall, they sometimes do not.

In 2018 BAT was issued additional income tax assessments to the value of $124 million for aggressive tax planning using debt financing structures in South Africa.

This is certainly not the only country where the giant has faced additional tax assessments: in their 2018 annual report BAT revealed how it is facing a $422 million income tax assessment in Brazil; a $1,155 million assessment related to intra-group transactions in the Netherlands; a VAT and duty dispute to the tune of $218 million in Bangladesh; and a $131 million tax assessment in Egypt. Altogether, the potential liabilities – should they fail to successfully challenge the assessments – total some $2,1 billion.[1] That's just for 2018.

In 2019 BAT was sued by the Dutch government for €1 billion for tax evasion.[2] It seems in 2017 £1,6 billion had flowed through its main holding company (British American Tobacco International Holdings BV) to the parent company in the United Kingdom, on which it paid a mere £1,6 million in tax (a tax burden of 0,1%).[3]

JTI does not disclose its tax disputes in its annual reports,[4] but PMI did in its 2018 annual report: aside from various customs and excise duty disputes, PMI also paid $243 million to settle an additional income tax assessment in Korea.[5] Imperial's annual report for 2018 notes that it was taken to task for transfer pricing to the value of £250 million in France; and anticipates possible further assessments of £74 million in Russia and as much as £300 million under the UK's Controlled Foreign Company regime.[6] That's just for 2018.

21. Avoidance, evasion and glass houses

Part of the problem in telling this story lies in the fact that these voluntary disclosures in annual reports are oftentimes the only insights we have into the more sophisticated schemes big tobacco gets embroiled in (because as we've seen, our tax and customs agencies are typically sworn to secrecy).

This means that just as big tobacco has historically managed to evade detection of their smuggling activities by keeping their supply chains almost entirely opaque, they have similarly been able to keep much of their other tax tomfooleries opaque through a simple lack of transparency.

At the BAT Plc annual general meeting in 2014 an activist asked, 'Mr. Chairman, I note that BAT reports on the amount of corporation tax paid in the UK (which appears to be zero) and the amount of corporation tax paid overseas, without providing a breakdown of the countries comprised within the overseas heading. The Sustainability Summary states that "Transparency is important to us". With the importance of transparency in mind could you let us know in what countries the company does pay corporation tax, and can you confirm whether the company would be open to providing a country-by-country breakdown of taxes paid in annual reports in the future?'

BAT's CEO responded simply and curtly that there was 'no need to report globally.'[7] I beg to differ, Mr Stevens — I think there is a very good reason for your company to start reporting on how much you pay in taxes in the different countries you operate in: so we know just to what extent we can trust you.

BAT SA is the second biggest listed company in South Africa — with a dual listing in the UK — and with a market cap that is three times bigger than that of behemoth Anglo American. And yet they pay a mere 0,8% of the corporate income tax SARS collects.[8]

BAT has its headquarters in the UK. Between 2011 and 2014 it did not pay one cent in profit taxes there. Not a cent. Imperial is similarly headquartered in the UK. Between the two, in 2016 they paid a paltry

£83 million in taxes. How does big tobacco claim the moral high ground when it is paying an effective tax rate of 3,5% in the UK (post 2014) while other companies pay on average somewhere between 20–28%?[9]

Why would the parent company of the largest publicly listed company in the world not pay a cent of corporate income tax in the United Kingdom? 'Because it didn't make any profit on its UK activities.' Instead, according to *The Guardian* newspaper through just one of its subsidiaries BAT shifted pre-tax profit to the tune of $942 million – and it has more than 100 subsidiaries.[10]

BAT's dispute with the taxman in South Africa – around 'debt structuring', a classic tax scheme – sits at close to R2 billion ($124 million). Low estimates put the annual loss in excise from contraband tobacco at around R3 billion a year. So BAT may well owe the equivalent in taxes of two thirds of what SARS loses to illicit tobacco. And that's just on corporate income tax, never mind on customs and excise duties, for which they subsequently also received an assessment to the tune of R214 million (around $15 million) for mismatches between their export declarations and what was actually in the containers, and some other alleged abuses around rebates. (And all of that's *before* Project Honey Badger could wrap up its investigation into BAT.)

The Tax Justice Network estimates that in Bangladesh BAT managed to shift $21 million in profits through royalties and IT charges, costing the country $5,8 million in taxes; in Indonesia they reportedly shifted $73 million through loans and royalties, costing the country $13,7 million in taxes. By booking Brazil's profits in Madeira they may have managed to shift $110 million out of the country, costing Brazil $33 million in tax revenues. In Kenya, by shifting dividend payments to the tune of $26 million, they reportedly avoided payment of $2,7 million in local taxes. For the record: media reports suggest that BAT disagrees with the analysis.[11]

They happily pay themselves royalties, management fees and IT

21. Avoidance, evasion and glass houses

charges; they lend themselves money; they send profits back home to investors.

And they get away with it all because '[While] the schemes involved are similar to those used in criminal activities . . . what prevents some of their activities being exposed as tax evasion is mainly because multinational companies can back up what they do with opinions from tax advisers that make it difficult to establish the intent necessary for a criminal offence.'[12]

But perhaps most curious of all of big tobacco's structures may well be this one, described to me by a seasoned tax investigator: they've devised what can only be described as fictitious transactions that are aimed at bolstering their trade volumes, by shipping the same containers from one country, to the next, on to another and then back to their country of origin. There is no commercial substance to these transactions – they just make the books look good; make it look like business is booming; making shareholders happy.[13] (You know who else tried doing that? Enron. And, by some accounts, Steinhoff too.)

When they're not shifting profits to the UK, they're hiding behind a veil of secrecy in Switzerland.

Switzerland is perhaps more traditionally known as the land of cheese and chocolate, but by some accounts its third biggest export is cigarettes.[14] (I wonder how robust Swiss tax inspections are?) Part of the answer perhaps lies in a claim contained in court papers filed in the Colombian Governors' lawsuit against PMI. 'Philip Morris has moved the records concerning many of its illegal activities worldwide to Switzerland so as to escape the surveillance of the governments which are victimized by Philip Morris' illegal activities.'[15]

Being based in a country like Switzerland has other benefits too: not only does the company pay reduced corporate income tax rates on what little profits remain, it also benefits from commercial secrecy laws that render its financial transactions and banking entirely opaque, and that effectively protects it from having to answer questions from pesky investigators. In response to an international investigation into wide-scale smuggling, RJ Reynolds noted, 'We'd like to help you but Swiss legislation on commercial secrecy prevents us.'

Big tobacco doesn't just keep its money in Switzerland – it makes cigarettes there too. I continue to be amazed at the number of cigarettes being exported from Switzerland – the country literally exports almost as many cigarettes as it does chocolates, producing nearly 2 billion packs a year (JTI alone makes 43 million cigarettes a day in Switzerland). Most of the local production – as much as 75% – is exported, most of it to Japan, Morocco and South Africa. I really couldn't tell you why South Africa is importing cigarettes from Switzerland, given its own domestic capabilities and its proximity to industry-powerhouse Zimbabwe, but in 2014, 74% of South Africa's imported cigarettes came from Switzerland – by 2018 this had increased to 87% (that makes for more than 3 000 tons of cigarettes imported into South Africa from Switzerland a year).[16]

Perhaps at least part of the reason why South Africa is such a popular export market for Swiss-made cigarettes lies in the fact that there may be a big – and I mean very big – incentive to do so, in the form of what appears to be a discount on the import duties and rates payable.

Under the European Free Trade Agreement, it seems that if you import cigars from Switzerland, you'd pay 14,3 cents per kilogram in import duties. Import them from somewhere else and it would cost you 110 cents for the same kilogram. The same goes for cigarettes: if imported from Switzerland, the rate of duty is 5,8%, but 45% if imported from somewhere else (except for transactions in the Southern African Customs Union, which are duty free).[17] So, importing tobacco from Switzerland is eight to nine times cheaper than doing so from anywhere else.

It's a bizarre discounted rate with what seems to be little commercial substance, seeming to give big tobacco yet another competitive advantage over its smaller competitors. (I asked SARS for comment but received no reply.)

21. Avoidance, evasion and glass houses

This isn't the only cushy deal they seem to have negotiated in South Africa: I have not been able to verify this, but a source tells me that they may have secured an unusually generous wastage allowance.[18]

Many governments give excise manufacturers what is called a wastage allowance – a small percentage of their production volumes on which they do not have to pay tax. On average perhaps around 0,5% of their production volumes are simply assumed to have not made it to market, because of 'spillage and clingage'.[19] However, most countries entirely exclude tobacco products from this allowance. So you can imagine my astonishment when my source said that (some) South African manufacturers appear to have informally negotiated for what is reportedly somewhere between a 5-20% wastage allowance[20] – for which I could not find a mandate in legislation, and which is certainly not in keeping with international good practice. Maybe my source is wrong, and I asked SARS for comment, but they did not reply.

Is this simply regulatory capture in action?

We also know that BAT is being investigated by UK tax authorities for what some have termed 'al-Qaeda-styled'[21] payments to its network of undercover agents.

I'd like to hear BAT explain how the alleged use of those Travelex cards to pay its network of agents does *not* amount to money laundering. The whole point was so that you didn't have to use normal payment channels that could be traced back to you, right? The use of these prepaid cards has been highlighted worldwide as a means for organised criminal networks to move money offshore and across jurisdictions, amounting to money laundering.

And remember that thumb drive I got in Rosebank? It also highlighted another potential problem for BAT: the VAT invoices it received from FSS for its 'services' had some peculiarities. The invoices – which correctly quote both BAT and FSS' VAT numbers and certainly purport to be VAT invoices – use a rather anomalous system. Instead of referring to transactions as being either zero rated or VAT-able, as is required on a VAT invoice, they refer to the line items as either an 's' or an 'e' (I assume the 'e' is meant to convey 'exempt'). Some 'disbursements' are marked with 'e's' and some not, and I have to wonder how the taxman would have been able to make sense of these differently-constructed VAT invoices.

And there is more: some invoice numbers appear to be duplicated. I'd love to know how these 'VAT invoices' were accounted for in both BAT and FSS' tax returns.

As big tobacco has reinvented itself, it has similarly evolved how it makes its profits.

Perhaps — and bear with me here — there is something of a moral equivalence between the alleged smuggling of packs of cigarettes by independent players like Delport, Amalgamated Tobacco, Carnilinx or Gold Leaf on the one hand, and big tobacco sending its untaxed profits offshore and laundering money on the other? Perhaps there is something of an equivalence when there seem to be billions of cigarettes unaccounted for being made by their very own members? Why do we frown on the smaller independent players trying to minimise their tax liabilities, but apparently cut cushy deals with big tobacco to import their cigarettes at a vastly discounted rate from Switzerland?

Big tobacco poses an entirely different, more complex risk — one that includes elements of illicit trade, but one that also goes far beyond just that. As outlined in the first chapters of this book, there is ample historical evidence of multi-national tobacco companies being involved in smuggling their own product; but what lies beneath that is a series of dark mills, of smoke and mirrors, that covers how they illegally spy on their competitors; how their structures allow them to pay virtually no corporate income tax; how they may inflate sales volumes through fictitious revenue schemes; how they abuse their relationship with tax agencies to secure even more preferential treatment that gives them even more of an edge over their smaller competitors; and aggressive tax planning.

21. Avoidance, evasion and glass houses

Ultimately, is the end result from these more sophisticated schemes – monies lost to the state, and you and I having to bear more of the tax burden – not the same?

We pay our taxes, you and I. And when some pay less than their fair share, we pay more. Whether they pay less through some ham-fisted smuggling effort, or through more sophisticated profit-shifting schemes, the result is the same – you and I are paying more tax than we should.

22. Blowing smoke

Of course, in time, much of the above may well become academic, as the tobacco business model is slowly evolving, moving from combustible cigarettes, to what the industry suggests may be healthier options that heat tobacco, instead of burning it.

There is no consensus amongst experts that these new devices *actually* reduce risk to smokers, and indeed industry itself is very careful to refer to these devices as '*potentially* reduced-risk' products. 'Potential' being in italics because even in internal industry documents the word is highlighted. There seems to be a bit of industry reluctance to *guarantee* harm reduction – perhaps because industry has learnt some lessons from its previous experiences promising healthier cigarettes.

Why? Because its very business model depends on it.

This book does not dwell on cigarettes from a health perspective, but it is still worth wondering what happened to the earlier 'healthier' versions? How are they different from what is being launched today?

It's an important conversation, not just from a health perspective, but because big tobacco is arguing that this new generation of products should receive a tax break. They argue that governments should be *encouraging* smokers to switch to these products, which requires some kind of special tax regime to make them more affordable. (And they've been quite successful in doing so. PMI notes in its annual report: 'To date, we have been largely successful in demonstrating to regulators that our reduced risk products are not cigarettes, and as such they are generally taxed either as a separate category or as other tobacco products, which typically yields more favourable tax rates than cigarettes.'[1])

A PMI executive once expected us to believe that, 'None of the things which have been found in tobacco smoke are at concentrations which can be considered harmful. Anything can be considered harmful. Apple sauce is harmful if you get too much of it.'[2]

They lied to us then, and it is quite conceivable that they may be lying to us today.

In 1954 industry told us, 'If we had any thought or knowledge that in any way we were selling a product harmful to consumers we would stop business tomorrow.'[3] In 1972 they promised, 'If our product is harmful we'll stop making it.'[4] By 1997 they were saying, 'We would shut manufacturing plants down instantly if scientists prove cigarettes cause cancer.'[5]

In 2017 they said, 'We know tobacco products pose real and serious health risks and the only way to avoid these risks is not to use them.'[6]

And it turns out the tobacco companies knew about the health risks all along. Internal industry documents note, in some detail, industry's acknowledgement of the fact that cigarettes are – and always were – undeniably harmful and cause disease, and that modifying conventional cigarettes is unlikely to be effective in harm reduction.

For 42 years Philip Morris noted in internal documents that the design of its filters led to small particles being dislodged during smoking, resulting in their consumers ingesting and inhaling non-degradable, toxin coated cellulose acetate fragments and carbon microparticles. And by all accounts Philip Morris did nothing about it, noting instead that 'the *illusion* of filtration is as important as the fact of filtration'.[7]

This is not the first time industry has sought to launch supposedly reduced risk products, or claim to have developed healthier alternatives:

In 1952 the US Federal Trade Commission slapped Philip Morris on the wrist for making false claims about its Di-Gl reducing irritation from smoking. In 1952 Lorillard introduced Kent cigarettes, boasting that its micronite filter offered 'the greatest health protection in cigarette history'. Its secret? It contained asbestos. In 1989 PMI spent $300 000 test-marketing a version of its next brand called 'De-Nic', which contained only 0,1 mg nicotine – apparently most sales were made to tobacco researchers who bought them for use in studies. In 1989 RJR released Premier, its smokeless cigarette, for test-marketing but abandoned it in the same year. In 1997 PMI launched its Accord smoking system. In 2000 RJR started marketing its Eclipse cigarette as a healthier alternative. In 2001 Brown & Williamson began test-marketing Advance, its 'reduced risk' cigarette. Much of this development appears to have come to a grinding halt in 2002, when a jury ordered PMI to pay $150 million for making misrepresentations about its 'light' cigarettes,[8] and when governments started insisting on disclosure of the actual ingredients of cigarettes. In 1989 the Canadian government started requiring cigarette manufacturers to list the additives for each brand, resulting in Reynolds temporarily withdrawing its brands and reformulating them. Philip Morris withdrew its cigarettes from the Canadian market entirely.[9]

In 1994 the tobacco industry released 'The List'. It showed that their cigarettes contained 599 additives.[10]

This new generation of cigarettes – heat-not-burn, electronic, vaping, whatever the adjective is – is more than just a new product line for tobacco companies. It offers them an opportunity to significantly change the way their products are taxed, by touting them as some sort of healthier alternative that governments should actually be *encouraging* their citizens to use.

And while this may change the landscape somewhat, the patterns and trends and rhetoric we've been exploring throughout this book will likely not.

Governments' failure to pre-empt and adopt a much stronger upfront policy position of their own on the taxation of these products may prove to be an Achilles heel. It is entirely conceivable that big tobacco may in the not too distant future find the majority of its revenues accruing from heated tobacco products, without the tax burden currently imposed on its traditional cigarettes, and it will be extremely difficult for governments to claw back the lost tax revenues. We'd better hope this new stuff really *is* 'reduced risk'.

Beyond simply lobbying for a friendlier tax regime for its products, the industry is now also painting a vision of what it calls a 'smoke-free future'.

PMI announced a $1 billion investment in a 'healthier future', and set up a 'Foundation for a Smoke-Free World'.[11] It sounds impressive but the funding is the equivalent of what the industry spends on advertising in three days, and represents just 0,1% of their annual revenue. (By contrast, a company like Mattel spends around 5% of their revenues on corporate social responsibility.) In 2018, PMI spent more on public relations ($5,2 million to Ogilvy, and $665 000 to Mercury) than on research, which doesn't really fit the image it is trying to paint of itself as a research-driven scientific body. PMI continues to be its only source of funding.[12] It's little more than a public relations arm of PMI.

This billion-dollar investment represents about one dollar for every person tobacco will kill this century.[13] The $80 million a year also pales in comparison to PMI's other sponsorships, for instance its annual spending on its longstanding sponsorship of Ferrari, which had been estimated to cost PMI in the region of $160 million annually.[14]

> 'Is anything less believable than big tobacco investing in a smoke-free future? It's the latest publicity gambit – a billion dollar lie – from PMI which is looking to rebrand themselves as fighting for health.'
> – Jose Castro, 'A billion dollar lie'[15]

The vast majority of PMI's effort, revenues, profits and brand equity seemingly continue to remain tied to combustible tobacco – with the billion dollars being nothing less than a tax-deductible marketing expense.

Are the promises of so-called 'reduced risk products' and the Foundation for a Smoke-Free World just industry again blowing smoke? I suspect perhaps so.

It doesn't really matter, though, for purposes of this book and the story it tells – what matters is that big tobacco will use the same tactics it used for its combustible cigarettes for its new stable of products. It will continue to be a merchant of disinformation; it will continue to use proxies to speak on its behalf; it will continue to misdirect our politicians; it will continue to lobby and capture; it will continue to use our enforcement agencies as their economic hitmen, and it will continue to keep its supply chains opaque. And you can bet that it will continue to pursue every possible avenue to dilute, delay, deflect and derail efforts aimed at better regulating it.

> 'The intricate, interlocking, and overlapping web of national and international organizations, committees, affiliations, conferences, research laboratories, funding mechanisms, and repositories for smoking and health information which defendants established, staffed, and funded in order to accomplish the following goals: counter the growing scientific evidence that smoking causes illnesses, avoid liability verdicts, and ensure the future economic viability of the industry . . . like an amoeba, the organization changed its shape to fit its current needs, adding organizations when necessary and eliminating them when they became obsolete. Whatever the shape or composition of the enterprise at any given time, again like an amoeba, its core purpose remained constant: survival of the industry.'
> – *Judge Gladys Kessler, United States Court of Appeals*[16]

Vintage big tobacco ad from the Stanford University catalogue

Brand: Kent
Manufacturer: Lorillard Tobacco Company
Campaign: Kent Classic
Year: 1954
Theme: Filter Safety Myths
Quote: More scientists and educators smoke Kent with the micronite filter
Comment: Part of a broader Kent campaign, with other ads in the series saying, 'Kent, with micronite filter, takes out far more nicotine and tars than any other filter cigarette, old or new.'; 'The difference in price is just a few pennies, the difference in protection is priceless!'; 'Gives you the greatest health protection.' In fact, the micronite filter contained asbestos, a potent carcinogen.[17]

23. Inconvenient truths

In the final analysis, big tobacco faces a number of inconvenient truths.

It will likely tell you that the illicit trade in cigarettes is attributable to smaller, low cost manufacturers, or organised crime syndicates. The inconvenient truth is that big tobacco itself has played a substantial role in creating and sustaining the black market, and there are numerous very well documented examples where illicit trade was not only condoned but formed an explicit part of big tobacco's business model across continents and spanning decades.

Big tobacco will tell you that illicit cigarettes are the result of high tax rates. The inconvenient truth is that study after study has shown that tax rate increases do not necessarily correlate with an increase in illicit trade, and that an upswing in illicit trade is more directly related to a lack of enforcement than to higher tax rates.

It will tell you that it is a significant tax revenue contributor and a key employer, which should earn it a seat at the policy-making table and government's protection against what it positions as illegal competitors. The inconvenient truth is that most of their income is typically channelled to a headquarters in a low tax jurisdiction, resulting in the payment of relatively marginal tax in most jurisdictions. And the inconvenient truth is that in most countries the tax contribution from tobacco companies only very barely covers the health costs associated with smoking, meaning that despite the relatively large tax payments, government is still mostly out of pocket.

23. Inconvenient truths

In South Africa the healthcare costs associated with smoking are estimated to amount to around R59 billion a year[1] – BAT, with 75% of local market share, claims a total tax contribution of R14 billion.[2] Who is paying for the shortfall? That's right – you are.

In the USA healthcare costs associated with tobacco are reportedly estimated at 17 times that of the tax contribution made by the industry.[3] For every dollar Bangladesh raises in income tax from BAT, it apparently loses $24 in economic damage caused by smoking.[4] All making arguments around being a significant revenue contributor somewhat moot.

The inconvenient truth is that tobacco's tax contributions nowhere near compensate for the environmental cost of cigarettes: they don't compensate for the 200 000 hectares of forests we lose every year; for the 175 tons of cigarette butts that are discarded every year (which are not biodegradable); for producing as much greenhouse gas as 1,5 million cars; for leaving us with more plastic waste than plastic bottles do.

Big tobacco will tell you that they are big employers, and that further regulation will result in divestment and job losses. The inconvenient truth is that tobacco farmers who handle crops are reportedly exposed to a substantial amount of nicotine – the equivalent of smoking 36 cigarettes a day; and that typical insecticides used in the production of tobacco leaf include a chemical that was used as a tear gas in World War I. The inconvenient truth is that many of the job losses at tobacco companies will likely have come from automation and process optimisation – and not from increased regulation. The inconvenient truth is that econometric analysis by the World Bank and others consistently suggests that very few countries would actually experience job losses as a result of reduced tobacco consumption, with the money simply being invested elsewhere to create jobs in other sectors of the economy (the same message is hidden in a footnote in an industry document).[5]

Big tobacco will suggest that 72 000 people stand to lose their jobs in South Africa as a result of the growth in the illicit market. But BAT only employs 2 187 people. The rest of the 70 000 includes 'indirect and induced' numbers,[6] which essentially includes the cashier at the fuel station who rings up your pack of cigarettes.

Big tobacco will tell you that illicit trade is becoming an increasingly big problem. They may be right. But the inconvenient truth is that they use their opaque industry-funded studies as a way of deflecting enforcement efforts away from them, instead using our enforcement agencies as economic hitmen to take out competitors as a way of maintaining their market dominance.

They will tell you that industry can't control where their cigarettes end up. The inconvenient truth is that they know exactly where their cigarettes are going, but don't care. The inconvenient truth is that they could use know-your-customer or commensurate demand policies to better secure their supply chains but apparently choose not to. The inconvenient truth is that other industries can track a log of wood from a forest in Indonesia to a teak chair in Europe; or know where a tube of toothpaste is anywhere in the global supply chain – but that the tobacco industry chooses not to do the same despite its products being more lethal and more susceptible to criminality.

Big tobacco will tell you that it has developed its own traceability solution that could be used to track cigarette packs through the supply chain. The inconvenient truth is that it was developed as part of a court ordered agreement, after big tobacco was found to have been supplying the black market in Europe. The inconvenient truth is that their solution is not secure and constitutes an extremely poor enforcement tool. The inconvenient truth is that even industry uses its own solution to track only a percentage of its packs. In law we talk about the 'reasonable man test'. When one looks at the body of evidence as a whole, what would a reasonable man believe? The inconvenient truth is that, with decades of evidence, any reasonable man would likely believe that big tobacco is, at a minimum, complicit in the illicit trade in tobacco, and is incapable of regulating its own supply chain and its own employees.

23. Inconvenient truths

Given the plethora of examples of the industry's involvement in the illicit trade in tobacco, spanning decades and continents, governments can't have confidence that industry records and control systems are adequate to enable the companies to meet their compliance obligations, and monitor their supply chains properly. There are no verifiable indications that big tobacco has made substantive, systemic changes to its processes, systems, policies and strategies to make a serious effort at ensuring they are no longer a complicit actor in the proliferation of illicit trade.

Any other industry with the same history of non-compliance and appetite for risk and blatant obfuscation and vulnerability to criminality would long since have been litigated out of existence, or at the very least had its supply chain regulated far more strictly. Think of Enron, Arthur Anderson and Bell Pottinger.[7] All gone. Volkswagen with their emissions scandal is paying over $20 billion in fines and their stock price took a beating. Big tobacco has arguably done more harm than all of them combined but has not so much as batted an eye and remain a great investment for the morally ambiguous.

Why? Because of their four pillars of power: they control what we read; they control what our politicians do; they control where our law enforcement agencies look; and they'll do mostly anything to ensure that their supply chains remain opaque. Making them, perhaps, too big to fail.

Vintage big tobacco ad from the Stanford University catalogue

Brand: Lucky Strike
Manufacturer: American Tobacco Company
Campaign: Mass Marketing Begins
Theme: Targeting Women
Quote: I'm a 'Lucky Girl' because I've found a new way to keep my figure trim. Whenever the desire for a sweet tempts me, I light up a Lucky Strike.
Comment: In 1928, Lucky Strike introduced its Cream of the Crop campaign, featuring celebrity testimonials from female smokers like Rosalie Nelson (poster girl and flapper), and then followed with Reach for a Lucky Instead of a Sweet in 1929, designed to prey on female insecurities about weight and diet. Rosalie Adele Nelson was the original poster girl for Lucky Strike. She is the all-American girl, perhaps because she smokes Lucky Strike cigarettes.[8]

24. Pebbles for government's David

What our governments are doing is having a limited impact – almost without exception. What successes they claim to have – usually an increase in the number of seizures – are having a negligible impact on the extent to which tobacco companies across the spectrum are paying the taxes and duties they should.

It's time for our governments to think more; read more; question more; do more and fundamentally re-think their overall strategy in combatting illicit trade. Because if they don't, they arguably become complicit in perpetuating the illicit trade in cigarettes.

It's time we give government's 'David' bigger pebbles to take on big tobacco's Goliath. It's time to see past the smoke and mirrors and wake up to big tobacco's magic show of misdirection and illusion.

It's time we understand how big tobacco controls what we think, by controlling what we read. This means maintaining a very strong sense of scepticism about anything we read or hear that relates to the tobacco industry and understanding that much of the messaging we are subjected to is meant to secure a pro-big tobacco view. Instead, we need to be far better about searching out evidence from independent, objective researchers and academics who haven't received funding from the tobacco industry.

It's time to stop buying industry rhetoric not supported by independent, objective research and analysis.

We need to understand the systemic weaknesses that allow big tobacco to control what our politicians and policy makers do. We need to introduce transparency and lobbyist registers; introduce rules that ensure that all engagements with the tobacco industry are recorded and the details made public; and lobby politicians and policy makers to understand that their acquiescence simply kills their constituents and adds considerable costs to government-funded healthcare spending.

But perhaps most importantly, we need to understand the very real risk from soft capture and be mindful not to substitute government prerogatives for industry rhetoric.

We have to understand that big tobacco has an interest in influencing where our enforcement agencies look. It is a way of rooting out competitors who eat into their market share. We need to be sceptical of intelligence provided by big tobacco. We shouldn't be relying on information provided by big tobacco that may well have been obtained illegally (or fabricated). We shouldn't be providing big tobacco access to information on their competitors or give them seats on illicit trade intelligence or enforcement forums.

We need to understand that big tobacco has an interest in keeping its supply chains opaque. And we need to introduce measures that make it less so. We should be managing the upstream inputs into tobacco production, like cigarette paper and filters far better. We should be controlling who is allowed to buy cigarette manufacturing equipment. We should be introducing more stringent production controls. We should be requiring manufacturers to introduce know-your-customer policies, and to provide commensurate demand calculations showing that there is a legitimate demand for their cigarettes in the countries they ship to. And we should be introducing measures that track cigarettes through the supply chain, so they end up where they are supposed to.

While all of this may be true for big tobacco, we still shouldn't be taking our eyes off the smaller tobacco players. Big tobacco created a niche market with huge profit margins and established smuggling routes and practices. While commercialised illicit trade may have started with them, they have simply created a blueprint for the other smaller players we see in the space today.

If you work in the tobacco industry, don't buy your own propaganda.

Big tobacco historically appears to have allowed an illicit trade stream to develop alongside its legitimate business, effectively resulting in two parallel enterprises, whilst ensuring that the legal side could engage with government with some semblance of integrity and could not be held legally liable for the dark underbelly of the company. I would like to think that many of the staff employed by the tobacco industry genuinely believe that they are working to reduce the harm caused by smoking; that their companies are the victims of illicit trade, and never the perpetrators.

If you fall in this category, don't drink the industry Kool-Aid. Understand the industry's history of unlawful behaviour. Understand the industry's credibility gap. Understand how the industry has historically manipulated research. Understand that a bottle of shampoo travels along a more secure supply chain than your highly-susceptible-to-criminality products do. Understand how your colleagues' use of corporate espionage and money laundering tactics expose your company to even more distrust. Understand why governments should be sceptical of your products and your messaging. Question more. Challenge more. And then do better.

If you work for an industry representative body, use transparent methods so we can actually engage with the substance of your calculations on issues like the size and prevalence of illicit trade. Be upfront about what research you've funded and which other bodies or proxies represent your interests.

As individuals, in whatever other official capacities we may hold, we *do* have power.

Even if you don't work at a government agency, and feel powerless to add your voice, you could invest in tobacco-free portfolios. In the 1990s Ben and Jerry's ice cream boycotted tobacco, by dropping tobacco-owned Oreo cookies from its ice cream in protest. Today consumers have an option to do something similar: Bronwyn King, a radiation oncologist, discovered that she was unknowingly supporting tobacco through her pension investments. A portion of her portfolio was invested in BAT, Imperial, PMI and Swedish Match. She founded Tobacco Free Portfolios, which collaborated with finance industry executives, resulting in over $2,5 billion having already been divested from tobacco stocks.[1]

We – you and I, people like us – have power. Because we know how industry plays its game. We know where its power lies and how it uses that power.

I am not a tobacco control activist. For me, it is an important distinction to make. There are many people in the tobacco control space for whom I have great respect and whose objectives I wholly support and who I count as colleagues and friends. But much of the tobacco control space is also fraught with paranoia and absolutes and extremist views. The tobacco control fraternity's absolute ban on any engagement with the tobacco industry is not something that sits well with me. I have always maintained that constructive engagement is possible even with the most recalcitrant of players – as long as you show up with a heavy dose of cynicism. I believe in giving credit where it is due, even when it is marred by a healthy dose of scepticism. I choose to believe that there are a handful of people working across the big tobacco companies, who I hope are genuinely making an effort to stamp out illicit trade, who are genuinely trying to better secure their supply chains.

I am entirely open to hearing how big tobacco has changed its spots, or what it has done to better secure its supply chain, or what steps it has taken to hold those purported rogue employees to account, or what percentage of their staff lay-offs are the result of process optimisation and automation (and not of illicit packs being sold by their smaller competitors).

Doing this – all of it – is the only way we'll get to a space where big tobacco is no longer too big to fail.

> 'This is the most important lesson you
> must learn about magic.
> There are many ways of seeing.
> Each has an element of truth,
> but none is the whole truth.
> If you limit yourselves to one way of seeing,
> one truth, you will limit your power.
> You must see in many ways.
> You must be flexible.
> You must be willing to learn from different sources. And you must always remember that
> the truths you see are incomplete.'
> – *Patricia C Wrede, American fantasy literature author*[2]

Vintage big tobacco ad from the Stanford University catalogue

Brand: Lucky Strike
Manufacturer: American Tobacco Company
Year: 1930
Theme: 20 679 Physicians
Quote: Toasting removes dangerous irritants that cause throat irritation and coughing
Comment: As the More Doctors Smoke Camels campaign theme demonstrated, one common technique wielded by the tobacco industry to reassure a worried public was to incorporate images of physicians in their ads. The doctors were never specific individuals, because physicians who engaged in advertising would risk losing their licence. These type of ads regularly appeared in medical journals such as the *Journal of the American Medical Association*. Most notable in this theme are the '20,679 Physicians' advertisements. The ads present no actual data.[3]

25. Too big to fail?

I've been dwelling a lot on the reasons why big tobacco continues to be so powerful, through its playbook of controlling what we read, controlling our politicians, directing where our law enforcement agencies look, and keeping their supply chains opaque.

But perhaps there is another reason – one that I almost prefer not to contemplate.

Over a cup of coffee with a highly respected investigator, we were exploring why nothing (public) had yet come of the UK's investigation into BAT Plc for its monkeyshines in South Africa. We know for a fact that they are investigating BAT Plc. We know with some certainty that the charges potentially include money laundering and corruption.

So, I called up somebody who is closely associated with the UK's investigation, who explained that part of their problem was the sheer volume of documents and evidence they had, which made piecing together a coherent story that could stand up to lawyerly scrutiny an absolutely herculean task.

But our conversation also yielded another, more startling thought:

Perhaps some companies are just too big to fail.

A veritable lifetime ago I was working on tax compliance programmes for one of the leading economies in the world. We were very pertinently advised not to target financial institutions, because exposing any weaknesses on their part could literally collapse the country's economy.

It was something we grappled with at SARS too: should a tax agency simply shut down unresponsive, recalcitrant non-compliant businesses? Or do they have a broader responsibility, as responsive regulators, to help those companies stay in business if the resultant job losses and economic impact would be disproportionately big?

Which button do you press – 'business rescue', or 'big stick'?

Which brings us to the little conundrum the world faces with a company like BAT Plc.

Wherever big tobacco is listed on a stock exchange, our pension funds and our governments are investing, and heavily so. This doesn't only give big tobacco a semblance of respectability; it gives them real power.

I tapped Moneyweb contributor Barbara Curson for some quick insights: In South Africa, at the time of writing the government employees' pension fund was holding 42 918 236 shares in BAT, at a current share price of R559,48. That gives them a R23 billion ($1,5 billion) stake in what happens to BAT. (More, actually: the pension fund also holds 23 126 707 shares in Reinet, which *also* holds shares in BAT. In fact, 48% of Reinet's investments are in . . . BAT.[1] So, if my calculations are correct, that means an additional R6,2 billion – $405 million – that is potentially at stake for the country's pensioners.)

If BAT goes bust in South Africa? South African pensioners stand to lose R30 billion (roughly $2 billion).

Indeed, one source notes how the South African Revenue Service was ostensibly ready to conduct a raid on BAT, and was told to stand down at the last moment by the President's office, and to settle the matter with BAT amicably.[2] (Another source disputes that this has ever happened at SARS, but when it comes to tobacco I wouldn't be surprised.)

And there's more: If everyone in South Africa were to give up smoking, government would have to find R17 billion a year somewhere else to plug its fiscal holes. 'In other words, they are delighted that smokers exist and are addicted,' South African journalist Ciaran Ryan quips.[3]

But worse: if BAT Plc were to be indicted on money laundering charges internationally, they would apparently be required to (temporarily) de-list on the stock exchange. The sheer chaos that would likely result may well topple markets.

In 2019 Canada, Imperial, Rothmans, Benson & Hedges and JTI all filed for court protection after a court ordered them to pay $15,5 billion in damages. They say they can't afford to pay it. They had to pay a $1 billion deposit, while court-appointed monitors review how to handle the financial crisis. They've asked for a period of immunity where the court order cannot be enforced against them, because they don't want to face bankruptcy procedures.[4] It must be nice when you can walk away from a $15,5 billion court judgement just because it would otherwise bankrupt you.

Knowing that – and having seen what happened to the SARS investigators who were stupidly brave enough to take on big tobacco (they all lost their jobs and faced trumped-up criminal charges) – if you were an investigator in the UK, or at OLAF, or any of the other bodies tasked with taking on the big boys, just how brave would you really be?

When it comes right down to it, I'm willing to bet the big boys club will negotiate another $1 billion fine to make criminal charges go away, and walk away with the same impunity they have displayed every single other time they have been caught with their hands in the cookie jar.

Are the big tobacco companies simply too big to fail? They just might be.

Conclusion

Holding big tobacco to account is daunting.

As tax sleuth – and victim of what has to be one of big tobacco's dirtiest campaigns – Johann van Loggerenberg ultimately explains in *Tobacco Wars*, 'Will tobacco companies and their employees implicated ultimately be held accountable? I very much doubt this. There's too much at stake: too much money, too much power, too many secrets held dear. On the whole there has been no recognition on their part of their true culpability. Life for them has mostly gone on as before, business as usual.'[1]

I asked him whether the fight was perhaps not a futile one. His reply? 'We never surrender and we never give up. We die in our boots.'

Let's hope it doesn't come to that. Because as he also says, 'The tobacco business is as dirty and nasty as it is dangerous.'

Addendum 1: What Project Honey Badger was investigating

Public copies of the letters SARS sent to tobacco manufacturers in South Africa as part of Project Honey Badger explain the various elements being covered under the investigation. The letters offer a good overview of the different types of tobacco-related frauds one is likely to encounter, not just in South Africa, but anywhere tobacco is being made, sold or traded in. The following is an extract from these letters:[1]

The following schemes have been identified as the most prevalent in this sector:

Under-valuation (in other words stating a lower price than what was really paid) of tobacco-related products imported into South Africa in order to pay lower excise duty and VAT.

Mis-declaration of tobacco-related products imported into South Africa by the following means: Declaring the products to SARS as something other than what they are and thereby paying a different tariff and duty; declaring the products to be destined for bond or in transit, supposedly for later export. Instead all or some of the products are diverted into the local market; 'round-tripping' and 'ghost exports'. In these activities, often state officials are coerced and corrupted to participate and facilitate the passing of fraudulent documentation.

Permutations of the above fraudulent declarations, such as mixing goods that fall under different tariff headings thereby making it difficult for customs officials to inspect and sort between the goods or mixing products intended for local and foreign markets, the so-called 'stock- or mixing-game'.

Various methods of straightforward smuggling, that is importing goods without making any declaration to SARS whatsoever, is evidently on the increase. Examples are:

- The use of couriers (i.e. small operators) in particular from Zimbabwe, to smuggle products into South Africa. Small 'bakkies', truck loads, and even individuals using public transport are used to bring low volumes of products into the country. Their smuggled goods are then purchased at particular points where they gather to sell them;
- Larger scale smuggling operations such as the use of trucks across non-designated ports; avoiding ports of entry entirely by crossing into the country via illegal pathways; and via private and commercial cargo on aircraft;
- On the manufacturing side within the country, similar scams exist, including mixing, under-valuation and mis-declaration. As manufacturers operate under licence, which entails more onerous compliance obligations, particular risks have been identified;
- Tax and customs when dealing with wastage and losses during the manufacturing process;
- Tampering with machinery;
- Unrecorded manufacturing;
- Stock control and accounting, and
- Mixing of stock.

At a retail and wholesale level it is concerning that some entities appear quite comfortable to purchase products that are obviously below market prices and therefore should indicate risk. Of equal concern is that manufacturers and suppliers, ostensibly compliant from a SARS perspective, are quite happy to continue trading with these entities.

SARS is a member of the Financial Action Task Force (FATF), an international inter-governmental body developing and promoting policies to combat money laundering and terrorist financing. The FATF has extended the definition of customs smuggling as predicate crime to money-laundering, to also include offences relating to mis-declaration and under-valuation. In addition, tax evasion has been included on the list of predicate offences to money-laundering. This means these schemes (e.g. smuggling, under- and mis-declaration), have been found to be indicative of money-laundering. In this regard SARS has identified the following areas of risk:

- Unrecorded cash transactions between suppliers, manufacturers and buyers;
- The use and creation of various means to create fictitious transactions or to keep financial transactions out of sight of SARS, which includes but are not limited to inter-company transactions, fraudulent invoices, loan account abuses and fraud, fraudulent inter-company agreements and international transactions;
- Income tax, VAT, PAYE and SDL transgressions;
- Non-compliance of directors and persons with commercial and financial interests in manufacturers, importers, clearing agencies, suppliers, transporters, professional services, storage and retailing in respect of their personal tax affairs;
- Non-compliance of the businesses in respect of corporate income tax, PAYE and payroll management, including UIF, SDL and VAT;
- Outstanding returns and tax debts among business and individuals. In some cases, traders have made no attempts to engage SARS with a view to rectify the situation.

As will be shown later in this letter, a great number of instances have been identified where persons receive cash payments from manufacturers who then fail to account for such payments for tax purposes. It seems to be common practice to deal with large cash sums in this manner precisely to avoid SARS scrutiny. More than 20 individuals have already been engaged in respect of their personal tax affairs, and in one instance a tax inquiry is reaching a point where one such person will be assessed for amounts exceeding R20 million. In other instances, only after SARS identified such transactions, did individuals come to the fore and admit having received significant cash payments from manufacturers who themselves failed to and continue to fail to account for these payments for tax purposes. Very worrying is that in one instance, such payments concern a listed company and the scale and number of people in these positions are not yet determined.

The tobacco sector is not immune to tax base erosion practices. A quick glance at transfer pricing disputes worldwide shows the tremendous size of the problem in the tobacco industry and suggests it lends itself to such practices quite easily. Instances of transfer pricing, 'treaty shopping' and thin capitalisation suggest estimated losses exceeding R1 billion alone. It is a lesser understood and even lesser talked about and publicised subject and often not considered to be on the same scale as smuggling and diversion tactics. The reality is however that tax base erosion in a developing state like South Africa has immense consequences beyond mere loss of tax-based income – it speaks directly to the culture and integrity of corporates and their commitment to a bright economic future.

Instances have been found where taxpayers appear to have been hiding their control of businesses so as to avoid scrutiny and obfuscate SARS actions. In some cases, SARS has become aware of taxpayers shifting their asset control to trusts and 3rd parties now that SARS has engaged them. It would be advisable for such persons to note that SARS now has the legal means to apply to court to have such assets preserved pending the outcome of financial investigations and SARS will not hesitate to utilise this when the situation demands this.

Complicated and unnecessary business transactions: It is astounding how in some cases evidence shows manufacturers and importers making use of complicated transactions that are at face value unnecessary. One can only conclude that they are done in such a manner so as to make it difficult for SARS to determine the true nature of the transactions. Numerous instances demonstrate this:

- Cash payments are made to practitioners, legal representatives, transporters and agents. The size of the payments is such that it does not appear to make obvious business sense to make such payments unless there were certain ulterior motives behind them. In one case a practitioner was found to have been paid R1 million in cash by a manufacturer which he failed to account for income tax purposes while he was actually undergoing a SARS audit at the time;
- Transporters are used as 'tag teams' which does not make any commercial sense. One transporter will be engaged to take a consignment to a location but only up to a point, to hand over to another. It defies any logic that would make business sense in respect of cost, efficiency and management of operations;
- Clearing agents appear to not consider the consequences of their actions and the fact that they are opening themselves to being held personally liable for non-compliance of their clients. It would appear as if clearing agents in general do not consider tobacco transactions to be high risk – something I would suggest they do at their own peril;
- The use of 'high sea sales' which are really just sham transactions have already been explained above;
- The same applies for the use of 'front companies' and the abuse of 'power of attorney' and 'nominees' where the proverbial 'persons or entities of straw' are used as the face of transactions. Effectively in these instances, culprits seek to make it difficult for SARS to identify high risk transactions and secondly to avoid the financial consequences if found out.

Addendum 2: Where the quoted internal industry documents come from

Through a number of lawsuits tobacco companies were required to disclose a large number of internal documents. A number of organisations leapt at the chance of digitally preserving their disclosures for posterity, providing detailed insights into what would otherwise have been very opaque business practices.[1]

> See for instance:
> www.hlth.gov.bc.ca/guildford
> www.tobaccotactics.org
> www.tobaccodocuments.org
> https://bat.library.ucsf.edu
> https://www.library.ucsf.edu/archives/tobacco/
> www.lorillarddocs.com
> www.cdc.gov/tobacco/industrydocs/ docsites.htm
> http://galen.library.ucsf.edu/tobacco

Of course, these repositories only contain a fraction of the documentation big tobacco would have documented over the course of decades, and many of the big tobacco companies managed to destroy incriminating documents before investigators could lay their hands on them,[2] as a result of which the true extent of smuggling activities may never be known.

(After the court judgements one internal BAT document noted,

'The Bogota office will be clean by Q3/94 in reference to DNP [duty not paid, i.e. smuggled] information.'[3])

Most of the internal industry documents we now have access to relate mostly to BAT, simply because PMI and other tobacco companies responded more narrowly to the courts' disclosure orders and appear to have taken greater care than BAT to avoid unnecessarily revealing any incriminating documents not specifically required under the lawsuits. As a result, while the examples quoted may create the impression that BAT may have been more active in establishing a contraband network, this may not be an accurate reflection and conceivably understates the involvement of other tobacco companies. Indeed PMI had to pay a lot more in EU settlements than BAT did.

As a result, the examples quoted conceivably understate the involvement of big tobacco companies in the illicit trade in cigarettes.

A number of other internal documents come from whistle-blowers, like Francois van der Westhuizen, like Luis Pestana, the South African voice behind @espionageafrica on Twitter,[4] and Paul Hopkins, who used to do BAT's dirty work in Africa.

Some of them were surreptitiously handed to me on a thumb drive in Rosebank, Johannesburg.

For more examples of the darker mills and schemes see also for instance the series of articles by the International Consortium of Investigative Journalists.[5] Just the headlines tell a story: 'Tobacco companies linked to criminal organizations in lucrative cigarette smuggling';[6] 'Philip Morris accused of smuggling, money-laundering conspiracy in racketeering lawsuit';[7] 'Cyprus: Big Tobacco's favorite smuggling hub into the UK';[8] 'Africa: Disguising BAT's involvement in cigarette smuggling';[9] 'In Latin America, Big Tobacco partners with money launderers, smugglers';[10] 'Philip Morris' Mafia connections';[11] 'BAT finds a partner in Asia's most notorious criminal organization';[12] 'Tobacco companies linked to criminal organizations in lucrative cigarette smuggling;'[13] and other pieces by the International Consortium of Investigative Journalists[14] and the Tobacco Underground.

Addendum 3: Counterfeits

Counterfeits globally only account for around 8%[1] of the illicit tobacco market – and in some countries as little as 2% – but they are often used as a red herring to get law enforcement agencies to focus on something other than the complicity of licensed, legitimate tobacco manufacturers.

Nonetheless, cigarettes are one of the most counterfeited products globally.[2] At EU borders fake cigarettes account for 24% of all seizures (most of them are Marlboro's).[3]

Most of the counterfeits come from China, which produces enough fake cigarettes to supply every US smoker with 460 packs a year. It is the source of 99% of US counterfeit cigarettes and up to 80% of those in the EU.[4]

It's particularly worrying because Chinese counterfeits on average release as much as 80% more nicotine and 130% more carbon monoxide than brand-name cigarettes, and often contain impurities like dust, insect eggs, asbestos and – yes – even human faeces.[5]

The counterfeiting business in China is something of a brotherhood – you're only allowed to work in production if your family tree can be traced to the area. But more than that, it goes to great lengths to avoid detection: factories are built to masquerade as People's Liberation Army compounds with workers dressed in cast-off military uniforms, doing fake army drills in the mornings; factories are built under local village temples or lakes or on ships; pig pens are built near factories to mask the smell of tobacco.[6]

(One trick to uncovering hidden factories lies in looking for locations with unusually high electricity consumption.)

Yunxiao produces 95% of China's cigarettes. Since the Qing Dynasty, Yunxiao has made cigarettes by hand, and almost every household has a manual cigarette machine. The whole village of Yunling Township is a giant fake factory. Yunxiao fake cigarettes are so renowned that counterfeiters are making fake copies of their fakes (a kind of double decoy).[7]

What had started out under stoves at home and in pig pens was moved to old forests of the mountains, local mines for production, or holes dug into the mountains, just like the tunnel wars during the War of Resistance Against Japanese Aggression. As enforcement activities were stepped up, counterfeiters moved back home, but this time making crawl spaces under toilets, or using hydraulic technology to remotely move entire hidden walls, or installing machines on the back of more mobile trucks.[8]

Every year several investigators are reportedly killed in efforts to penetrate the Chinese counterfeit trade. Raids have been known to use as many as 5 000 officers because they are typically met with armed resistance. Many private security companies refuse to participate in tobacco investigations and raids because the risks are simply too big.[9]

Of course not all counterfeits come from China:

In North Korea the production of counterfeits and the involvement of diplomats in illicit trade is widely assumed to be government-approved. Counterfeits are legal in North Korea, and as regulations have started tightening in China, counterfeit cigarette factories have started moving to cities like Pyongyang and Hoeryong, using North Korean labour, and Chinese raw materials and distribution channels. In the space of three years, US law enforcement officials found counterfeit Marlboros from North Korea 1 300 times. Since around 2016, high-quality counterfeit Marlboros have been seized at least twice in Manila and Malta, hidden in shipments of legal North Korean cigarettes, and suspected to be destined for sale in Syria and Turkey.[10]

Addendum 4: Illicit whites

Cheap whites (sometimes called illicit whites) are relatively new to the illicit tobacco world: they're cigarettes that are legally produced for the sole purpose of being exported and sold on the illicit market, where they compete simply on price. In essence, they are cigarettes that are specifically made to be smuggled or sold on the black market. Cheap whites are generally produced openly and quite legally, at known locations and often exported legally – very commonly in free trade zones in places like Kaliningrad, Ukraine, Cyprus and the United Arab Emirates.[1] They only become contraband once they hit their destination market.

Illicit whites are arguably not necessarily all bad for big tobacco: because they are cheaper, they stop poorer smokers from quitting, and pave the road to smoking for younger smokers, both of which are potential customers to eventually upgrade to more expensive premium brands over time.

Illicit whites / cheap whites are increasing in prominence: In 2009 they accounted for 12% of all illicit consumption in Europe; by 2015 this had increased to 35%[2] – constituting a significant market loss for the bigger companies.

At one point, the best known illicit white brand in Europe was Jin Ling,[3] made in the Kaliningrad free trade zone in Russia. Jin Lings don't have a legal market in Europe – they aren't advertised and aren't openly offered for sale in shops. The Russian-run Jin Ling factory was able to produce the equivalent of 7% of legal EU cigarette imports. A container would cost you $100 000, which you could sell (tax free) for an enormous $2 million profit. In the UK the potential profit would be up to three times higher.[4]

Jin Lings are particularly interesting because the organisation behind it – the Baltic Tobacco Factory (BTF) of Kaliningrad, Russia – apparently has some links to big tobacco: its factory network in Russia and Ukraine was previously owned and run by subsidiaries of JTI; and it got high quality tobacco leaf from BAT ('an oversight', BAT called it). Dig a bit more and you'll find that, at some point, the Baltic Tobacco Factory was owned by a company called PRT Ltd. Which was reportedly owned by Britain's Gallaher. Which ended up being owned by JTI[5] – in what can surely only be described as an unfortunate coincidence.

While Jin Lings and one or two other players may have dominated the illicit whites market some years ago, we are now beginning to see a veritable proliferation of many other smaller players vying for market share. Where Jin Lings accounted for 39% of the market in 2009, they now account for only 8%.[6] The number of cheap white brands has increased by 12%, with many smaller players now contributing smaller volumes, making it even more difficult to target the source of illicit packs.

Addendum 5: A short history of tobacco smuggling[1]

Tobacco-related evasion and the smuggling of tobacco is by no means a new phenomenon – it's a practice dating back centuries.

To understand how far tobacco regulation has come – and what went wrong – let's start at the beginning:

In 1492 Christopher Columbus threw the tobacco leaves he got from the indigenous Arawak tribe as a gift overboard, unsure what to do with them. He may not have appreciated the gift, but many others subsequently did, setting in motion the growth of an industry that continues to thrive today.

Rodrigo de Jerez was one of the first Europeans known to have smoked. In 1492 his Spanish neighbours were so petrified of the smoke coming out of his mouth that he was arrested by the Holy Inquisition for being possessed and imprisoned for seven years.

A number of countries simply adopted an outright ban on tobacco use: China in 1612; Russia under the Romanoffs in 1613; Japan in 1620; and Switzerland in 1657.

But there were also some more curious restrictions on smoking: in 1647 America's Connecticut banned public smoking, with citizens only being allowed to smoke once a day, and 'not in company with any other'. In 1634 Russia introduced a tobacco ban, albeit exempting foreigners in Moscow. In 1650 in Connecticut smoking was only allowed on order of a physician. In 1675 Switzerland's Berne town council established a special *Chambres de Tabac* to deal with smokers, who faced the same penalties as adulterers. And in 1830 the Prussian government enacted a law that cigars had to be smoked in a wire-mesh device designed to prevent sparks setting fire to ladies' crinoline hoop skirts (the mix of horse hair and cotton was highly flammable).

Over time, punishments for tobacco use became more severe: in 1617 the Mongolian Emperor introduced the death penalty for using tobacco; Shah Sefi from the Ottoman Empire punished two merchants for selling tobacco by pouring hot lead down their throats; and by 1633 Turkey had also introduced the death penalty for smoking, executing as many as 18 people a day (ostensibly as a fire-prevention- and anti-plague measure). In 1634 Russia's Czar Alexis introduced transportation to Siberia as punishment for smoking – a second offence warranted execution; and by 1638 smoking had become punishable with decapitation in China.

Across the pond, in 1629 new American settlers were not allowed to plant tobacco during their first year of residence, and settlers in general were not allowed to plant more than 2 000 tobacco plants per family member (Virginia's settlers had been growing so much tobacco that they weren't planting any food crops).

Of course, much of government regulation was aimed at securing monopolies and government revenues: As far back as 1604 England's King James I realised that taxes on tobacco could be enormously profitable. Trying to stamp out smoking, he increased taxes on tobacco by 4 000%, which indeed stopped people from smoking, but also dried up the King's funds. James slashed taxes and the money poured in. In 1620 King James introduced new restrictions: limiting tobacco sales to 100 weight of tobacco per person; and establishing stamps or seals to be placed on tobacco to confirm the quality of the tobacco. In 1625 he introduced a royal monopoly: no tobacco could be imported except from Virginia; a £15 annual royal licence was required to sell tobacco; and no tobacco cultivation was allowed in England (except in herb gardens for medicinal purposes). By 1698 Russia's Peter the Great had established a similar trade monopoly with the English.

Cuba under Spanish rule introduced a tobacco monopoly in 1717. To minimise the risk of contraband, Spanish officials offered to pay tobacco growers prices that largely matched those paid by contrabanders and pirates. The strategy was smart but ineffective. Farmers resented state control of their industry and opposed Spain's plan to purchase Cuban tobacco at low prices only to sell it on the European market at inflated prices. Farmers revolted, destroying crops, and eventually prompting the 'first violent expulsion of a Captain General' in Cuban colonial history.

Very little of the early regulation efforts were focused on the health impact of smoking, aside perhaps from a complaint in 1603 from doctors in England that tobacco was being used without a physician's prescription. In fact, somewhat curiously, when the Great Plague hit Europe in 1665, smoking was made compulsory at Eton to ward off infection, with tobacco thought to have a protective effect.

England's mercantile system meant that American tobacco growers and traders could only sell their tobacco leaf to the government, which would process the leaves and sell them to the rest of the world. To keep profits in England, Charles II issued the Navigation Acts in 1651, prohibiting the export of tobacco except to English ports, in turn incentivising Scottish and Dutch sea captains to evade authorities and export fees. (The famed Boston Tea Party was the culmination of 60 years of outright dissatisfaction with England's mercantile policy, causing Americans to smuggle as a matter of principle.)

Indeed, smuggling from colonial America was rife: around 1716 as many as 2 400 Anglo-Americans are believed to have worked as pirates.

By the 1700s smuggling had already become big business in France (mostly in salt and tobacco), effectively turning smuggling into a profession across virtually all of the country. By 1707 more than 70% of tobacco produced in the Lorraine area was estimated to have been smuggled.

By the 1730s 're-landing' accounted for the majority of smuggling (today we'd call it 'round tripping'). Cheap tobacco was exported legally from one of the French ports, with papers showing its destination as a port in Italy or Spain. Once out of the harbour the ship's master would unload his cargo onto a smaller boat, which would re-land the tobacco back in France and sell it on the local black market. When the ship's master returned to his port of origin, he would submit forged papers, claiming that he had unloaded his cargo at the originally-declared destination.

Eighteenth century tobacconists would buy contraband tobacco, mix it with legal government-monopoly tobacco (along with fillers like rosewood powder, tan, rotten wood, powdered brick and cinders), and sell the new mix to consumers at the monopoly price, making a hefty profit in the process.

Aristocrats on the Breton Coast would regularly travel to Jersey and Guernsey to collect contraband tobacco, illegally importing around 15 000 pounds a month (so Jersey and Guernsey's reputations as tax havens in fact go back centuries).

On occasion smuggling was perhaps quite simply justified: In 1632 the French tax rate more than tripled, from two *livres* to seven. Tax collection was outsourced to the highest bidder, who then added their own 32% profit margin for collecting taxes due. It cost taxpayers 90 000 *livres* to pay the King 70 000 *livres* in taxes. Traders dealing in commodities like tobacco also had to pay import and export duties; internal regional tariffs; tolls; transit fees; river tolls; and entry taxes at city gates. Cargo on the river Loire between Orleans and Nantes – which is not far – had to make transit fee payments at 20 different points along the river.

Addendum 6: Selected extracts from the BBC Panorama's story: 'The secret bribes of big tobacco'[1]

We know about the bribes because of Paul Hopkins. [He] served in the Irish special forces. He then worked for BAT in Africa for 13 years. He ran security and anti-smuggling operations but also arranged BAT's bribe payments. He fell out with the company and was made redundant. Now he's turned whistle-blower.

[A] local MP sits on an important parliamentary committee [that] was writing a report on a rival tobacco company, and BAT wanted to see it. BAT agreed to pay the MP.

Paul Hopkins: 'To see the report would cost 5 000. The payment was done by a third party . . . we received a copy of the draft report.'

[The MP] said BAT could amend the report in return for more cash. 'For this to happen, it would cost 20 000.' The contractor said BAT paid the bribe, the MP changed his report and BAT got what it wanted.

PH: 'I was a commercial hit man. My job was to ensure that the competition never got a breathing space.'

Interviewer: 'Were you surprised by the sort of things that BAT expected you to do?'

PH: 'No. They're quite shocking in this environment, but, as it was explained to me, in Africa that's the cost of doing business.'

BAT describes payments to three officials linked to the [WHO's] tobacco convention as 'unlawful bribes'. So in these previously unpublished documents, the company admits they WERE illegal payments.

Mastermind Tobacco in Kenya's capital, Nairobi [is] one of BAT's main rivals in East Africa ... and BAT paid bribes to discover its secrets. Paul also arranged bribes to get public officials to hand over details of Mastermind's tax affairs.

Interviewer: 'How much money's worth of black ops is here?'

PH: 'To cover you, a couple of hundred thousand pounds? Minutes of the marketing meeting. This would be the most useful. I got to see it usually 12 or 14 hours after it happened.'

Interviewer: 'But if you hadn't paid any money, how many files would we have in front of us?'

Hopkins: 'Oh, none. BAT is bribing people, and I'm facilitating it.'

Interviewer: 'BAT managers knew you were bribing people?'

PH: 'Yes.'

The whistle-blower isn't the only former employee who says BAT paid bribes. Documents submitted to court suggest BAT did make illegal payments. They show BAT paid MPs in Uganda's Parliament to undermine a proposed anti-tobacco law. Minutes of a meeting between BAT and the MP say he supported having most of our views accommodated in the proposed tobacco law. Just to be clear, an MP who is the poster boy for the anti-tobacco lobby was being secretly bribed by BAT.

The problem for BAT is the evidence of illegal behaviour keeps coming.

'We owe him 3 000 but this is also an exchange for the draft tobacco control bill that the Minister has.'

BAT have admitted that this counts as illegal bribery.

We first asked BAT about the bribery allegations three months ago. We've sent 16 emails to the chief executive, but he hasn't answered any of our questions about the bribe payments we uncovered.

Addendum 7: Big tobacco's rogue's gallery – additional detail

1990s: Colombia: Colombia was losing as much as $305 million a year to tobacco smuggling in the 1990s.[1] Evidence shows how BAT executives detail in their 'Colombian Group Meeting Minutes' their cigarette marketing in Colombia, indicating the per-pack, no-tax price they charge in pesos, at a time when the company had virtually no legal cigarette exports to the country. The minutes note that the company would begin selling 'duty paid' – i.e., legally imported cigarettes on which taxes are paid – only in the coming year. BAT was integrally involved in setting the pricing, organising distribution routes and marketing of cigarettes to distributors in Colombia[2] at a time when 95% of its cigarettes in the country was contraband. (Smuggling in Colombia was not attributable just to BAT though: PMI's 'Latin America Region Strategic Plan' included prices for its 'duty-free' customers in La Guajira and Aruba, at a time when it apparently had virtually no legal imports into Colombia.)[3]

> 'Whether the company could continue with duty paid and duty not paid in parallel and be seen as a clean and ethical company at the same time.'
>
> – Fax query from BAT's headquarters to its branch office in Venezuela[4]

1990s: Canada: Illicit cigarette consumption accounted for 30% of the total Canadian market. The majority of these illicit cigarettes were legally produced in Canada by major manufacturers,[5] exported untaxed to the

United States and then smuggled back into Canada. Criminal charges and civil lawsuits were brought against Imperial Tobacco, Rothmans, Benson & Hedges, JTI, and RJ Reynolds, resulting in the payment of $1,7 billion in criminal fines and civil restitution for their role in smuggling schemes.[6]

> 'Really the options were limited. The no-brainer in the equation becomes: We have to enter the black market. We have to enter the black market. We've got to pursue this tax-free environment through the illegal smuggling efforts back into Canada.'
> – Les Thompson, Sales Executive, RJ Reynolds[7]

1993: USA: An investigation reveals an undisclosed $500 000 given by Philip Morris to the ACLU between 1987 and 1992; and $975 149 given to the US GOP in 'soft' dollars, and $841 120 in contributions to the tobacco industry PACs and Republican members of Congress.

1996: Italy: Eleven PMI executives face tax fraud charges for failing to pay taxes on tobacco import fees and royalty payments, with a tax liability of $400 million.[8]

1997: South Africa: Philip Morris faces a smuggling charge by the Rembrandt Group: PMI is accused of using smugglers to get a foothold in the lucrative South African market, violating an exclusive licence held by Rembrandt to make and sell Philip Morris products in South Africa.[9]

1998: Hong Kong: A BAT executive in Hong Kong is convicted of taking bribes from a cigarette smuggling syndicate.[10] 'Management of BAT(HK) was aware duty-not-paid cigarettes would ultimately be smuggled in China and other countries. There could be no other explanation for this enormous quantity of duty-not-paid cigarettes worth billions and billions of dollars. BAT's irresponsible behaviour amounted to assisting criminals in transnational crime,' Justice Wally Yeung Chun-Kuen found.[11]

1999: USA: The New York Lobbying Commission hits Philip Morris with the largest fine in commission history – $75 000; and forbids its chief representative from lobbying for three years.

> 'With the tobacco industry under siege in recent years, New York State has offered cigarette manufacturers a legislative safety zone. Such a smoke-friendly atmosphere does not appear by accident. In fact, the tobacco industry, particularly Philip Morris, has been plying the state's lawmakers with gifts and goodies including dinners and tickets to sports events like the Indianapolis 500. Philip Morris has now been forced to acknowledge that it violated New York State's lobbying law by underreporting the extent of its gift-giving.'
> – *New York Times editorial*[12]

1999: Canada sues the three biggest manufacturers over smuggling issues.

2000: Russia sues Philip Morris for damaging its economy.

2000: Newspaper exposes BAT's smuggling activities – UK and beyond: *The Guardian* newspaper exposes how BAT's own documents revealed that the company had 'condoned tax evasion and exploited the smuggling of billions of cigarettes in a global effort to boost sales and lure generations of new smokers.' The article suggests that senior BAT executives supplied huge numbers of cigarettes a year to wholesalers and distributors, intending that they would find their way onto black markets after being smuggled across borders, without duty being paid; and knowingly advertised and promoted smuggled cigarettes to improve its market share. Documents show how euphemisms like 'duty not paid', 'general trade' and 'transit' are used to describe 'unorthodox' cigarette sales channels, as an alternative to legal 'duty paid' sales.[13]

2000: Colombia: BAT faces serious racketeering charges in Colombia 'arising from its involvement in organised crime in pursuit of a massive, ongoing smuggling scheme'[14] and facilitating illegal trade. BAT confirms it knew that some of its products were being 'handled other than through official channels'.[15]

2000: EU: The inflow of illicit cigarettes to Europe suddenly declines after the European Commission files a civil action against PMI and RJ Reynolds, accusing the companies of being involved in smuggling cigarettes.[16]

2001: Geneva: Court pleadings filed against BAT show how as much as $200 million allegedly made its way to Geneva in one year alone, funded by smuggling.[17]

2001: BAT issues a profit warning to its shareholders, informing analysts that profits were expected to plummet by up to £500 million as it was being forced to clamp down on illegal trafficking.[18]

2001: UK: Imperial Tobacco is challenged on roundtripping. The company is accused of exporting huge quantities of Regal and Superking cigarettes to countries where Imperial has no market share. They are then illegally imported back into the UK through smuggling networks. As much as 65% of the 12 billion Regal and Superkings exported by Imperial are cited as having been illegally smuggled back into the UK.[19]

> 'One comes to the conclusion that you are either crooks or you are stupid, and you do not look very stupid. How can you possibly have sold cigarettes to Latvia, Kaliningrad, Afghanistan

and Moldova in the expectation that those were just going to be used by the indigenous population or exported legitimately to neighbouring countries, and not in the expectation they would be smuggled? You must know – you only have to read a newspaper every day, a member of the public could tell you – these are places which are linked to organised crime, that the drugs trade passes through all of these countries. Did you not know that?'

– *George Osborne, member of the UK Parliament's Public Accounts Committee, during questioning of the CEO of Imperial Tobacco*[20]

2002: South Africa: A private detective confirms BAT spied on competitors. Local tobacco company Apollo alleged that BAT conspired with tax agency officials, using private detectives and bugging devices, to obtain confidential information about Apollo's business operations. Raids on BAT offices turn up incriminating documents, and a private detective testifies that he was paid by BAT to tap Apollo's phones and admits attending meetings between BAT and the tax agency to discuss the phone-tapping operation. (Interestingly this was the first case where a private company secured a search warrant to trawl the tax agency's offices for evidence of collusion with its competitors.)[21]

2004: EU: Philip Morris is accused of oversupplying low-tax markets with its own products, allowing the surplus to be smuggled into countries with higher taxes, where they are sold cheaply. It pays the European Union $1,25 billion to settle tobacco smuggling charges.[22]

2005: UK/Aruba: BAT is investigated for supplying millions of cigarettes to its agents in Aruba, to be smuggled into neighbouring Colombia. The investigation ends inconclusively, and its findings are kept secret – only for it to later emerge that BAT's lawyers admit that certain allegations of BAT's involvement in smuggling are true. The lawyers' letter warns that BAT's directors face potential problems over the company's internal documents, and need to be careful how they testify, with evidence suggesting that BAT had deliberately used smuggling channels in Latin America 'with a view to securing market share'.[23] A whistle blower later noted how, by 1998, BAT's transit trade through Aruba included 45 000 cases a month. Each case contained 10 000 cigarettes.[24]

2005: Cameroon: BAT is accused of orchestrating the unjustifiable delay by customs of a competitor's raw materials at the port, causing the competitor big losses in product damage.[25]

2008: Canada: Imperial Tobacco and Rothmans Benson & Hedges are fined $1,15 billion for producing cigarettes in Canada, and shipping them to smugglers and black market distributors in the United States, who bring them back into Canada for illegal sale.[26]

2008: Africa: The BBC's documentary *Bannatyne Takes on Tobacco* reveals how BAT breaks the rules in Nigeria, Malawi and Mauritius.[27]

2009: West Africa: The United Nations Office on Drugs and Crime (UNODC) publishes its report entitled 'Transnational Trafficking and the Rule of Law in West Africa: A Threat Assessment'. The report does not mention BAT by name but argues that there are only few individuals in the region with the capacity to organise operations of the scale that UNODC had uncovered. BAT then unwittingly exposed itself with a number of documents suggesting the importance of smuggling as a component of BAT's business strategy, mainly to compete with other transnational tobacco companies and circumvent local import restrictions.[28]

2009: Sudan and Birao: Internal BAT documents describe BAT's relationship with shadowy transporters in Sudan and Birao who are described as 'indispensable in negotiating border crossings'.[29]

2009: Nigeria: BAT is accused of using distributors to minimise its tax liabilities. The distributors, acting as middlemen, purchase cigarettes from BAT (UK) and supply them to transiteers (smugglers who physically transport contraband). The distributors serve to insulate BAT from direct contact with the transiteers, reducing the risk of detection and prosecution. To avoid detection of smuggled cigarettes, cigarette consignments are mis-declared, for example as matches. Plans to conceal cigarettes among other merchandise and falsify documents on the origin of the stock were known to BAT. The same modus operandi is used for smuggling cigarettes from Equatorial Guinea, to North Cameroon and Chad, and for concealing smuggled cigarettes sent to Sierra Leone. BAT is accused of not only being engaged in smuggling, but also relying heavily on under-invoicing to minimise duties.[30]

> 'General trade [illicit] movements to this end market will remain a priority throughout the period. Both legal and transit importing (smuggling) would be required to properly – and profitably – develop the brand. Legal imports would be loss making and significantly under invoiced because of Nigeria's high duty rates.'
> – BAT Nigeria[31]

2010: EU: BAT pays the European Commission $200 million to settle 'smuggling-related' issues.[32]

2010: Canada: Five tobacco companies (Imperial owned by BAT, JTI, Rothmans owned by JTI, and RJ Reynolds partly owned by BAT) plead guilty to 'aiding persons to sell or be in possession of tobacco products manufactured in Canada that were not packaged and were not stamped in conformity with the Excise Act.'[33]

2011: Russia and Middle East: The Organised Crime and Corruption Reporting Project reveals that Russia and the Middle East are the 'hub of smuggling by JTI distributors' and that the company 'did almost nothing when faced with reports . . .'[34]

2012: Djibouti: Prepaid contraband apparently goes missing, raising tensions over who should incur the loss. Transiteers reportedly threaten to cease moving BAT's contraband.[35]

2012: Guinea: BAT is said to become concerned that its 'transiteers' are also smuggling competitors' products and establishes its own staff on the ground to do what the smugglers were doing. As described by BAT staff in an internal memo, 'Our objective now is to preserve the façade that S. represents between us and the sensitive markets of Togo, Benin, Niger and Equatorial Africa.'[36]

2012: Spain: PMI faces an EU lawsuit for 'involvement in organised crime in pursuit of a massive, ongoing smuggling scheme'.[37]

2012: Canada: The Canadian government files a racketeering lawsuit against RJ Reynolds, to the tune of $1 billion, for smuggling between Canada and the US. The case was dismissed on a technicality.[38]

2012: Colombia: PMI is sued for $3 billion in damages for smuggling, money-laundering, conspiracy and racketeering[39] in Colombia – where, over a period of ten years, employees are said to have laundered drug money as part of a smuggling operation, in the process creating a trail of third-party payments and Swiss bank accounts.

'Defendants created a circuitous and clandestine distribution chain for the sale of cigarettes in order to facilitate smuggling. The decision to establish and maintain this distribution chain was made at the highest executive level of PMI. Defendants have collaborated with smugglers, encouraged smugglers, and sold cigarettes to smugglers, either directly or through intermediaries, while at the same time supporting the smugglers' sales through the establishment and maintenance of so-called "umbrella [cover] operations" in the target jurisdictions.'[40]

2012: EU: The European Union investigates whether JTI violated its Syrian sanctions with the sale of cigarettes to Syria's state-owned tobacco company, and to a firm linked to Syrian President Bashar al-Assad, to finance his crackdown on the Syrian uprising. The sales involving millions of cartons to the Syrian state tobacco company would have provided the regime with a cash infusion at a time of growing economic isolation. In addition, the Assad government is believed to have used cigarettes as a form of payment for military forces and militias, who had a central role in its violent crackdown. Syria could have reaped profits of more than $100 million if it resold the cigarettes for around $3 a pack (the common price in the region at the time). Analysts noted it isn't unusual for companies to sell products in developing nations at low prices to build brand recognition but questioned how JTI could make any money selling cigarettes so cheaply.[41]

2012: Ecuador: The government files a Racketeer Influence and Corrupt Organizations (RICO) Act Charge Against PMI, BAT and RJ Reynolds.[42]

2012: Zimbabwe: Zimbabwe is said to be investigating economic espionage charges against BAT, the Tobacco Institute of Southern Africa and a firm of private detectives, involving an estimated $10 million worth of cigarettes local companies reportedly lost to armed syndicates in transit to South Africa. It emerges that BAT Zimbabwe adopted a formal industrial espionage strategy some years earlier, with its own 'marketing intelligence system (MkIS)'.[43]

2013: Russia: Criminal charges are reportedly laid against BAT for tax evasion in Russia, to the tune of $10,7 million.[44]

2013: Kenya: Allegations surface that BAT bribed a former Kenyan Minister of Justice with £50 000 to prevent an independent cigarette track and trace system tender being awarded. Media reports suggest cash donations to the political campaign were 'falsely listed in BAT accounts as payments for management fees or as expenses incurred in anti-smuggling operations'.[45] Whistle-blower Paul Hopkins has since also gone on to claim that this allowed BAT to have 'the contract deliberately delayed while they secretly lobbied to get their own system chosen'.[46]

2014: EU: BAT is reportedly fined £650 000 for oversupplying tobacco in low-tax European jurisdictions. The practice of flooding low-tax foreign markets with more tobacco than they are capable of consuming, sparks concerns that much of the product is able to find its way back into the highly taxed UK without payment of duties. Her Majesty's Revenue and Customs estimates that the actual supply of some brands exceeded legitimate demand by 240%.[47]

2014: No fewer than 15 pages of BAT's Annual Report are dedicated to listing contingent liabilities for lawsuits it is defending across the globe, including South Africa.[48]

2014: USA: PMI is challenged for defrauding the government by failing to sell cigarettes to military vendors at the lowest price.[49]

2015: South Africa: BAT handsomely paid an attorney who chairs a tobacco association group to feed them intelligence on some of their competitors who she represents in her capacity as an attorney.[50]

2013-15: South Africa: Recordings and documents show how BAT appears to be committing industrial espionage on a grand scale, running a large network of agents placed to spy inside rival organisations. The claim is corroborated by affidavits, audio and video recordings, copies of financial transactions and the accounts of five cigarette manufacturers, a state informant, sources close to the agency and one of BAT's senior agents.[51]

2015: UK/South Africa: The British tax agency discovers that BAT paid agents using Travelex cards registered overseas in other people's names. Over 11 months BAT seemingly paid one agent in question a total of £30 500. BAT either gave her cash or loaded the money on to Travelex cards registered in the name of a BAT employee in the UK. The agent was then given the cards and used them to withdraw cash from ATMs in South Africa. A request from the tax and customs authority in the UK states that the agency identified at least eight South Africans who had a 'peculiar relationship with BAT' and received payments from BAT through 'concealed transactions'. UK tax authorities are investigating these payments that have been described as an 'al-Qaeda-styled' method of payment. Correspondence between the agent and BAT shows she became worried about BAT's payment methods. A senior BAT employee assured her that the same method of payment is used by BAT UK around the globe for payment of other agents.[52]

2016: Thailand: PMI reportedly faces a $3,15 billion fine in Thailand for tax evasion to the value of around $791,4 million in taxes, for under-declaring import prices for cigarettes from the Philippines.[53]

2016: Somalia: Evidence emerges of BAT promoting sales of its cigarettes in some of the most fragile and unstable countries in Africa and the Middle East, starting from around 2008. The documents describe how cartons of cigarettes are distributed in black bags in Somalia after Al-Shabaab banned sales. They tell of an unmapped town in eastern DRC, allegedly created by BAT to produce and process tobacco leaf, where millions of dollars are said to have been smuggled into the country to pay farmers and staff. The case is being investigated by the UK Serious Fraud Office.

2017: South Korea: South Korea levies more than $260 million in additional taxes on PMI and BAT for pocketing profits by illegally hoarding cigarettes. South Korea hiked its cigarette prices by 2 000 won starting in January 2015. BAT and PMI – aware of the expected price hike beforehand – are understood to have stocked up on their tobacco at warehouses before the price was raised and released them in the market afterwards, avoiding taxes on the resulting $178 million profits.[54]

2017: USA: UPS is accused of shipping over 683 000 cartons of contraband cigarettes to unlicensed wholesalers and retailers and was ordered to pay nearly $247 million in damages and penalties for illegally shipping large volumes of untaxed cigarettes.[55]

2017: Argentina: PMI and Inexto are accused of corruption, collusion, bribery, conspiracy, illegal trade practices and falsifying records (showing losses that have not been incurred) in Argentina. Evidence suggests manipulation of the company's internal control systems, in the process defrauding shareholders, and possibly money laundering. Arguments suggest that Codentify/Inexto is merely a PMI puppet, allowing the company to falsify accounting information, and hide and/or simulate losses, and manipulate the amount of taxes payable.[56] (Inexto says the charges were trumped up by a competitor.)

2017: Thailand/Philippines: PMI is accused of under-valuing cigarettes imported from Indonesia, facing a fine of $562 million, on top of alleged fraudulent import practices on cigarettes from the Philippines where they apparently face 272 counts of fraud and a penalty of $2,29 billion.[57]

2017: Africa: A former special forces soldier employed by BAT from 2001 to 2014 reveals how he personally made at least five illegal cross-border trips in Africa, to make substantial money drops to what are believed to be illegal BAT production locations (at one point dressed as a priest with a weapon under his cassock to deliver $2 million in a ruck sack). He provides evidence that the operations were authorised from London, along with other documents confirming BAT used private security firms in Africa as intermediaries to conduct what are called 'deniable operations'. He also reveals how he was asked by BAT's local corporate and regulatory affairs department to arrange for the bribery of officials in Rwanda, Burundi and the Comoros Islands to impede implementation of the WHO's Framework Convention on Tobacco Control, paying out £20 000 in total.[58]

2017: UK: The UK Serious Fraud Office launches an investigation into BAT's behaviour in, amongst others, Kenya, Burundi, Rwanda and the Comoros Islands after a BAT whistle-blower tells a British newspaper he paid bribes on the company's behalf to the Kenya Revenue Authority for information BAT could use against a competitor. The whistle-blower also alleges links between prominent opposition Kenyan politicians and BAT Kenya. He also claims BAT paid bribes to government officials in Burundi, Rwanda and the Comoros Islands to undermine tobacco control regulations. Leaked material formed the basis of BBC Panorama's *The Secrets of Big Tobacco*.[59]

Addendum 8: Email from JTI manager on doing nothing[1]

From: Reynolds, David A
Sent: Saturday, April 10, 2010 12:11 AM
To: r....s...@jt.com
Cc: h...y...@jt.com; a...k...@jt.com; k..m..@jt.com
Subject: Urgent Brand Integrity Issues of Concern
Importance: High
Sensitivity: Confidential

...After I was promoted to run the Global Brand Integrity Operations my team progressively uncovered numerous cases of smuggling and unauthorized sales outside of Asia. Regretfully, we have increasingly encountered both reticence on the part of senior JTI officers in these regions and in Geneva to follow up on our findings and even open hostility towards the Brand Integrity program overall ...

In particular, in recent months members of my team have been directed not to investigate several instances of smuggling related to specific JTI distributors and the possible involvement of JTI employees with known smugglers. We likewise have encountered repeated instances where evidence we have developed on smuggling by distributors simply has not been acted upon in a correct, timely, and forceful manner and in a few cases sensitive information from BI investigations has even been passed back to the smugglers themselves by unknown persons in the company . . . Shipments to unauthorized buyers have reached a massive scale exposing the company to fines potentially of around EUR 30 million.

We have repeatedly reported our findings to JTI management including Chief Compliance and the General Manager for the Russia Market but have yet to elicit any concerted effort to halt these diversions. Even more of concern the latter stated that he was not troubled by the diversions given the amount of money the market was generating from sales of these brands.

The obstruction my team has been facing recently culminated with a concerted effort by certain senior JTI officers to break into and steal documents from email accounts used by Brand Integrity, our service providers, and even some of the firm's competitors and law enforcement agencies.

In all these cases, JTI management has not lived up to the 'zero-tolerance' policy . . . and, in those cases that touch on smuggling into or via the European Union, has specifically and repeatedly violated Article 9.1 of the EC-JTI Agreement of December 14, 2007, which calls for the company to proactively report all instances relating to 'illegal products'. There is substantial evidence that JTI has not been doing so.[2]

Addendum 9: Extracts from affidavits on BAT's espionage ring in South Africa[1]

Affidavit of Francois van der Westhuizen, an ex-murder and robbery cop, who was hired by Forensic Security Services (FSS), the company that worked as the contracted security arm of BAT for an estimated R150 million ($10,3 million per year). His statements are corroborated by documentary evidence posted – and still available at the time of writing this – on a Twitter account @espionageafrica. He was responsible for the development of a project management plan ('the PMP') for BATSA:

8. Having now realised that my employment with FSS and BATSA was plagued with unlawful conduct, I decided to resign from my employ with FSS and BATSA and convey the facts of my deployment to the relevant parties.

36. I prepared the project management plan (PMP) in and around January 2014. The PMP was circulated to BATSA and FSS management and approved by BATSA. [Note: a copy of the PMP was attached to his affidavit.]

37. I was always told by FSS as well as BATSA that the only way for BATSA to successfully suppress competitors such as Carnilinx would be to employ a strategy of falsely suggesting that the competitors (including Carnilinx) are selling and marketing their cigarettes unlawfully . . . The allegations of non-payment of excise duties and that the products were counterfeit, was simply an excuse to be employed by the law enforcement agent who was task [sic] to seize the goods, to disrupt Carnilinx's business.

38. Although there was never proof of any illicit trading, the project was aimed establishing a campaign of effective and ongoing disruption to Carnilinx's business. Whether or not there was proof of Carnilinx trading in breach of its obligations to the Commissioner of Customs and Excise was quite irrelevant to BATSA.

39. The constantly emphasised object of the project was to disrupt the trading activities of Carnilinx to such an extent so as the make it unfeasible for Carnilinx to operate. Ultimately, the aim was to squeeze Carnilinx out of the market, and if that was not possible, to at least prohibit its growth in order to guard the overwhelming near-monopoly share held by BATSA. Even if no prosecution commenced and even if these was never a conviction, all that was required is the maximum disruption of Carnilinx's business on an ongoing basis. To this end, FSS agents, with BATSA's knowledge, often fed false information of alleged illicit trading by Carnilinx, to lure law enforcement agents who were paid by BATSA discreetly to seize cigarette stock emanating from Carnilinx on-route to the distributors. BATSA devised a cunning system of rewarding informants for information, which filtered through to law enforcement agents: If there was no reporting from the informants, they would not get '*rewarded.*' Often this forced the informants to fabricate allegations of illicit cigarettes transport [sic] by Carnilinx just so that they could '*rewarded.*' BATSA knew that the informants would fabricate stories and feed it to the law enforcement agencies because they wanted to be rewarded. It was expedient for BATSA to allow that, and it did.

41. BATSA knew well that such a result, i.e. of reducing Carnilinx's distribution to 50% would be unattainable unless law enforcement agents such as the SAPS, JMPD and SARS were part of the collective strategy employed against Carnilinx. For that reason, BATSA always encouraged us to allege illegality on the part of Carnilinx as a basis to lure law enforcement agents. However, FSS was never able to show trading in illicit cigarettes by either a non-payment of customs and excise

duty on the part of Carnilinx or dealing in counterfeit goods by Carnilinx's customers.

42. That there is and always was an unholy alliance between BATSA and the law enforcement agencies which comprises a concerted practice and cooperation between government officials and BATSA, is identified in the PMP as follows:

'Client has the authority to make decisions and may provide funding / finance.' This is a reference to BATSA having the final authority to make decisions and to provide funding including payments to relevant law enforcement agencies.

It also stated that 'Client has the potential to overcome political and socio-economic obstacles that might have a direct influence of certain aspects of the project management goals.' This is a reference to the political connections, which members and directors of BATSA have cemented within the senior members of the South African law enforcement circles.

44. I was required to submit weekly progress reports, the project sponsor being BATSA, who was at all stages fully aware of and directed the project. The objective of the project was to manipulate the facts to ensure that a perception of illicit trade is created in the minds of law enforcement agents so that they could justify to their superiors and to the prosecution whatever was being done for BATSA. The stated objective for the project is expressed as follows: 'The benefit to be derived from this project will be to level the playing field for the client [BATSA] and at the same time to increase the client's market share.'

45. The PMP also states that the success will be measured through the amount of positive detentions that are to be made.

46. In order to raise the threshold to one of near impossibility for the release of goods, BATSA implemented a threshold that cigarette stock will not be released until confirmation is received that the invoice presented can be accounted for by SARS. In other words, if the vehicle is intercepted late on a Friday afternoon, it will result in the detention

of the truck and its driver because there would be no way of physically checking that the invoice has been accounted for by SARS until the next week.

48. The PMP has as its primary objective the elimination of Carnilinx, as a competitor. The objective is not the masquerading impression of seeking to cut alleged illicit cigarette trade down. It is to eliminate Carnilinx from the market and to prevent its distributors from dealing with it, irrespective of whether or not it pays its taxes.

50. The extent to which BATSA instructed FSS to undermine Carnilinx's ability to trade and hence eliminate it from the market is quite shameful. In the PMP it is recorded that one of the means by which the objectives of eliminating Carnilinx from the market is to be achieved is, 'To cause animosity between retailer / distributor, all persons relates to the top structure of the plant as well as the different organisations to which they belong.'

51. It is clear that the objective was not to stop illicit trade. It was to stop Carnilinx from trading, whether lawfully or otherwise. It was to disrupt its activities through in-house fighting at its director level. In short, disruption meant unlawful interference with the business of Carnilinx, using State resources and law enforcement agents to achieve that objective.

52. The ongoing nature of the campaign of harassment and disruption of Carnilinx' business was constantly monitored by BATSA.

54. BATSA was paranoid that its unlawful strategy would be exposed by law enforcement agents and this required that only a few selected 'trusted officials' be dealt with. In this case 'trusted' would mean police officers who have good relationships with BATSA and are willing to play its game. Since the activities of BATSA and FSS were unlawful, not every law enforcement agent would participate or cooperate with its plan. For this reason, it was recorded in the PMP: 'correct evaluation and channelling of communication through a structured base. The correct screening of individuals and law enforcement agents and role

players'. There was thus a very specific directive to discriminate against law enforcement agents to whom the complaint may be lodged because in the ordinary course a law enforcement agent acting within the purview of the law would not take seriously some of the frivolous complaints orchestrated by BATSA. However, a cooperating law enforcement agent who is being rewarded would be glad to assist.

60. The PMP, which is obviously meant to be an internal confidential document, records that law enforcement agents are to be paid up to R5 000 a month for cooperating with FSS and BATSA in disturbing Carnilinx's trading operations.

61. Thus, each law enforcement agent, whether it is from SARS, JMPD or SAPS, would be on BATSA's informal payroll, receiving a minimum of R2 000 each per month up to R5 000 each per month. Effectively, this was a bribe by BATSA to corrupt police officials who it regarded as trusted.

62. In order to breach Carnilinx's privacy, the PMP records that 'surveillance equipments [sic] for example drones, beacons . . . and the use of black widow specialist technical equipment, PT606 camera to be aligned with Intel Ops and logistics to be possibility [sic] engaged'.

63. That there was a clear breach of law which was ordered by BATSA is apparent from the express working [sic] of the PMP: 'The hiring of temporary surveillance agents in areas where FSS personnel cannot entrance and / or might be prohibited to do so by law.'

66. BATSA authorised FSS to employ a substantial number of spies for the sake of spying on Carnilinx and other competitors . . . There were, to my knowledge, in the region of 171 such spies . . . They were paid by BATSA through FSS as a conduit. The payments were made in cash so that there was no direct link to BATSA. I point out that BATSA was directly responsible for the employment of these agents. BATSA would approve each of their employments and determine what these spies were paid. The primary objectives of these spies and the purpose of their employment were made clear to them. They were required

to: spy on Carnilinx . . . by intercepting their phone calls, by placing hidden cameras at their homes and businesses; . . . steal important documents such as production sheets and production schedules; . . . sabotaging machinery, for instance placing an old rag in the working components so that the machines were jammed and were damaged; instigating staff members within the Carnilinx factory to sabotage the factory and / or work at a slower pace.

67. Payment to each of these spies was made in cash only, with the specific instructions from BATSA that there must be no link of any bank account from either BATSA or FSS to any of these spies in case they turned against BATSA or FSS. In each instance, the payment of the cash amount to the information was specifically reviewed and the most senior management of the anti-illicit trading division of BATSA approved the reward. If they provided any information and an arrest took place, irrespective of whether or not the arrest and detention was meritorious, the spy would be paid a reward. This strategy was designed to induce fabricated reports of illicit activity resulting in arrests and detentions.

In another affidavit Van der Westhuizen also comments:[2]

18. During these discussions the aforementioned individuals all boasted about their close relationship and the special cooperation they shared with each other which results in successful investigations against Carnilinx Tobacco Company.

19. It was obvious during this interaction that the individuals were all very well acquainted and knew each other for many years.

20. . . . Spoke fondly about the intervention at Muldersdrift on Carnilinx Tobacco goods. All the individuals were well aware of a tracking beacon that was placed on the Carnilinx vehicle and in fact, they all recalled how x placed the beacon on the Carnilinx truck by pretending to be lost in the Carnilinx basement.

21. It was peculiar to note that Hennie Niemann (a Colonel in the

South African Police Service and member of the Tobacco Task Team) got very upset that he was often asked to cover up for MP of British American Tobacco South Africa. It was patently clear that Niemann was receiving instructions from BAT.

22. During the braai, I learnt that Piet Swart (a SARS investigator) was very grateful to Derrick Vosloo for passing on important information which allowed him to make successful SARS interventions against Carnilinx.

We cannot change
what we are not aware of.
Once we are aware,
we cannot help but change.
– *Sheryl Sandberg*

Sources

PROLOGUE
1. Minutes of Evidence, Hearings into tobacco smuggling involving UK companies, UK Parliament, Public Account, http://www.publications.parliament.uk/pa/cm200203/cmselect/cmpubacc/143/2061901.htm
2. The Tobacco Atlas, 6th Edition, 2018, *WHO*, https://tobaccoatlas.org/topic/illicit-trade/
3. The illicit trade in tobacco products, *WHO*, http://applications.emro.who.int/docs/Fact_Sheet_TFI_2014_EN_15313.pdf?ua=1&ua=1; UK considering formal investigation into cigarette smuggling, *International Consortium of Investigative Journalists*, https://www.icij.org/investigations/big-tobacco-smuggling/uk-considering-formal-investigation-cigarette-smuggling/
4. Key to the Future: BAT and Cigarette Smuggling in China, Kelley Lee and Jeff Collin, http://journals.plos.org/plosmedicine/article?id=10.1371/journal.pmed.0030228#sd001; https://bat.library.ucsf.edu; https://www.ncbi.nlm.nih.gov/pmc/articles/PMC1502159/
5. SARS wars: Suspension of the last remaining key official jeopardises tobacco war cases, *Daily Maverick*, https://www.dailymaverick.co.za/article/2017-02-10-SARS-wars-suspension-of-the-last-remaining-key-official-jeopardises-tobacco-war-cases/; SARS target of tobacco industry backlash, *IOL*, https://www.iol.co.za/news/south-africa/gauteng/SARS-target-of-tobacco-industry-backlash-1728457; Industry prepared the ground for illicit cigarette trade, *African Tobacco Control Alliance*, http://atca-africa.org/en/south-africa-tobacco-industry-prepared-the-ground-for-illicit-cigarette-trade
6. Illicit cigarette trade in South Africa: 2002 – 2017, Nicole Vellios, https://tobaccocontrol.bmj.com/content/early/2019/08/05/tobaccocontrol-2018-054798
7. The illicit tobacco trade in Zimbabwe and South Africa, *Atlantic Council*, https://www.atlanticcouncil.org/images/publications/The_Illicit_Tobacco_Trade_in_Zimbabwe_and_South_Africa.pdf
8. Counterfeit tobacco trade in *South Africa*, *Mondaq*, http://www.mondaq.com/southafrica/x/292288/Copyright/Counterfeit+Tobacco+Trade+In+Southern+Africa
9. PMI Corporate Affairs Presentation, https://www.reuters.com/investigates/special-report/pmi-who-fctc/
10. Philip Morris: Corporate Affairs Approach, https://www.documentcloud.org/documents/3892762-2014-Corporate-Affairs-Approach-and-Issues.html
11. Son of a bitch memo, *Source Watch*, https://www.sourcewatch.org/index.php/R.J._Reynolds_Son-of-a-Bitch_memo

12. Global illicit cigarette trade: What's next, *International Consortium of Investigative Journalists*, https://www.icij.org/investigations/big-tobacco-smuggling/global-illicit-cigarette-trade-whats-next/
13. Minutes of Evidence, Hearings into tobacco smuggling involving UK companies, UK Parliament, Public Account, http://www.publications.parliament.uk/pa/cm200203/cmselect/cmpubacc/143/2061901.htm

1. THE BIRTH OF BIG TOBACCO

1. *Smoking, Culture and Economy in The Middle East: The Egyptian Tobacco Market*, Relli Schechter, IB Taurus
2. Father of the modern cigarette, William Kremer, https://www.bbc.com/news/magazine-20042217; https://library.duke.edu/rubenstein/uarchives/history/articles/james-buchanan-duke; http://museumofdurhamhistory.org/beneathourfeet/people/DukeBJames
3. See e.g. Five things you didn't know about Philip Morris, Dan Caplinger, https://www.fool.com/investing/2017/09/06/5-things-you-didnt-know-about-philip-morris-intern.aspx; PMI Key Milestones, PMI website, https://www.pmi.com/who-we-are/key-milestones; History of Philip Morris, *Source Watch*, https://www.sourcewatch.org/index.php/History_of_Philip_Morris
4. The China National Tobacco Corporation: From domestic to global dragon?, US National Library of Medicine, https://www.ncbi.nlm.nih.gov/pmc/articles/PMC5553430
5. Obituary: Anton Rupert, *The Guardian*, https://www.theguardian.com/news/2006/jan/23/guardianobituaries.smoking
6. Our South African History, BAT website, http://www.batsa.co.za/group/sites/BAT_A2ELAD.nsf/vwPagesWebLive/DO9YABCW
7. The illicit tobacco trade in Zimbabwe and South Africa, *Atlantic Council*, https://www.atlanticcouncil.org/images/publications/The_Illicit_Tobacco_Trade_in_Zimbabwe_and_South_Africa.pdf
8. Framework Convention on Tobacco Control, *WHO*, https://www.who.int/fctc/text_download/en/

2. THE COMPETITION: 'CHEAP AND NASTY'

1. African king of the cheapie ciggie, Linda van Tilburg, https://www.biznews.com/undictated/2019/08/06/african-king-of-the-cheapie-ciggie-extract-from-tobacco-wars
2. *WHO* Fact Sheet on Smoking, 2019, https://www.who.int/news-room/fact-sheets/detail/tobacco
3. The illicit tobacco trade in Zimbabwe and South Africa, *Atlantic Council*, https://www.atlanticcouncil.org/images/publications/The_Illicit_Tobacco_Trade_in_Zimbabwe_and_South_Africa.pdf
4. Belinda Walter affidavit, https://twitter.com/espionageafrica; https://drive.google.com/file/d/0B0gfZnd_OvzdWTZ4Z0FuZ25Md0E/view
5. Tycoon hits back at SARS, *News24*, https://www.news24.com/Archives/Witness/Tycoon-hits-back-at-SARS-20150430
6. The illicit tobacco trade in Zimbabwe and South Africa, *Atlantic Council*, https://www.atlanticcouncil.org/images/publications/The_Illicit_Tobacco_Trade_in_Zimbabwe_and_South_Africa.pdf

7. https://twitter.com/FITA_sa/status/1095318088281669634
8. Tobacco wars turn deadly, *Moneyweb*, https://www.moneyweb.co.za/news/south-africa/tobacco-wars-turn-deadly/
9. Controlling Illicit Tobacco Trade: International Experience, Hana Ross, https://tobacconomics.org/wp-content/uploads/2015/05/Ross_International_experience_05.28.15.pdf
10. Project Sun: 2017 Report, *KPMG*, https://assets.kpmg.com/content/dam/kpmg/uk/pdf/2017/07/project-sun-2017-report.pdf
11. Ukraine's lost cigarettes flood Europe, *International Consortium of Investigative Journalists*, https://www.icij.org/project/tobacco-underground/ukraines-lost-cigarettes-flood-europe
12. Russians capture cigarette smuggling drone, *Arstechnica*, https://arstechnica.com/tech-policy/2014/05/russians-capture-cigarette-smuggling-drone/
13. Slovaks find railway smuggling tunnel to Ukraine, *Reuters*, https://www.reuters.com/article/us-slovakia-ukraine-tunnel/slovaks-find-railway-smuggling-tunnel-to-ukraine-idUSBRE86I0ZO20120719
14. Interview with head of a leading tax and customs agency
15. Tobacco manufacturing machinery for sale on Alibaba, see e.g. https://www.alibaba.com/products/tobacco_machinery.html?spm=a2700.galleryofferlist.scGlobalHomeHeader.314.52954e033jJNYD&IndexArea=product_en
16. Interview with person frequently associated with contraband tobacco in Southern Africa
17. Ibid
18. Arrests Again Point to Paraguay President's Contraband Cigarettes, *Insight Crime*, https://www.insightcrime.org/news/brief/arrests-point-paraguay-president-contraband-cigarettes/
19. Montenegrin PM accused of link with tobacco racket, *The Guardian*, https://www.theguardian.com/world/2003/jul/11/smoking.internationalcrime
20. From illegal markets to legitimate businesses: the portfolio of organised crime in Europe, *Transcrime*, https://www.int-comp.org/media/1997/ocp-full-report.pdf
21. The neglected mega problem of illicit trade in normally licit goods, https://cco.ndu.edu/News/Article/980844/12-the-neglected-mega-problem-illicit-trade-in-normally-licit-goods/
22. Diplomats arrested for cigarette smuggling, *Reuters*, https://www.reuters.com/article/us-northkorea-odds/diplomats-arrested-for-cigarette-smuggling-idUSTRE5AJ2Z420091120
23. China cigarette order goes up in smoke, *Reuters*, https://www.reuters.com/article/idUSPEK124354
24. Jordanians sceptical of corruption crackdown, *The National*, https://www.thenational.ae/world/mena/jordanians-sceptical-of-corruption-crackdown-1.757914
25. Investigative journalist Olivera Lakic shot in Montenegro, *The Guardian*, https://www.theguardian.com/world/2018/may/08/investigative-journalist-olivera-lakic-shot-montenegro
26. Interview with source
27. BAT internal report, India Domestic Markets, 31 March 1994. See, also, BAT Bates No. 503964700, BAT Bates No. 503964664
28. Tobacco smugglers are patriots, *SBS News*, https://www.sbs.com.au/news/tobacco-smugglers-are-patriots-senator

29. The world's most widely smuggled legal substance, *International Consortium of Investigative Journalists*, https://www.icij.org/project/tobacco-underground/worlds-most-widely-smuggled-legal-substance
30. From illegal markets to legitimate businesses: the portfolio of organised crime in Europe, *Transcrime*, https://www.int-comp.org/media/1997/ocp-full-report.pdf; Organized crime in Europe: A country-by-country breakdown, *The Mob Museum*, https://themobmuseum.org/blog/organized-crime-in-europe-a-country-by-country-breakdown/
31. Tobacco industry lobbying: the scandal of the century, *EU Observer*, https://euobserver.com/opinion/131592; NY cigarette-smuggling ring may have terror link, *CNN*, http://edition.cnn.com/2013/05/17/us/new-york-cigarette-ring/index.html; The WCO Illicit Trade Report 2012, WCO, http://dx.doi.org/10.1787/9789264251847-en; Charting illicit trade, *OECD*, http://www.keepeek.com/Digital-Asset-Management/oecd/governance/charting-illicit-trade_9789264251847-en#page153
32. The illicit tobacco trade in Zimbabwe and South Africa, *Atlantic Council*, https://www.atlanticcouncil.org/images/publications/The_Illicit_Tobacco_Trade_in_Zimbabwe_and_South_Africa.pdf
33. From illegal markets to legitimate businesses: the portfolio of organised crime in Europe, *Transcrime*, https://www.int-comp.org/media/1997/ocp-full-report.pdf; Organized crime in Europe: A country-by-country breakdown, *The Mob Museum*, https://themobmuseum.org/blog/organized-crime-in-europe-a-country-by-country-breakdown/; http://uk.reuters.com/article/2013/04/17/uk-eu-tobacco-idUKBRE93G0Q020130417; Illicit Trade Report 2012, *WCO*, http://www.cites.org/fb/2013/wco_illicit_trade_report_2012; The world's most widely smuggled legal substance, *International Consortium of Investigative Journalists*, https://www.icij.org/project/tobacco-underground/worlds-most-widely-smuggled-legal-substance

3. 'BIGGER THAN DRUGS'

1. Jacques Pauw, *The President's Keepers*, Tafelberg, 2017
2. Ibid
3. How British American Tobacco exploited war zones to sell tobacco, *The Guardian*, https://www.theguardian.com/world/2017/aug/18/british-american-tobacco-cigarettes-africa-middle-east
4. Key to the Future: British American Tobacco and Cigarette Smuggling in China, Kelley Lee, Jeff Collin, http://europepmc.org/articles/pmc1502159
5. See e.g. How smuggling helps lure generations of new smokers, Maud Beelman, https://www.theguardian.com/uk/2000/jan/31/duncancampbell
6. ICIJ, Exposed: How billions of cigarettes end up on black markets, https://www.icij.org/investigations/big-tobacco-smuggling/exposed-how-billions-cigarettes-end-black-markets/
7. Tobacco Smuggling, *Tobacco Tactics*, http://www.tobaccotactics.org/index.php/Tobacco_Smuggling; Tobacco industry lobbying: the scandal of the century, *EU Observer*, https://euobserver.com/opinion/131592
8. Illegal cigarettes burn up SA's money, *Eyewitness News*, ewn.co.za/2014/11/26/Illegal-cigarettes-burn-up-SAs-money
9. See e.g. Cough up, SARS tells BAT, https://www.financialgazette.co.zw/cough-up-SARS-tells-bat-sa/; letter sent to BAT seen by author

10. British American Tobacco bribed police, *News24*, https://www.news24.com/SouthAfrica/News/british-american-tobacco-bribed-police-a davit-20160816; https://www.zimeye.net/2016/09/04/profile-bat-whistle-blower-still-under-threatened/; Founding affidavit submitted by DF van der Westhuizen, Carnilinx v BAT, FSS et al, in particular paragraphs 90, 92, 93
11. Tobacco Institute of Southern Africa website, https://www.tobaccosa.co.za, as at 22 February 2020
12. The illicit tobacco trade in Zimbabwe and South Africa, *Atlantic Council*, https://www.atlanticcouncil.org/images/publications/The_Illicit_Tobacco_Trade_in_Zimbabwe_and_South_Africa.pdf

4. DEAD EASY TO CHEAT
1. The contribution of British American Tobacco South Africa to the South African economy, 2016, http://www.batsa.co.za/group/sites/bat_a2elad.nsf/vwPagesWebLive/DOA2LJ7R/$FILE/medMDAG2LAG.pdf?openelement
2. The illicit tobacco trade in Zimbabwe and South Africa, *Atlantic Council*, https://www.atlanticcouncil.org/images/publications/The_Illicit_Tobacco_Trade_in_Zimbabwe_and_South_Africa.pdf
3. http://www.tobacco.org/tagged/south-africa
4. UK considering formal investigation into cigarette smuggling, *International Consortium of Investigative Journalists*, https://www.icij.org/investigations/big-tobacco-smuggling/uk-considering-formal-investigation-cigarette-smuggling/
5. Exposed: How billions of cigarettes end up on black markets, *International Consortium of Investigative Journalists*, https://www.icij.org/node/460/exposed-how-billions-cigarettes-end-black-markets
6. BAT letter dated 25 August 1989. BAT Bates No. 302000021
7. Venezuelan Market Definitions and Assumptions, BAT Bates No. 500025647
8. Review of Asia-Pacific Market, BAT Bates No. 502628801

5. SMUGGLING: A ROGUE'S GALLERY
1. Key to the Future: British American Tobacco and Cigarette Smuggling in China, Kelley Lee, Jeff Collin, http://journals.plos.org/plosmedicine/article?id=10.1371/journal.pmed.0030228#sd001; https://www.ncbi.nlm.nih.gov/pmc/articles/PMC1502159/; https://bat.library.ucsf.edu
2. Sales: Mission statement, BAT. Bates No. 500323451–500323468, http://bat.library.ucsf.edu/data/j/n/t/jnt01a99/jnt01a99.pdf
3. A report on its China trade structure for the British-American Tobacco Group: section 3, BAT. Bates No. 201813538–201813643, http://bat.library.ucsf.edu/data-/f/b/p/fbp02a99/fbp02a99.pdf
4. Purpose, BAT. Bates No. 301130954–301131002; http://bat.library.ucsf.edu/data-/k/t/n/ktn41a99/ktn41a99.pdf
5. A report on its China trade structure for the British-American Tobacco Group: section 1, BAT Bates No. 201813661–201813751, http://bat.library.ucsf.edu/data-/h/b/p/hbp02a99/hbp02a99.pdf
6. Secret: BAT organisation in China, Bates No. 201813500–201813508; http://bat.library.ucsf.edu/data/r/a/p/rap02a99/rap02a99.pdf
7. B&W internal document, BAT Bates No. 500014760
8. Secret: BATCo preview, Bates No. 502639056–502639062 http://bat.library.ucsf.edu/data/q/j/h/qjh30a99/qjh30a99.pdf

9. Distribution initiatives within PRC, BAT Bates No. 500014779–500014780. Guildford Depository
10. In 1982, BAT declared that it was exporting 811 million sticks to China – but only declared 202 million sticks on import into China. By 2004, BAT's customs declarations suggested it was exporting 113 919 million sticks to China – but only 2 134 million sticks were actually declared as having been imported into China. Salter R. BATCo. Plan 1991–1995. British American Tobacco. Bates No. 201761791, http://bat.library.ucsf.edu/pageview?a=img&tid=knv20a99&total=2
11. Country summary – Hong Kong, BAT Bates No. 201764651–201764653, http://bat.library.ucsf.edu/data/p/h/v/phv00a99/phv00a99.pdf
12. BATCo. Plan 1991-1995, BAT. Bates No. 201761791, http://bat.library.ucsf.edu/pageview?a=img&tid=knv20a99&total=2
13. A report on its China trade structure for BAT Group: section 1, Bates No. 201813661–201813751; http://bat.library.ucsf.edu/data/h/b/p/hbp02a99/hbp02a99.pdf
14. BATCo. Plan 1991-1995, Bates No. 201761791. http://bat.library.ucsf.edu/pageview?a=img&tid=knv20a99&total=2
15. Philip Morris to Help Colombia Halt Cigarette Smuggling, *Dow Jones News Service*; The multi-million dollar trade route, *International Consortium of Investigative Journalists*, https://www.icij.org/investigations/big-tobacco-smuggling/multi-million-dollar-trade-route/; Big tobacco, *The Nation*, https://www.thenation.com/article/big-tobacco/
16. Tobacco's Other Secret, *CBS 60 Minutes*, https://www.cbsnews.com/news/tobaccos-other-secret/; Controlling Illicit Tobacco Trade: International Experience, Hana Ross, https://tobacconomics.org/wp-content/uploads/2015/05/Ross_International_experience_05.28.15.pdf
17. Italian prosecutors accuse Philip Morris of tax evasion, *The Wall Street Journal*, https://www.wsj.com/articles/SB836775941251927000
18. International business rival asserts PMI smuggles in South Africa, *New York Times*, http://www.nytimes.com/1997/11/22/business/international-business-rival-asserts-philip-morris-smuggles-in-south-africa.html
19. Hong Kong Tobacco Exec Gets 3-Year Jail Term for Bribery, *Dow Jones News Service*; HK Top Court Restores Ex-Tobacco Exec's Conviction, *Reuters*
20. Tobacco's Other Secret, *CBS 60 Minutes*, https://www.cbsnews.com/news/tobaccos-other-secret/
21. Illegal pathways to illegal profits, *Tobacco Free Kids*, https://www.tobaccofreekids.org/assets/global/pdfs/en/Illegal_profits_to_illicit_profit en.pdf; The tobacco industry rallies against illicit trade but have we forgotten about its complicity?, *The Conversation*, http://theconversation.com/tobacco-industry-rallies-against-illicit-trade-but-have-we-forgotten-its-complicity-38760; Tobacco giant implicated in global smuggling schemes, *The Guardian*, https://www.theguardian.com/uk/2000/jan/31/kevinmaguire.duncancampbell
22. The tobacco industry rallies against illicit trade but have we forgotten about its complicity?, *The Conversation*, http://theconversation.com/tobacco-industry-rallies-against-illicit-trade-but-have-we-forgotten-its-complicity-38760
23. https://www.industrydocumentslibrary.ucsf.edu/docs/#id=qphp0219
24. Progress in combating cigarette smuggling: controlling the supply chain, Luk Joossens, https://tobaccocontrol.bmj.com/content/17/6/399
25. Tobacco giants to pay up to 1.15bn over contraband sales, *CBC News*, http://www.

cbc.ca/news/canada/tobacco-giants-to-pay-up-to-1-15b-over-contraband-sales-1.701089
26. Tobacco giant, British American Tobacco, caught in intensive smuggling, corporate espionage, *Premium Times*, http://www.premiumtimesng.com/business/5939-investigation-tobacco-giant-british-american-tobacco-caught-in-intensive-smuggling-corporate-espionage.html
27. The tobacco industry rallies against illicit trade but have we forgotten about its complicity?, *The Conversation*, http://theconversation.com/tobacco-industry-rallies-against-illicit-trade-but-have-we-forgotten-its-complicity-38760; UK considering formal investigation into cigarette smuggling, *International Consortium of Investigative Journalists*, https://www.icij.org/investigations/big-tobacco-smuggling/uk-considering-formal-investigation-cigarette-smuggling/
28. Tobacco giant, British American Tobacco, caught in intensive smuggling, corporate espionage, *Premium Times*, http://www.premiumtimesng.com/business/5939-investigation-tobacco-giant-british-american-tobacco-caught-in-intensive-smuggling-corporate-espionage.html
29. Ibid; Sorepex letter, BAT Bates No. 301773794
30. Ibid
31. Africa: Disguising BAT's involvement in cigarette smuggling, *International Consortium of Investigative Journalists*, https://www.icij.org/investigations/big-tobacco-smuggling/africa-disguising-bats-involvement-cigarette-smuggling/; British American Tobacco and the 'insidious impact of illicit trade' in cigarettes across Africa, E LeGresley, https://tobaccocontrol.bmj.com/content/tobaccocontrol/17/5/339.full.pdf
32. Assessment of the European Union's illicit trade agreements with the four major Transnational Tobacco Companies, Luk Joossens, https://tobaccocontrol.bmj.com/content/25/3/254
33. US District Court. European Community complaint against Philip Morris, RJ Reynolds and Japan Tobacco. New York: United States District Court, Eastern District of New York, 2000, http://uniset.ca/other/cs6/150FSupp2d456.html
34. Dubai diplomat accused of smuggling BAT cigarettes, *The Guardian*, https://www.theguardian.com/uk/2001/dec/17/britishamericantobaccobusiness.smoking
35. Assessment of the European Union's illicit trade agreements with the four major Transnational Tobacco Companies, Luk Joossens, https://tobaccocontrol.bmj.com/content/25/3/254
36. For an in-depth analysis on the effectiveness of the agreement, see some of the work done by e.g. Luk Joossens.
37. Upfront payments of $12,7 billion; and more than $183 billion to be paid in annual instalments ($4,5billion in 2000, $6,5 billion in 2002 and 2003, $8,14 billion from 2008 to 2017, and from 2017 on $9 billion to be paid per year, in perpetuity).
38. The tobacco industry rallies against illicit trade but have we forgotten about its complicity?, *The Conversation*, http://theconversation.com/tobacco-industry-rallies-against-illicit-trade-but-have-we-forgotten-its-complicity-38760
39. http://www.premiumtimesng.com/business/5939-investigation-tobacco-giant-british-american-tobacco-caught-in-intensive-smuggling-corporate-espionage.html; BATUKE letter, Bates No. 301626956
40. Tobacco firms used suspected drug traffickers, EU lawsuit claims, *International Consortium of Investigative Journalists*, https://www.icij.org/investigations/big-tobacco-smuggling/tobacco-firms-used-suspected-drug-traffickers-eu-lawsuit-claims/

41. Ibid
42. Ibid; Philip Morris accused of smuggling, money-laundering conspiracy in racketeering lawsuit, *International Consortium of Investigative Journalists*, https://www.icij.org/investigations/big-tobacco-smuggling/philip-morris-accused-smuggling-money-laundering-conspiracy-racketeering-lawsuit/
43. EU Probes Cigarette Deal That May Have Aided Syria, *The Wall Street Journal*, https://www.wsj.com/articles/SB10000872396390444233104577595221220332192; Smuggling, the tobacco industry, and plain packs, Luk Joossens, https://www.cancerresearchuk.org/sites/default/files/smuggling_fullreport.pdf
44. Tobacco firms used suspected drug traffickers, EU lawsuit claims, *International Consortium of Investigative Journalists*, https://www.icij.org/investigations/big-tobacco-smuggling/tobacco-firms-used-suspected-drug-traffickers-eu-lawsuit-claims/
45. BAT fined for oversupplying tobacco in low tax European jurisdictions, *The Guardian*, https://www.theguardian.com/business/2014/nov/16/bat-fined-for-oversupplying-tobacco-in-low-tax-european-jurisdictions; The tobacco industry rallies against illicit trade but have we forgotten about its complicity?, *The Conversation*, http://theconversation.com/tobacco-industry-rallies-against-illicit-trade-but-have-we-forgotten-its-complicity-38760; Tobacco industry lobbying: the scandal of the century, *EU Observer*, https://euobserver.com/opinion/131592
46. British American Tobacco 'bribed' Kenyan politician Martha Karua to stop action against cigarette smuggling, *The Independent*, http://www.independent.co.uk/news/uk/crime/british-american-tobacco-bribed-kenyan-politician-martha-karua-to-stop-action-against-cigarette-a6779236.html
47. The tobacco industry by the numbers, *The Mail and Guardian*, http://mg.co.za/article/2012-05-18-the-tobacco-industry-by-the-numbers
48. Philip Morris, BAT fined $260 million for illegal cigarette hoarding, *The Korea Times*, http://www.koreatimes.co.kr/www/tech/2017/02/694_223714.html; Philip Morris, BAT Korea Face Multi-billion Fine for Tax Evasion, Business Korea, http://businesskorea.co.kr/english/news/industry/16760-tax-evasion-philip-morris-bat-korea-face-multi-billion-fine-tax-evasion
49. Gravísima denuncia contra Philip Morris por fraude, *Periodico Tribuna*, http://periodicotribuna.com.ar/18065-gravisima-denuncia-contra-philip-morris-por-fraude-.html; https://whyitisbad.wordpress.com
50. Thailand Slaps Philip Morris With More Tax Evasion Charges, *The Wall Street Journal*, https://www.wsj.com/articles/thailand-slaps-philip-morris-with-more-tax-evasion-charges-1487090584
51. The Serious Fraud Office is investigating British American Tobacco for bribery, *Business Insider Singapore*, http://www.businessinsider.sg/british-american-tobacco-bribery-charges-serious-fraud-office-inquiry-2017-8/?r=UK&IR=T
52. The illicit tobacco trade in Zimbabwe and South Africa, *Atlantic Council*, https://www.atlanticcouncil.org/images/publications/The_Illicit_Tobacco_Trade_in_Zimbabwe_and_South_Africa.pdf
53. New migraine for British American Tobacco, *Financial Mail*, https://www.businesslive.co.za/fm/opinion/editors-note/2019-04-11-rob-rose-new-migraine-for-british-american-tobacco/
54. BBC Panorama, The secret bribes of big tobacco, https://www.bbc.co.uk/news/av/uk-34970163/panorama-the-secret-bribes-of-big-tobacco
55. How British American Tobacco exploited war zones to sell tobacco, *The Guardian*,

https://www.theguardian.com/world/2017/aug/18/british-american-tobacco-cigarettes-africa-middle-east
56. Ibid
57. The BBC documentary is available for viewing here: https://www.bbc.com/news/business-34964603
58. COM(2017) 235 final – Progress report on the implementation of the Commission Communication Stepping up the fight against cigarette smuggling and other forms of illicit trade in tobacco products – a comprehensive EU strategy
59. Tobacco industry's elaborate attempts to control a global track and trace system and fundamentally undermine the Illicit Trade Protocol, Anna Gilmore, https://tobaccocontrol.bmj.com/content/28/2/127

6. JAM ON THEIR FACE AND STILL THEY DO NOTHING
1. BTC 'Restricted' memo, Monthly Review, BAT Bates No. 503932405
2. Illegal pathways to illegal profits, *Tobacco Free Kids*, https://www.tobaccofreekids.org/assets/global/pdfs/en/Illegal_profits_to_illicit_profit_en.pdf; Notes of Meeting with SUTL at SUTL Offices in Singapore, BAT memo, BAT Bates No. 500045568; Restricted, Visit of Sir Patrick Sheehy, BAT memo, BAT Bates No. 500017305; BAT Bates No. 503914283
3. UK considering formal investigation into cigarette smuggling, *International Consortium of Investigative Journalists*, https://www.icij.org/investigations/big-tobacco-smuggling/uk-considering-formal-investigation-cigarette-smuggling/
4. European Union v. RJR Nabisco Inc. et al., United States District Court, Eastern District of New York, Docket No. 1-00- 06617-NGG, www.tobacco.org/Documents/001103euvpm,rjr.html; BAT Bates No. 503095363
5. BAT Bates No. 500028732, BAT memo. BAT Bates No. 500017305
6. Philip Morris accused of smuggling, money-laundering conspiracy in racketeering lawsuit, *International Consortium of Investigative Journalists*, https://www.icij.org/investigations/big-tobacco-smuggling/philip-morris-accused-smuggling-money-laundering-conspiracy-racketeering-lawsuit/
7. Tobacco's Other Secret, *CBS 60 Minutes*, https://www.cbsnews.com/news/tobaccos-other-secret/
8. Ibid
9. Big tobacco, *The Nation*, https://www.thenation.com/article/big-tobacco/
10. Africa: Disguising BAT's involvement in cigarette smuggling, *International Consortium of Investigative Journalists*, https://www.icij.org/investigations/big-tobacco-smuggling/africa-disguising-bats-involvement-cigarette-smuggling/
11. Philip Morris accused of smuggling, money-laundering conspiracy in racketeering lawsuit, *International Consortium of Investigative Journalists*, https://www.icij.org/investigations/big-tobacco-smuggling/philip-morris-accused-smuggling-money-laundering-conspiracy-racketeering-lawsuit/; Global illicit cigarette trade: What's next, *International Consortium of Investigative Journalists*, https://www.icij.org/investigations/big-tobacco-smuggling/global-illicit-cigarette-trade-whats-next/
12. Europe Turning to U.S. to Fight Illicit Cigarettes, *The New York Times*, 08 May 1998; EU complaint, 32(t)
13. UK Parliament, Public Account – Minutes of Evidence, Hearings into tobacco smuggling involving UK companies, http://www.publications.parliament.uk/pa/cm200203/cmselect/cmpubacc/143/2061901.htm
14. Cigarette giant still mum on year-long corruption claims, *Cape Talk*, http://www.

capetalk.co.za/articles/266827/cigarette-giant-still-mum-on-year-long-corruption-claims
15. Industry Lobbying of the Public Sector and other Tactics, Yusuf Saloojee for *WHO*, https://www.who.int/tobacco/media/en/YUSSUF2000X.pdf
16. One of Europe's biggest cigarette dealers, now retired
17. Cigarette makers are seen as aiding rise in smuggling, *The New York Times*, https://www.nytimes.com/1997/08/25/business/cigarette-makers-are-seen-as-aiding-rise-in-smuggling.html
18. Big trouble at big tobacco: Brand Integrity Group Investigations Report https://www.reportingproject.net/troubleswithbigtobacco/documents/OCCRP_tobacco_1.pdf
19. Email from David Reynolds to JTI, dated 10 April 2010, https://www.reportingproject.net/troubleswithbigtobacco/documents/OCCRP_tobacco_10.pdf
20. Email exchange between David Reynolds and and Jean-Luc Perreard, https://www.reportingproject.net/troubleswithbigtobacco/documents/OCCRP_tobacco_12.pdf
21. Big trouble at big tobacco, https://www.reportingproject.net/troubleswithbigtobacco/
22. Ibid
23. Court pleadings, Gallaher and Tlais, https://www.reportingproject.net/troubleswithbigtobacco/documents/OCCRP_tobacco_11.pdf
24. Project Sun Report 2017, *KPMG*, https://assets.kpmg/content/dam/kpmg/lt/pdf/project-sun-2017-report.pdf
25. Tobacco industry's elaborate attempts to control a global track and trace system and fundamentally undermine the Illicit Trade Protocol, Anna Gilmore, https://tobaccocontrol.bmj.com/content/28/2/127
26. Tobacco industry lobbying: the scandal of the century, *EU Observer*, https://euobserver.com/opinion/131592

7. THEY PLAY A WEAK DEFENSE
1. Philip Morris: Corporate Affairs Approach, https://www.documentcloud.org/documents/3892762-2014-Corporate-Affairs-Approach-and-Issues.html
2. Gangsters prey on young women to smuggle cigarettes, *The Guardian*, https://www.theguardian.com/uk/2009/sep/06/cigarette-smuggling-uk-organised-crime
3. The world's most widely smuggled legal substance, *International Consortium of Investigative Journalists*, https://www.icij.org/project/tobacco-underground/worlds-most-widely-smuggled-legal-substance
4. Compliance Programme 2012-2017, SARS, http://www.SARS.gov.za/AllDocs/SARSEntDoclib/Ent/SARS-Strat-07-G02%20-%20Compliance%20Programme%202012%202013%20to%202016%202017%20-%20External%20Guide.pdf
5. Using data from www.who.int/tobacco/economics/illicittrade.pdf, based on a) Euromonitor estimates, b) World Customs Annual Report
6. Austin Rowan, head of cigarette fraud investigations for the EU's Anti-Fraud Office (OLAF); China's Marlboro country, Organised Crime and Corruption Reporting Project, https://www.reportingproject.net/underground/index.php%3Foption%3Dcom_content%26view%3Darticle%26id%3D9%26Itemid%3D22
7. A study of the illicit cigarette market in the European Union: Project Sun, *KPMG*, https://assets.kpmg/content/dam/kpmg/uk/pdf/2018/07/project_sun_executive_summary_2018.pdf
8. Illicit trade: Converging criminal networks, *OECD*, http://dx.doi.

org/10.1787/9789264251847-en; http://www.keepeek.com/Digital-Asset-Management/oecd/governance/charting-illicit-trade_9789264251847-en#page153; OECD Task Force on Countering Illicit Trade (TF-CIT), OECD, http://www.oecd.org/gov/risk/oecdtaskforceoncounteringillicittrade.htm
9. Presentation at the Tax Stamp Forum in Berlin, 2017
10. http://documents.worldbank.org/curated/en/677451548260528135/pdf/133959-REPL-PUBLIC-6-2-2019-19-59-24-WBGTobaccoIllicitTradeFINALvweb.pdf
11. Illicit trade in tobacco products, *Euromonitor*, http://www.euromonitor.com/illicit-trade-in-tobacco-products/report
12. See e.g. Illicit cigarette trade in the Maghreb region
13. Stepping up the fight against cigarette smuggling and other forms of illicit trade in tobacco products, *European Commission*, https://ec.europa.eu/anti-fraud/sites/antifraud/files/docs/body/communication_en.pdf; "Project Sun Report 2017", KPMG, https://assets.kpmg.com/content/dam/kpmg/uk/pdf/2017/07/project-sun-2017-report.pdf
14. The illicit trade in tobacco products, *WHO*, http://applications.emro.who.int/docs/Fact_Sheet_TFI_2014_EN_15313.pdf?ua=1&ua=1
15. Using data from www.trademap.org
16. Tobacco smugglers pay median fine of $17 000, *Financial Review*, https://www.afr.com/news/policy/tax/tobacco-smugglers-pay-median-fine-of-17000-20170824-gy35xo
17. *The Insider*, https://www.imdb.com/title/tt0140352/characters/nm0762466
18. According to the US Federal Trade Commission, Tobacco industry spends nearly 1 million an hour marketing tobacco products, https://truthinitiative.org/news/new-report-tobacco-industry-spends-nearly-1-million-hour-marketing-tobacco-products

8. TOOTHPASTE, FISH AND FIG LEAVES

1. https://en.wikipedia.org/wiki/Maryland_Tobacco_Inspection_Act_of_1747
2. Progress in combating cigarette smuggling: controlling the supply chain, Luk Joossens, http://tobaccocontrol.bmj.com/content/tobaccocontrol/early/2008/09/10/tc.2008.026567.full.pdf
3. Counterfeit focus sheet, *UNODC*, http://www.unodc.org/documents/counterfeit/FocusSheet/Counterfeit_focussheet_EN_HIRES.pdf; "OCTA 2011: EU Organised Crime Threat Assessment, Europol, https://www.europol.europa.eu/sites/default/files/ publications/octa2011.pdf.
4. UK Parliament, Public Account – Minutes of Evidence, Hearings into tobacco smuggling involving UK companies, http://www.publications.parliament.uk/pa/cm200203/cmselect/cmpubacc/143/2061901.htm
5. Colombian Governors Lawsuit vs. Philip Morris et al., 37(i)
6. Driving operational performance, *PMI* website, https://www.pmi.com/docs/default-source/pmi-sustainability/driving-operational-excellence.pdf
7. Anti-diversion governance committee report, *PMI*, https://www.stopillegal.com/docs/default-source/anti-diversion/anti-diversion-governance-comittee-report-2016-17.pdf?sfvrsn=b8973d7_2
8. Ibid
9. Environmental and supply chain management, BAT website, https://www.bat.com/group/sites/UK__9D9KCY.nsf/vwPagesWebLive/DO9QEGXN

10. Ibid
11. Driving operational excellence, *PMI*, https://www.pmi.com/docs/default-source/pmi-sustainability/driving-operational-excellence.pdf
12. The Tobacco Atlas, 6th Edition, 2018, *WHO* https://tobaccoatlas.org/topic/illicit-trade/
13. Codentify brochure, PMI website, http://www.pmi.com/eng/documents/Codentify_E_Brochure_English.pdf (since deleted); The transnational tobacco companies' strategy to promote Codentify, their inadequate tracking and tracing standard, Luk Joossens, http://tobaccocontrol.bmj.com/content/early/2013/03/11/tobaccocontrol-2012-050796; http://www.iticnet.org/file/document/watch/3616 (since deleted); https://en.wikipedia.org/wiki/Codentify
14. Why governments cannot afford Codentify to support their track and trace solutions, Hana Ross, https://tobaccocontrol.bmj.com/content/27/6/706
15. Ibid
16. British American Tobacco 'bribed' Kenyan politician Martha Karua to stop action against cigarette smuggling, *The Independent*, http://www.independent.co.uk/news/uk/crime/british-american-tobacco-bribed-kenyan-politician-martha-karua-to-stop-action-against-cigarette-a6779236.html
17. Transnational Tobacco Company Influence on Tax Policy, Anna Gilmore, https://www.ncbi.nlm.nih.gov/pmc/articles/PMC2040352/?fbclid=IwAR1RLYRF1Ybio3jpT_m8tZGHQBeVol803qyLxbMkiWerivlDXk_dT9OcmJc
18. Tobacco giant recalls 8 billion faulty cigarettes, *The New York Times*, https://www.nytimes.com/1995/05/27/us/tobacco-giant-recalls-8-billion-faulty-cigarettes.html
19. The best investment of the past 35 years? Sadly, it was cigarettes, *The Guardian*, https://www.theguardian.com/money/2019/jan/26/the-best-investment-of-the-past-35-years-sadly-it-was-cigarettes
20. www.thisfish.info
21. www.harvestmark.com
22. Indonesian teak farmers achieve traceability to the tree stump, *The Guardian*, https://www.theguardian.com/sustainable-business/indonesian-teak-farmers-traceability
23. Data science the key to Monsanto improving its supply chain, *CIO*, https://www.cio.com/article/3214664/data-science-key-to-monsanto-improving-its-supply-chain.html; Creating a digital supply chain: Monsanto's journey, Slideshare, https://www.slideshare.net/BCTIM/creating-a-digital-supply-chain-monsantos-journey; Monsanto CIO Jim Swanson leads a digital revolution of the world's oldest industry, *Forbes*, https://www.forbes.com/sites/peterhigh/2016/02/01/monsanto-cio-jim-swanson-leads-a-digital-revolution-of-the-worlds-oldest-industry/#6eecc2f15a86
24. P&G reaffirmed as a Gartner 2018 supply chain master, P&G Website, https://news.pg.com/blog/Gartner2018; https://rctom.hbs.org/submission/pg-end-to-end-supply-chain-model/; https://www.gtnexus.com/resources/blog-posts/how-supply-chain-transformation-saved-pg-12-billion
25. Customs trade partnership against terrorism, US Customs and Border Protection, https://www.cbp.gov/border-security/ports-entry/cargo-security/ctpat
26. Conflict diamonds, De Beers website, https://www.debeersgroup.com/building-forever/our-impact/confidence/conflict-diamonds
27. No curative power is claimed, Stanford University description of Philip Morris ad, http://tobacco.stanford.edu/tobacco_main/images_body.php?token1=fm_img2636.php
28. Research into the impact of tobacco advertising, Stanford University, http://tobacco.stanford.edu/tobacco_main/images.php?token2=fm_st012.php&token1=fm_

img2756.php&theme_file=fm_mt002.php&theme_name=For%20your%20Throat&subtheme_name=Johnny%20Calls%20for%20Philip%20Morris

9. A PLAYBOOK FOR PROFIT

1. *Fraud Examiners Manual*, 2003 US Edition, http://www.fraud-magazine.com/article.aspx?id=4294967799
2. Corporate comebacks: Marlboro, *Minyanville*, http://www.minyanville.com/businessmarkets/articles/MO-MAN-health-Cigarettes-MARLBORO/4/14/2009/id/21972?page=full; Marlboro's brand still one of world's best, *CNN*, https://money.cnn.com/2015/05/27/news/companies/marlboro-brand-tobacco-cigarettes/index.html
3. How big tobacco has survived death and taxes, https://www.theguardian.com/world/2017/jul/11/how-big-tobacco-has-survived-death-and-taxes
4. Tobacco stocks on fire despite proposed cigarette tax hikes, *CNBC*, https://www.cnbc.com/2016/09/22/tobacco-stocks-on-fire-despite-proposed-cigarette-tax-hikes.html
5. Own analysis; http://www.statisticbrain.com/tobacco-cigarette-industry-sales-statistics/; https://data.worldbank.org/indicator/NY.GNP.ATLS.CD?year_high_desc=false
6. America's best stock over, *CNN*, https://money.cnn.com/2015/02/19/investing/americas-best-stock-ever/
7. Ibid
8. Understanding the vector in order to plan effective tobacco control policies: An analysis of contemporary tobacco industry materials, US National Library of Medicine, https://www.ncbi.nlm.nih.gov/pmc/articles/PMC3705181/
9. Altria: This tobacco stock still looks like a quality income investment, *Guru Focus*, https://www.gurufocus.com/news/775899/altria-this-tobacco-stock-still-looks-like-a-quality-income-investment
10. BAT's profit soars, *Tobacco Reporter*, https://www.tobaccoreporter.com/2018/07/bats-profit-soars/
11. The best investment of the past 35 years? Sadly, it was cigarettes, *The Guardian*, https://www.theguardian.com/money/2019/jan/26/the-best-investment-of-the-past-35-years-sadly-it-was-cigarettes

10. MERCHANTS OF DISINFORMATION

1. Philip Morris: Corporate Affairs Approach, https://www.documentcloud.org/documents/3892762-2014-Corporate-Affairs-Approach-and-Issues.html
2. *The Unseen Power: Public Relations: A History*, by Scott M Cutlip
3. Tobacco industry efforts on subverting international agency for research on cancer's second-hand smoke study, *Research Gate*, https://www.researchgate.net/publication/12546928_Tobacco_industry_efforts_subverting_International_Agency_for_Research_on_Cancer's_second-hand_smoke_study and https://www.ncbi.nlm.nih.gov/pubmed/10770318
4. New report: Tobacco industry spends nearly $1 million an hour marketing tobacco products, US Federal Trade Commission, https://truthinitiative.org/news/new-report-tobacco-industry-spends-nearly-1-million-hour-marketing-tobacco-products
5. Tobacco *Atlas*, *WHO*, https://www.who.int/tobacco/en/atlas24.pdf
6. Tobacco tax the most effective and least used tool in public health, *Medium*, https://medium.com/@Union_TBLH/tobacco-tax-the-most-effective-least-used-tool-in-public-health-997a769f7372
7. Handling An Excise Tax Increase, Bates No. 2022216179/6180

Sources

8. Cigarette Smuggling in Europe: Who Really Benefits? Luk Joossens, Tobacco Control, http://tc.bmjjournals.com/cgi/content/full/7/1/66
9. Ballot bullies: The big spenders, *Capital and Main*, https://capitalandmain.com/ballot-bullies-infographic-the-big-spenders-1024
10. PMI Annual Report 2018, http://www.annualreports.com/HostedData/AnnualReports/PDF/NYSE_PM_2018.pdf
11. The Tobacco Atlas, 6th Edition, 2018, *WHO*, http://www.tobaccoatlas.org/topic/prices/http://www.tobaccoatlas.org/secondary-topic-tax/policy/
12. Tobacco cost increase without tax, *CBC*, http://www.cbc.ca/news/health/tobacco-cost-increase-without-tax-1.4475796
13. *WHO* webpage on tobacco, http://www.who.int/tobacco/en/index.html; Illicit trade, *WHO* website, www.who.int/tobacco/economics/illicittrade.pdf
14. Cigarette Smuggling in Europe: Who Really Benefits?
15. See e.g. South Africa in top 5 of illegal cigarette smuggling, *BizCommunity*, https://www.bizcommunity.com/Article/196/307/129276.html; Allegations that South Africa's revenue service loses millions from illicit tobacco, *ATIM*, https://www.atim.co.za/2017/08/allegations-that-south-africas-revenue-service-loses-millions-from-illicit-tobacco/; South Africa is one of the world's top five markets for illicit cigarettes, *Defence Web*, https://www.defenceweb.co.za/security/border-security/south-africa-is-one-of-worlds-top-five-markets-for-illicit-cigarettes/; Most illegal tobacco products manufactured in SA, *FTW Online*, http://www.ftwonline.co.za/article/103804/Most-illegal-tobacco-products-manufactured-in-SA#!
16. Standardised packaging: Report of the independent review undertaken by Sir Cyril Chantler, Australian Government, www.kcl.ac.uk/health/10035-TSO-2901853-Chantler-Review-ACCESSIBLE.PDF TobaccoTactics: KPMG, http://www.tobacco-tactics.org/index.php?title=KPMG
17. Tobacco industry lobbying: the scandal of the century, *EU Observer*, https://euobserver.com/opinion/131592
18. Tobacco industry manipulation of data on and press coverage of the illicit tobacco trade in the UK, Andy Rowell, http://tobaccocontrol.bmj.com/content/23/e1/e35.abstract?sid=6600e4c1-6c8e-4aa7-abda-6828a1128b3f
19. Did the tobacco industry inflate estimates of illicit cigarette consumption in Asia? An empirical analysis, Jing Chen, http://tobaccocontrol.bmj.com/content/24/e2/e161.full.pdf+html?sid=6600e4c1-6c8e-4aa7-abda-6828a1128b3f
20. Contrasting academic and tobacco industry estimates of illicit cigarette trade: evidence from Warsaw, Poland, Michal Stoklosa, http://tobaccocontrol.bmj.com/content/23/e1/e30.abstract?sid=6600e4c1-6c8e-4aa7-abda-6828a1128b3f
21. Illicit trade, tobacco industry-funded studies and policy influence in the EU and UK, Gary Jonas Fooks, http://tobaccocontrol.bmj.com/content/23/1/81.extract?sid=81d659f3-f091-49c5-87c0-df1b55e5e3a1
22. Report, 1 000 packs of illegal cigarettes sold each minute in Malaysia, *Malay Mail*, https://www.malaymail.com/news/malaysia/2019/06/21/report-1000-packs-of-illegal-cigarettes-sold-each-minute-in-malaysia/1764180
23. Illicit cigarette trade study funded by tobacco industry, Dr Ulysses Dorotheo, https://www.nst.com.my/opinion/letters/2019/08/516230/illicit-cigarette-trade-study-funded-tobacco-industry?fbclid=IwAR3Hhn_P5xVt3YUGfT8vhWz-4bs4DRgCKrx8YfFYBIgpApvTahEzL-sxchw

24. Measuring changes in the illicit cigarette market using government revenue data: the example of South Africa, Prof Corne van Walbeek, http://tobaccocontrol.bmj.com/content/23/e1/e69.abstract?sid=6606588d-12d4-408e-8392-d99b83a40db3
25. Is the illicit cigarette market really growing? The tobacco industry's misleading math trick, Michal Stoklosa, http://tobaccocontrol.bmj.com/content/early/2015/05/22/tobaccocontrol-2015-052398.extract
26. The Tobacco Atlas, 6th Edition, 2018, *WHO*, http://www.tobaccoatlas.org/topic/illicit-cigarette-trade/
27. Tobacco industry prepared ground for illicit cigarette trade, *ATCA*, http://atca-africa.org/en/south-africa-tobacco-industry-prepared-the-ground-for-illicit-cigarette-trade
28. Illicit cigarette trade, The Tobacco Atlas, ibid
29. Ibid
30. Study finds 'serious flaws' in EU report on illicit tobacco, Bath University, http://www.bath.ac.uk/news/2014/01/22/illicit-tobacco/; Research paper: Towards a greater understanding of the illicit tobacco trade in Europe: a review of the PMI funded 'Project Star' report, Prof Anna Gilmore, http://tobaccocontrol.bmj.com/content/early/2013/12/11/tobaccocontrol-2013-051240.full
31. Euromonitor data on the illicit trade in cigarettes, Evan Blecher, http://tobaccocontrol.bmj.com/content/24/1/100.extract?sid=42f842b4-a588-4f87-9b2c-ee9324197025
32. Smuggled Zimbabwean cigarettes in SA costing jobs, *Bulawayo24*, http://www.bulawayo24.com/index-id-news-sc-africa-byo-13276-article-Smuggled+Zimbabwean+cigarettes+in+SA+costing+jobs.html#sthash.x16uIIbp.dpuf; Contraband cigarettes swarm into South Africa, *CapitalFM*, https://www.capitalfm.co.ke/business/2012/03/contraband-cigarettes-swarm-into-south-africa/
33. Tobacco: the R125bn question, *Fin24*, http://www.fin24.com/Economy/Tobacco-the-R125bn-question-20130901; Who is to blame for the flourishing illegal cigarette trade?, *HealthE*, https://www.health-e.org.za/2013/06/13/who-is-to-blame-for-flourishing-illegal-cigarette-trade/
34. http://www.tobaccosa.co.za/TISA/userfiles/file/AIT_Conference_%202014-Print_and_On-line_Media_Coverage.pdf (accessed February 2019, since deleted)
35. PMB a hub for cigarette smuggling, *News24*, https://www.news24.com/SouthAfrica/News/PMB-a-hub-for-cig-smuggling-20150704
36. UK Parliament, Public Account – Minutes of Evidence, Hearings into tobacco smuggling involving UK companies, http://www.publications.parliament.uk/pa/cm200203/cmselect/cmpubacc/143/2061901.htm
37. Annual report 2018, BAT website, https://www.bat.com/group/sites/UK__9D9KCY.nsf/vwPagesWebLive/DOAWWGJT/$file/Annual_Report_and_Form_20-F_2018.pdf
38. Tobacco overview, *WHO* website, https://www.who.int/tobacco/media/en/TobaccoExplained.pdf
39. Brown and Williamson Smoking and health proposal, Truth Tobacco Industry Documents, https://www.industrydocumentslibrary.ucsf.edu/tobacco/docs/#id=psdw0147
40. Industry Lobbying of the Public Sector and other Tactics, Yusuf Saloojee for *WHO*, https://www.who.int/tobacco/media/en/YUSSUF2000X.pdf
41. Ballot bullies: Big tobacco goes all out to kill proposition 56, *Capital and Main*,

https://capitalandmain.com/ballot-bullies-big-tobacco-goes-all-out-to-kill-proposition-56-1025; Catch Me If You Can: Big Food Using Big Tobacco's Playbook? Applying the Lessons Learned from Big Tobacco to Attack the Obesity Epidemic, Harvard University Library, http://nrs.harvard.edu/urn-3:HUL.InstRepos:8965631; Coal industry feeling cornered peeks at big tobacco playbook, *The New York Times*, https://www.nytimes.com/2016/08/17/science/coal-industry-feeling-cornered-peeks-at-big-tobacco-playbook.html?_r=0
42. Ibid

11. ASTROTURF, GHOST WRITERS AND BOTS
1. Death and taxes: The framing of the causes and policy responses to the illicit tobacco trade in Canadian newspapers, Julia Smith, https://www.cogentoa.com/article/10.1080/23311886.2017.1325054.pdf
2. Activism in the 90s: changing roles for public relations, *Public Relations Quarterly*, 1991, Vol. 36, No.3
3. Philip Morris: Corporate Affairs Approach, https://www.documentcloud.org/documents/3892762-2014-Corporate-Affairs-Approach-and-Issues.html
4. Tobacco industry successfully prevented tobacco control legislation in Argentina, EM Sebrié, https://tobaccocontrol.bmj.com/content/tobaccocontrol/14/5/e2.full.pdf
5. Institute of Economic Affairs, *Tobacco Tactics*, https://www.tobaccotactics.org/index.php/Institute_of_Economic_Affairs
6. IEA funding scandal shows neither Europe nor Britain immune to tobacco industry playbook, *Eurasia Times*, https://www.eurasiatimes.org/en/05/06/2019/iea-funding-scandal-shows-neither-europe-nor-britain-immune-to-tobacco-industry-playbook/
7. How big tobacco has survived death and taxes, *The Guardian*, https://www.theguardian.com/world/2017/jul/11/how-big-tobacco-has-survived-death-and-taxes
8. Smoke and Mirrors: How Cigarette Makers Keep Health Question 'Open' Year After Year, *Wall Street Journal*, February 11, 1993. Bates No. TI10441486-TI10441519
9. Towards a greater understanding of the illicit tobacco trade in Europe: a review of the PMI funded 'Project Star' report, Anna Gilmore, https://www.ncbi.nlm.nih.gov/pubmed/24335339
10. Illicit trade, tobacco industry-funded studies and policy influence in the EU and UK, Gary Jonas Fooks, http://tobaccocontrol.bmj.com/content/23/1/81
11. Big Tobacco lobby group quits smoking industry, *Financial Times*, https://www.ft.com/content/6ca7f490-3c73-11e7-821a-6027b8a20f23
12. The tobacco industry and the illicit trade in tobacco products, *WHO*, http://www.who.int/fctc/publications/The_TI_and_the_Illicit_Trade_in_Tobacco_Products.pdf
13. In some countries this may be referred to as curatorship
14. A green corporate image – more than a logo, Presentation to Green Marketing Conference 1990, A. Little, http://www.tobaccotactics.org/index.php/Third_Party_Techniques
15. Tobacco overview, *WHO* website, https://www.who.int/tobacco/media/en/TobaccoExplained.pdf
16. Tobacco industry interference with tobacco control, *WHO*, http://apps.who.int/iris/bitstream/10665/83128/1/9789241597340_eng.pdf
17. Tobacco Tactics: KPMG, *Tobacco Tactics*, http://www.tobaccotactics.org/index.php?title=KPMG; Illicit trade: Converging criminal networks, *OECD*, http://dx.

doi.org/10.1787/9789264251847-en and http://www.keepeek.com/Digital-Asset-Management/oecd/governance/charting-illicit-trade_9789264251847-en#page153
18. Tobacco Tactics: Ghost writing, *Tobacco Tactics*, http://www.tobaccotactics.org/index.php/Influencing_Science:_Ghost_Writing
19. http://www.who.int/fctc/publications/The_TI_and_the_Illicit_Trade_in_Tobacco_Products.pdf
20. Tobacco Tactics: Third party techniques, *Tobacco Tactics*, http://www.tobaccotactics.org/index.php?title=Third_Party_Techniques; Tobacco Tactics: Front groups, Tobacco Tactics, http://www.tobaccotactics.org/index.php?title=Front_Groups
21. Tobacco Tactics: Astroturfing, *Tobacco Tactics*, http://www.tobaccotactics.org/index.php?title=Astroturfing
22. Tobacco Tactics: Alliance of Australian Retailers, *Tobacco Tactics*, http://www.tobaccotactics.org/index.php/Alliance_of_Australian_Retailers
23. A proposal for the establishment of the consumer tax forum, Truth Tobacco Industry Documents, https://www.industrydocumentslibrary.ucsf.edu/tobacco/docs/#id=ftyx0111
24. takebackthetax.org
25. keepit-100.co.za
26. handsoffmychoices.co.za
27. Professionals coopted to back tobacco giants, *Daily Maverick*, https://www.dailymaverick.co.za/article/2018-08-19-professionals-co-opted-to-back-tobacco-giants/
28. Tackling illicit trade a quick fix for treasury's cash shortfall, *Pretoria News*, https://www.iol.co.za/pretoria-news/opinion/tackling-illicit-trade-a-quick-fix-for-treasurys-cash-shortfall-13661824; Fawu marches to SARS over illegal tobacco trade, *The New Age*, http://www.thenewage.co.za/fawu-marches-to-SARS-over-illegal-tobacco-trade/
29. The contribution of British American Tobacco South Africa to the South African economy, BAT website, http://www.batsa.co.za/group/sites/bat_a2elad.nsf/vwPagesWebLive/DOA2LJ7R/$FILE/medMDAG2LAG.pdf?openelement
30. Codentify brochure, PMI website, http://www.pmi.com/eng/documents/Codentify_E_Brochure_English.pdf (since deleted); The transnational tobacco companies' strategy to promote Codentify, their inadequate tracking and tracing standard, Luk Joossens, http://tobaccocontrol.bmj.com/content/early/2013/03/11/tobaccocontrol-2012-050796; http://www.iticnet.org/file/document/watch/3616 (since deleted); https://en.winikipedia.org/wiki/Codentify
31. Cigarette tracking rules risk being derailed by lobbyists, *EU Observer*, https://euobserver.com/health/138135; DCTA technology ownership transferred to Inexto, an affiliate of Impala Group, press release, http://www.dcta-global.com/docs/DCTA_Press%20Release_1June2016.pdf; Big Tobacco suspected of dodging EU anti-smuggling rules, *EU Observer*, https://euobserver.com/economic/133899; UK House of Commons Hansard transcript, December 2016, Volume 618, https://hansard.parliament.uk/Commons/2016-12-20/debates/FF51202E-34FA-48C7-B002-28DB6AF473AA/ChristmasAdjournment#contribution-2494C922-BC37-458E-A0E8-246FC3551B09; Gravísima denuncia contra Philip Morris por fraude, Periodico Tribuna, http://periodicotribuna.com.ar/18065-gravisima-denuncia-contra-philip-morris-por-fraude-.html; Tobacco Control Movement unanimous

in opposition to Inexto, Patch, https://patch.com/virginia/ashburn/tobacco-control-movement-unanimous-opposition-inexto
32. Tobacco industry's elaborate attempts to control a global track and trace system and fundamentally undermine the Illicit Trade Protocol, Anna Gilmore, https://tobaccocontrol.bmj.com/content/28/2/127; https://www.tax-stamps.org/userfiles/files/ITSA%20Positioning%20Statement%20on%20Codentify.pdf
33. The transnational tobacco companies' strategy to promote Codentify, their inadequate tracking and tracing standard, Luk Joossens, http://tobaccocontrol.bmj.com/content/23/e1/e3.full?sid=aad20569-7f16-4e29-a6f4-5b07ea0e9658; SEC Investigating PMI and Inexto for Corruption in Argentina, Why It Is Bad, https://whyitisbad.wordpress.com; Codentify – Interview with a Tobacco Industry Insider, https://youtu.be/XQ7gZ_D_WMM; Big tobacco, Interpol & Codentify: potential problems with industry product tracking systems, *Tobacco Control Blog*, http://blogs.bmj.com/tc/2015/06/17/big-tobacco-interpol-codentify-potential-problems-with-industry-product-tracking-systems/?q=w_tc_blog_sidetab; Combating tobacco industry tactics: state of play and a way forward, http://www.who.int/fctc/mediacentre/news/2016/remarks-head-fctc-high-level-conference-brussels/en/; Protocol to eliminate the illicit trade in tobacco, *WHO*, http://apps.who.int/iris/bitstream/10665/80873/1/9789241505246_eng.pdf; World Health Organization is the Solution for Codentify, https://whyitisbad.wordpress.com/2016/02/29/world-health-organization-is-the-solution-for-codentify/; Big Tobacco squares up as EU rules aim to track every cigarette, *Reuters*, http://uk.reuters.com/article/us-tobacco-tracking-insight-idUSKBN0ET0I720140618; Major flaws discovered in the Codentify track and trace systems, *TobaccoFact*, http://www.tobaccofact.org/blog/major-flaws-discovered-in-the-codentify-track-and-trace-system; Tobacco Control Movement unanimous in opposition to Inexto, Patch, https://patch.com/virginia/ashburn/tobacco-control-movement-unanimous-opposition-inexto
34. Interview with Michael Eads, October 2019
35. BAT's tactics to influence track and trace tender, *Tobacco Tactics*, https://tobaccotactics.org/index.php?title=Kenya-_BAT's_Tactics_to_Influence_Track_and_Trace_Tender
36. On industry spending see e.g. Ballot bullies: big spenders, *Capital and Main*, https://capitalandmain.com/ballot-bullies-infographic-the-big-spenders-1024
37. Bots are automated programs that run over the Internet. Common examples include web crawlers, chat room bots, and malicious bots that are used to create 'fake news'
38. Research finds bots dominating discussion about ecigarettes on Twitter, *Forbes*, https://www.forbes.com/sites/victoriaforster/2018/08/07/research-finds-bots-dominating-discussion-about-e-cigarettes-on-twitter/#4e763e214e25

12. HASHTAGS, HEADLINES AND IPSOS
1. Illicit tobacco trade: Cheap manufacturer fights back, https://www.moneyweb.co.za/news/industry/illicit-tobacco-trade-cheap-manufacturer-fights-back/
2. TISA take-back-the-tax campaign: Bhekisisa responds, *Bhekisisa*, https://bhekisisa.org/article/2018-09-20-00-TISA-take-back-the-tax-campaign-tobacco-bhekisisa-responds
3. Gold Leaf Tobacco v Yusuf Abramjee, Replying affidavit of EA Adamjee, High Court of South Africa, Gauteng Division, case number 11743/2019
4. Johann van Loggerenberg, *Tobacco Wars*, Tafelberg, 2019
5. South Africa: Tobacco industry prepared the ground for illicit cigarette trade, *ATCA*,

http://atca-africa.org/en/south-africa-tobacco-industry-prepared-the-ground-for-illicit-cigarette-trade;TISA take-back-the-tax campaign: Bhekisisa responds, Bhekisisa, https://bhekisisa.org/article/2018-09-20-00-TISA-take-back-the-tax-campaign-tobacco-bhekisisa-responds
6. R10 illegal cigarette pack becomes SA's top seller, https://www.iol.co.za/news/south-africa/western-cape/r10-illegal-cigarette-pack-becomes-sas-top-seller-18292543
7. Unpublished Nielsen report. Data from tweet by @FITA_sa https://twitter.com/fita_sa/status/1113390987101995010
8. Tobacco giant British American Tobacco caught in intensive smuggling, corporate espionage, FITA website, http://f-ita.co.za/investigation-tobacco-giant-british-american-tobacco-caught-in-intensive-smuggling-corporate-espionage/

13. LIPSTICK ON A PIG

1. TobaccoTactics: CSR Strategy, *Tobacco Tactics* http://www.tobaccotactics.org/index.php?title=CSR_Strategy
2. University accepts tobacco 'blood money', *The Guardian*, https://www.theguardian.com/uk/2000/dec/05/highereducation.education
3. Manipulation 101: Big tobacco exposed, Minnesota Department of Health, https://www.slideshare.net/bethecatalyst/m101-20-presentation
4. http://3pk43x313ggr4cy0lh3tctjh.wpengine.netdna-cdn.com/wp-content/uploads/2015/03/TA5_2015_WEB.pdf
5. http://www.pmdocs.com/PDF/2085292292_2298_0.PDF
6. Tobacco lobby scored again, Manila Standard, http://manilastandard.net/news/-main-stories/top-stories/217390/tobacco-lobby-scored-again.html
7. Social Responsibility in Tobacco Production? Tobacco Companies Use of Green Supply Chains to Obscure the Real Costs of Tobacco Farming, US National Library of Medicine, https://www.ncbi.nlm.nih.gov/pmc/articles/PMC3155738/
8. Tobacco Industry Interference Index 2016, *SEATCA*, https://seatca.org/dmdocuments/TII%20Index%202016.pdf
9. Social Responsibility in Tobacco Production? Tobacco Companies Use of Green Supply Chains to Obscure the Real Costs of Tobacco Farming, US National Library of Medicine, https://www.ncbi.nlm.nih.gov/pmc/articles/PMC3155738/; Eliminating Child Labour in Malawi: A British American Tobacco Corporate Responsibility Project to Sidestep Tobacco Labour Exploitation Tobacco Control. 2006 March:224 – 30
10. Tobacco farmers in Bangladesh: Exploitation at the hand of the tobacco companies; Tobacco and poverty: Observations from India and Bangladesh, PATH Canada; https://www.ncbi.nlm.nih.gov/pmc/articles/PMC4669730/; Social Responsibility in Tobacco Production? Tobacco Companies Use of Green Supply Chains to Obscure the Real Costs of Tobacco Farming, https://www.ncbi.nlm.nih.gov/pmc/articles/PMC3155738/; Environmental harm, Tobacco Atlas, 6th Edition, 2018, *WHO*, http://www.tobaccoatlas.org/topic/environmental-harm/; Tobacco environment: WHO report, *CNN*, https://edition.cnn.com/2017/05/31/health/tobacco-environment-who-report/index.html; 5 ways cigarette litter impacts the environment, *Truth Initiative*, https://truthinitiative.org/news/5-ways-cigarette-litter-impacts-environment
11. Social responsibility in tobacco production?, Marty Otañez, Stanton a Glantz
12. http://archive.tobacco.org/Documents/dd/ddwereallyneed.html; and Public Health

Advocacy and Tobacco Control: Making Smoking History, Simon Chapman, http://www.wiley.com/remtitle.cgi?ISBN=0470691638
13. Big tobacco sought to enhance own image by fighting AIDS, study says, *National Post*, http://nationalpost.com/health/big-tobacco-sought-to-enhance-own-image-by-fighting-aids-study-says
14. 'Public enemy no. 1': Tobacco industry funding for the AIDS response, *Taylor and Francis Online*, https://www.tandfonline.com/doi/full/10.1080/17290376.2016.1164617; Julia Smith, https://www.ncbi.nlm.nih.gov/pmc/articles/PMC5068916/
15. Global: Big Tobacco sought to enhance own image by fighting AIDS, study says, *SEATCA*, https://seatca.org/?p=7711
16. Global Tobacco Interference Index 2019, http://exposetobacco.org/wp-content/uploads/2019/10/GlobalTIIIndex_Report_2019.pdf
17. Research into the impact of tobacco advertising, Stanford University, http://tobacco.stanford.edu/tobacco_main/images.php?token2=fm_st067.php&token1=fm_img1551.php&theme_file=fm_mt004.php&theme_name=Scientific%20Authority&subtheme_name=Pseudoscience

14. CAPTURED

1. PMI Internal industry corporate affairs presentation
2. Governance of regulators, *OECD*, http://www.oecd.org/gov/regulatory-policy/Flyer-Governance-of-regulators.pdf
3. Several of the data elements required for track and trace can only be supplied by the industry at the actual time of manufacture. This additional data has limited use in terms of investigating illicit trade, and yet it is required by law
4. Inside PMI's campaign to subvert the global anti-smoking treaty, Aditya Kalra, https://www.reuters.com/investigates/special-report/pmi-who-fctc/
5. Tracking and tracing the tobacco industry: potential tobacco industry influence over the EU's system for tobacco traceability and security features, *Tobacco Control Journal*, https://tobaccocontrol.bmj.com/content/early/2019/08/30/tobaccocontrol-2019-055094
6. The contribution of British American Tobacco South Africa to the South African economy, BAT website, http://www.batsa.co.za/group/sites/bat_a2elad.nsf/vwPagesWebLive/DOA2LJ7R/$FILE/medMDAG2LAG.pdf?openelement
7. BAT Bates number http://bat.library.ucsf.edu/data/h/f/k/hfk11a99/hfk11a99.pdf
8. Tobacco industry seeking to control anti-smuggling measures, say critics, *The Guardian* https://www.theguardian.com/society/2018/jun/14/tobacco-industry-seeking-to-control-anti-smuggling-measures-say-critics
9. How corruption became 'state capture' in South Africa, *Financial Times*, https://www.ft.com/content/36895cd6-a907-11e7-93c5-648314d2c72c
10. Return on Investment: The Hidden Story of Soft Money, Corporate Welfare and the 1997 Budget & Tax Deal, Bates No. TI36241005-TI36241007
11. https://www.ncbi.nlm.nih.gov/pubmed/17297056
12. Transnational Tobacco Company Influence on Tax Policy, Anna Gilmore, https://www.ncbi.nlm.nih.gov/pmc/articles/PMC2040352/?fbclid=IwAR1RLYRF1Ybio3jpT_m8tZGHQBeVol803qyLxbMkiWerivlDXk_dT9OcmJc
13. Tobacco giant gets free police protection, *City Press*, https://city-press.news24.com/News/Tobacco-giant-gets-free-police-protection-20150719
14. Document from source

15. Italy's tainted tobacco industry, Luca Muzi, https://www.theguardian.com/global-development/2019/may/31/i-had-pain-all-over-my-body-italys-tainted-tobacco-industry
16. How to spot a fake, Shellee Geduld, https://www.iol.co.za/news/south-africa/western-cape/how-to-spot-a-fake-1004629
17. Threats, bullying, lawsuits: tobacco industry's dirty war for the African market, *The Guardian*, https://amp-theguardian-com.cdn.ampproject.org/c/s/amp.theguardian.com/world/2017/jul/12/big-tobacco-dirty-war-africa-market
18. Since when do we believe the tobacco industry?, *Daily Maverick*, http://www.dailymaverick.co.za/opinionista/2014-11-25-since-when-do-we-believe-the-tobacco-industry/#.VYdoK4e5Lds

15. POLITICAL PATRONAGE

1. Industry Lobbying of the Public Sector and other Tactics, Yusuf Saloojee for *WHO*, https://www.who.int/tobacco/media/en/YUSSUF2000X.pdf
2. Philip Morris: Corporate Affairs Approach, https://www.documentcloud.org/documents/3892762-2014-Corporate-Affairs-Approach-and-Issues.html
3. Tweet by @JoossensLuk 29 March 2019
4. IEA funding scandal shows neither Europe nor Britain immune to tobacco industry playbook, *Eurasia Times*, https://www.eurasiatimes.org/en/05/06/2019/iea-funding-scandal-shows-neither-europe-nor-britain-immune-to-tobacco-industry-playbook/
5. Tobacco's Special Friend, *NPR*, https://www.npr.org/2019/06/17/730496066/tobaccos-special-friend-what-internal-documents-say-about-mitch-mcconnell
6. https://www.documentcloud.org/documents/5991154-1996-03-28-Philip-Morris-Memo-Re-Political.html#document/p2/a499615
7. Big soda and the ballot: Soda industry takes cues from tobacco to combat taxes, *NPR*, https://www.npr.org/sections/thesalt/2018/11/05/664435761/big-soda-and-the-ballot-soda-industry-takes-cues-from-tobacco-to-combat-taxes
8. Global Tobacco Interference Index 2019, http://exposetobacco.org/wp-content/uploads/2019/10/GlobalTIIndex_Report_2019.pdf
9. How big tobacco has survived death and taxes, https://www.theguardian.com/world/2017/jul/11/how-big-tobacco-has-survived-death-and-taxes; Tobacco: Philip Morris delays EU legislation, *The Guardian*, https://www.theguardian.com/business/2013/sep/07/tobacco-philip-morris-millions-delay-eu-legislation
10. Big tobacco leads the way, *John Uustal*, https://www.johnuustal.com/docs/big-tobacco-leads-the-way-by-John-Uustal.pdf
11. Behind the smokescreen BAT's tax woes mount, *Times Live*, http://www.timeslive.co.za/businesstimes/2015/04/26/behind-smokescreen-bat-s-tax-woes-mount
12. Tobacco's Other Secret, *CBS 60 Minutes*, https://www.cbsnews.com/news/tobaccos-other-secret/; Tobacco industry tactics for resisting public policy on health, Yusuf Saloojee, https://www.who.int/bulletin/archives/78%287%29902.pdf
13. Industry Lobbying of the Public Sector and other Tactics, Yusuf Saloojee for *WHO*, https://www.who.int/tobacco/media/en/YUSSUF2000X.pdf
14. Tobacco industry interference with tobacco control, *WHO*, http://apps.who.int/iris/bitstream/10665/83128/1/9789241597340_eng.pdf; PMI Worldwide regulatory affairs: issues review, prospects and plans, Truth Tobacco Industry Documents, http://legacy.library.ucsf.edu/tid/jww95a00

15. Industry Lobbying of the Public Sector and other Tactics, Yusuf Saloojee for *WHO*, https://www.who.int/tobacco/media/en/YUSSUF2000X.pdf
16. Ibid; Implementation of *WHO* Framework Convention on Tobacco Control Article 6 in ASEAN Countries, SEATCA, https://seatca.org/dmdocuments/SEATCA%20TOBACCO%20TAX(17SEPT15)WEB.pdf
17. Industry Lobbying of the Public Sector and other Tactics, Yusuf Saloojee for *WHO*, https://www.who.int/tobacco/media/en/YUSSUF2000X.pdf
18. Tobacco industry: Trump administration ties, *The Guardian*, https://www.theguardian.com/world/2017/jul/13/tobacco-industry-trump-administration-ties
19. Threats, bullying, lawsuits: tobacco industry's dirty war for the African market, *The Guardian*, https://amp-theguardian-com.cdn.ampproject.org/c/s/amp.theguardian.com/world/2017/jul/12/big-tobacco-dirty-war-africa-market
20. The law was actually drafted by us but the Government is to be congratulated on its wise actions: British American Tobacco and public policy in Kenya, Preeti Patel, https://www.ncbi.nlm.nih.gov/pmc/articles/PMC2598451/
21. Global Tobacco Interference Index 2019, http://exposetobacco.org/wp-content/uploads/2019/10/GlobalTIIIndex_Report_2019.pdf
22. British diplomat lobbied on behalf of big tobacco, *The Guardian*, https://amp.theguardian.com/uk-news/2017/sep/09/british-diplomat-lobbied-big-tobacco-bat-bangladesh-unpaid-vat
23. Ibid
24. Tobacco Industry Interference Index 2016, SEATCA, https://seatca.org/dmdocuments/TII%20Index%202016.pdf
25. Ibid
26. Pauw, *The President's Keepers* and The smuggler, the spook and the grabber, Amabhungane, https://amabhungane.org/stories/the-smuggler-the-spook-and-the-grabber/.
27. The illicit tobacco trade in Zimbabwe and South Africa, *Atlantic Council*, https://www.atlanticcouncil.org/images/publications/The_Illicit_Tobacco_Trade_in_Zimbabwe_and_South_Africa.pdf
28. See also The illicit tobacco trade in Zimbabwe and South Africa, *Atlantic Council*, https://www.atlanticcouncil.org/images/publications/The_Illicit_Tobacco_Trade_in_Zimbabwe_and_South_Africa.pdf
29. The tobacco tycoon's birthday bash and his policemen guests at table 9, https://select.timeslive.co.za/news/2018-02-13-the-tobacco-tycoons-birthday-bash-and-his-policemen-guests-at-table-9/
30. The illicit tobacco trade in Zimbabwe and South Africa, *Atlantic Council*, https://www.atlanticcouncil.org/wp-content/uploads/2019/09/The_Illicit_Tobacco_Trade_in_Zimbabwe_and_South_Africa.pdf
31. Sikhakhane Report, SARS website, https://www.SARS.gov.za/AllDocs/Documents/Adhoc/Sikhakhane%20Report.pdf
32. The illicit tobacco trade in Zimbabwe and South Africa, *Atlantic Council*, https://www.atlanticcouncil.org/images/publications/The_Illicit_Tobacco_Trade_in_Zimbabwe_and_South_Africa.pdf

16. VICTIMS AND SAVIOURS
1. Big tobacco sought to enhance own image by fighting AIDS, study says, *National Post*, http://nationalpost.com/health/big-tobacco-sought-to-enhance-own-image-by-fighting-aids-study-says
2. The tobacco industry and the illicit trade in tobacco products, *WHO*, http://www.

who.int/fctc/publications/The_TI_and_the_Illicit_Trade_in_Tobacco_Products.pdf
3. Government tricked into promoting tobacco, *FITA*, http://f-ita.co.za/govt-tricked-into-promoting-tobacco/
4. Big tobacco, Interpol & Codentify: potential problems with industry product tracking systems, *Tobacco Control Blog*, http://blogs.bmj.com/tc/2015/06/17/big-tobacco-interpol-codentify-potential-problems-with-industry-product-tracking-systems/?q=w_tc_blog_sidetab; The transnational tobacco companies' strategy to promote Codentify, their inadequate tracking and tracing standard, Luk Joossens, http://tobaccocontrol.bmj.com/content/23/e1/e3.full?sid=aad20569-7f16-4e29-a6f4-5b07ea0e9658; Cigarette tracking rules risk being derailed by lobbyists, *EU Observer*, https://euobserver.com/health/138135; https://en.wikipedia.org/wiki/Codentify
5. Document provided by source
6. Document provided by source
7. From @espionageafrica e.g. https://drive.google.com/file/d/0B6h7NrhWigQ7TmJxY0JrclpzUU0/view
8. The Tobacco Atlas, 6th Edition, 2018, *WHO*, https://tobaccoatlas.org/topic/illicit-trade/

17. SEX, LIES AND VIDEOTAPE

1. The Secret Bribes of Big Tobacco, *BBC*, https://www.youtube.com/watch?v=wETSRZyUTeE; 'The secret bribes of big tobacco paper trail,' *BBC*, https://www.bbc.co.uk/news/business-34944702
2. Ibid
3. BAT's takeover of Twisp wins approval, *Reuters*, https://af.reuters.com/article/investingNews/idAFKCN1V31CK-OZABS
4. The illicit tobacco trade in Zimbabwe and South Africa, *Atlantic Council*, https://www.atlanticcouncil.org/images/publications/The_Illicit_Tobacco_Trade_in_Zimbabwe_and_South_Africa.pdf
5. EspionageSA whistleblower uncovered, *News24*, https://www.news24.com/SouthAfrica/News/espionagesa-whistleblower-uncovered-20160923; SARS Wars: Fresh controversy hits Moyane's new investigative unit, *Daily Maverick*, https://www.dailymaverick.co.za/article/2016-11-22-SARS-wars-fresh-controversy-hits-moyanes-new-investigative-unit/
6. From @espionageafrica, https://drive.google.com/file/d/0B6h7NrhWigQ7VjRaeWZ1bmJ1UkE/view; see also https://drive.google.com/file/d/0B6h7NrhWigQ7emFYWDBOdkZ2anc/view and https://drive.google.com/file/d/0B6h7NrhWigQ7WmQxemdLVk8wd2M/view and https://drive.google.com/file/d/0B6h7NrhWigQ7aUNxS1BEX1ZGQ2c/view and https://drive.google.com/file/d/0B6h7NrhWigQ7aUNxS1BEX1ZGQ2c/view
7. From @espionageafrica, https://drive.google.com/file/d/0B0gfZnd_OvzdWTZ4Z-0FuZ25Md0E/view
8. Interview with source
9. https://drive.google.com/file/d/0B6h7NrhWigQ7TmJxY0JrclpzUU0/view
10. https://drive.google.com/file/d/0B6h7NrhWigQ7TmJxY0JrclpzUU0/view
11. BAT used state agency to spy on competitors, *ATCA*, https://atca-africa.org/en/south-africa-exclusive-british-american-tobacco-used-state-agency-to-spy-on-competitors
12. https://drive.google.com/file/d/0B6h7NrhWigQ7TmJxY0JrclpzUU0/view

13. Several documents provided by source
14. Troubles with big tobacco, https://www.reportingproject.net/troubleswithbigtobacco/documents/OCCRP_tobacco_6.pdf
15. Document provided by source
16. https://drive.google.com/file/d/0B0gfZnd_OvzdWTZ4Z0FuZ25Md0E/view
17. Document provided by source
18. https://drive.google.com/file/d/0B0gfZnd_OvzdWTZ4Z0FuZ25Md0E/view
19. Documents provided by source
20. Documents provided by source; https://drive.google.com/file/d/0B6h7NrhWigQ7TmJxY0JrclpzUU0/view
21. Document provided by source
22. Document provided by source
23. Van Loggerenberg, *Tobacco Wars*
24. Pauw, *The President's Keepers*
25. BAT accused of corporate espionage in South Africa, *The Independent*, https://www.independent.co.uk/news/world/africa/british-american-tobacco-accused-of-corporate-espionage-in-south-africa-a6900731.html
26. BATSA severs ties with forensic firm FSS, *Eyewitness News*, https://ewn.co.za/2016/09/07/BATSA-severes-ties-with-forensic-firm-FSS
27. Several documents provided by source
28. https://drive.google.com/file/d/0B6h7NrhWigQ7TmJxY0JrclpzUU0/view
29. https://drive.google.com/file/d/0B6h7NrhWigQ7TmJxY0JrclpzUU0/view
30. Supplementary section 204 statement, Daniel Francois van der Westhuizen, dated 21 December 2016. See also Affidavit dated 2 February 2016, https://drive.google.com/file/d/0B6h7NrhWigQ7VjRaeWZ1bmJ1UkE/view; see also https://drive.google.com/file/d/0B6h7NrhWigQ7emFYWDBOdkZ2anc/view and https://drive.google.com/file/d/0B6h7NrhWigQ7WmQxemdLVk8wd2M/view and https://drive.google.com/file/d/0B6h7NrhWigQ7aUNxS1BEX1ZGQ2c/view
31. Document provided by source
32. Document provided by source
33. Document provided by source
34. https://drive.google.com/file/d/0B6h7NrhWigQ7TmJxY0JrclpzUU0/view
35. Document provided by source
36. Document provided by source
37. https://drive.google.com/file/d/0B0gfZnd_OvzdWTZ4Z0FuZ25Md0E/view
38. https://drive.google.com/file/d/0B0gfZnd_OvzdWTZ4Z0FuZ25Md0E/view
39. Document provided by source
40. Affidavits by Daniel Francois van der Westhuizen, dated 2 February 2016, https://drive.google.com/file/d/0B6h7NrhWigQ7VjRaeWZ1bmJ1UkE/view; see also https://drive.google.com/file/d/0B6h7NrhWigQ7emFYWDBOdkZ2anc/view and https://drive.google.com/file/d/0B6h7NrhWigQ7WmQxemdLVk8wd2M/view and https://drive.google.com/file/d/0B6h7NrhWigQ7aUNxS1BEX1ZGQ2c/view
41. Document provided by source
42. Document provided by source
43. https://drive.google.com/file/d/0B6h7NrhWigQ7TmJxY0JrclpzUU0/view
44. https://drive.google.com/file/d/0B0gfZnd_OvzdWTZ4Z0FuZ25Md0E/view
45. https://drive.google.com/file/d/0B0gfZnd_OvzdWTZ4Z0FuZ25Md0E/view
46. I have only seen a draft of this affidavit, and do not know if it was ever signed

47. Various documents provided by source
48. https://drive.google.com/file/d/0B6h7NrhWigQ7TmJxY0JrclpzUU0/view
49. Judgement, Carnilinx v TISA and others, Western Cape High Court case number 4928/2015, http://saflii.org/za/cases/ZAWCHC/2016/101.html
50. As is evident when all of the documents posted by @espionageafrica are read together in context
51. Confirmed by sources at OLAF, and see also Britain probes British American Tobacco for corruption in Africa, https://ewn.co.za/2017/08/01/britain-probes-british-american-tobacco-for-corruption-in-africa
52. BAT asked to come clean on spying allegations, *Moneyweb*, https://www.moneyweb.co.za/news/companies-and-deals/british-american-tobacco-asked-to-come-clean-on-spying-allegations/
53. Ibid
54. Van Loggerenberg, *Tobacco Wars*
55. BAT Zim spying on competitors, The Independent, https://www.theindependent.co.zw/2012/11/16/bat-zim-spying-on-competitors/

18. FROM TAXMAN TO HITMAN
1. https://drive.google.com/file/d/0B0gfZnd_OvzdWTZ4Z0FuZ25Md0E/view
2. Porritt, Bennett backtrack on Tigon trial, *Moneyweb*, https://www.moneyweb.co.za/news/south-africa/porritt-bennett-backtrack-on-tigon-trial-boycott/
3. Judgement: SARS v Apollo, SARS website, http://www.SARS.gov.za/AllDocs/LegalDoclib/Judgments/LAPD-DRJ-HC-2009-18%20-%20Apollo%20Tobacco%20CC%2028%20December%202009.pdf
4. Van Loggerenberg, *Tobacco Wars*
5. See e.g. BAT-sucked in alleged industrial espionage, *The Herald*, https://www.herald.co.zw/bat-sucked-in-alleged-industrial-espionage/
6. Judgement: SARS v Apollo, ibid
7. Van Loggerenberg, *Tobacco Wars*
8. As is evident when all of the documents posted by @espionageafrica is read together in context
9. See e.g. the commentary at http://atca-africa.org/en/south-africa-tobacco-industry-prepared-the-ground-for-illicit-cigarette-trade
10. Project Honey Badger letter sent to FITA and TISA, November 2013, addendum 1

19. UNHOLY ALLIANCES AND FRIENDS IN EVEN HIGHER PLACES
1. https://drive.google.com/file/d/0B0gfZnd_OvzdWTZ4Z0FuZ25Md0E/view
2. Interview with source; Van Loggerenberg, *Tobacco Wars*
3. State capture: All roads lead to tobacco, some to Marius Fransman, *Daily Maverick*, https://www.dailymaverick.co.za/article/2017-01-23-state-capture-all-roads-lead-to-tobacco-some-to-marius-fransman/; *Daily Maverick*'s 28 questions for the Hawks, *Daily Maverick*, https://www.dailymaverick.co.za/article/2016-08-24-daily-mavericks-28-questions-for-the-hawks/; The real rogues, Rob Rose, https://www.pressreader.com/south-africa/financial-mail/20160901/281865822900693
4. https://drive.google.com/file/d/0B6h7NrhWigQ7TmJxY0JrclpzUU0/view
5. Document, unsigned, dated April 2015, compiled by Walter herself
6. https://drive.google.com/file/d/0B6h7NrhWigQ7TmJxY0JrclpzUU0/view

7. Interview with source
8. Interview with source; https://drive.google.com/file/d/0B6h7NrhWigQ7TmJxY0JrclpzUU0/view
9. https://drive.google.com/file/d/0B6h7NrhWigQ7TmJxY0JrclpzUU0/view
10. Big tobacco in bed with SA law enforcement agencies, *The Mail and Guardian*, https://mg.co.za/article/2014-03-20-big-tobacco-in-bed-with-sa-law-enforcement-agencies
11. Sikhakhane Report, SARS website, https://www.SARS.gov.za/AllDocs/Documents/Adhoc/Sikhakhane%20Report.pdf

20. BAT'S CHRISTMAS PRESENT TO THE UNDERWORLD?

1. Interview with Johann van Loggerenberg, December 2019
2. Copy in author's possession, redacted here for the sake of brevity, and also referenced in media articles e.g. Spies v SARS, The Citizen, https://www.pressreader.com/south-africa/the-citizen-gauteng/20190520/281479277874706
3. https://www.iol.co.za/news/flashback-now-hawks-take-aim-at-gerrie-nel-1993942; https://www.pressreader.com/south-africa/business-day/20180410/281483571957100; https://ewn.co.za/2015/05/17/Another-twist-in-the-Sars-rogue-unit-scandal
4. Spies v SARS, *The Citizen*, https://www.pressreader.com/south-africa/the-citizen-gauteng/20190520/281479277874706
5. Tobacco excise revenue plunge shows SARS collection up in smoke, *Business Day Live*, https://www.businesslive.co.za/bd/national/2018-05-29-tobacco-excise-revenue-plunge-shows-SARS-collection-up-in-smoke/
6. The illicit tobacco trade in Zimbabwe and South Africa, *Atlantic Council*, https://www.atlanticcouncil.org/images/publications/The_Illicit_Tobacco_Trade_in_Zimbabwe_and_South_Africa.pdf
7. In South Africa, illicit cigarettes are a smoking gun on corruption, *Atlantic Council*, https://www.atlanticcouncil.org/blogs/new-atlanticist/in-south-africa-illicit-cigarettes-are-a-smoking-gun-on-corruption#.XNmMLqiuokI.twitter
8. Research into the impact of tobacco advertising, Stanford University, http://tobacco.stanford.edu/tobacco_main/images.php?token2=fm_st090.php&token1=fm_img2312.php&theme_file=fm_mt017.php&theme_name=Movie%20Stars&subtheme_name=Movie%20Stars%20-%20Men

21. AVOIDANCE, EVASION AND GLASS HOUSES

1. Ashes to ashes: How BAT avoids taxes in low and middle income countries, *Tax Justice Network*, https://www.taxjustice.net/wp-content/uploads/2019/04/Ashes-to-ashes_How-British-American-Tobacco-Avoids-Tax-in-Low-and-Middle-Income-Countries_Tax-Justice-Network_2019.pdf
2. https://www.nrc.nl/nieuws/2019/09/19/fiscus-eist-miljard-van-tabaksgigant-bat-a3973963
3. Ibid
4. Annual Report 2018, JTI website, https://www.jti.com/sites/default/files/global-files/documents/jti-annual-reports/jt-annual-report-2018.pdf
5. Annual Report 2018, PMI website, http://www.annualreports.com/HostedData/AnnualReports/PDF/NYSE_PM_2018.pdf
6. Annual Report 2018, Imperial, https://www.imperialbrandsplc.com/content/dam/imperial-brands/corporate/investors/annual-report-and-accounts/2018/pdfs/

annual-report-2018.pdf
7. Taxing questions at British American Tobacco AGM, *Share Action*, https://shareaction.org/shareaction-british-american-tobacco-agm/
8. These are the 25 biggest companies in South Africa, *BusinessTech*, https://businesstech.co.za/news/business/233451/these-are-the-25-biggest-companies-in-south-africa/
9. Major tobacco companies pay almost no corporation tax despite massive profits, Bath University, https://www.bath.ac.uk/announcements/major-tobacco-companies-pay-almost-no-corporation-tax-despite-massive-profits/
10. Tobacco firm BAT costs developing countries 700m in tax, *The Guardian*, https://www.theguardian.com/business/2019/apr/30/tobacco-firm-bat-costs-developing-countries-700m-in-tax; Ashes to ashes: How BAT avoids taxes in low and middle income countries, ibid
11. Ashes to ashes: How BAT avoids taxes in low and middle income countries, ibid
12. https://www.uneca.org/publications/base-erosion-and-profit-shifting-africa-reforms-facilitate-improved-taxation
13. Interview with source
14. The blazing success of Swiss cigarettes in Africa, *PublicEye*, 2019, quoting KPMG report from 2017, http://stories.publiceye.ch/tobacco/
15. Colombian Governors Lawsuit vs. Philip Morris et al., 37(v)
16. https://www.trademap.org
17. https://tradelogistics.co.za/wp-content/uploads/2016/09/Import-Duty-Look-Up.pdf
18. Interview with source
19. Allowances applied in certain member states for losses due to the nature of excise goods during movements under duty suspension, *European Commission*, https://ec.europa.eu/taxation_customs/sites/taxation/files/docs/body/ced710_rev6_en.pdf
20. Interview with source
21. BAT's smoke and mirrors war on rivals, *Sunday Times*, https://www.pressreader.com/south-africa/sunday-times/20140330/282299613130796/TextView

22. BLOWING SMOKE
1. Annual Report 2018, PMI website, http://www.annualreports.com/HostedData/AnnualReports/PDF/NYSE_PM_2018.pdf
2. Tobacco explained, *WHO* website, https://www.who.int/tobacco/media/en/TobaccoExplained.pdf
3. Philip Morris announcement to spend nearly $1 billion to end smoking sounds like fake news, *The Truth Initiative*, https://truthinitiative.org/news/philip-morris-announcement-spend-nearly-1-billion-end-smoking-sounds-fake-news
4. Failed promises of the cigarette industry and its effect on consumer misperceptions about the health risks of smoking, KM Cummings, https://tobaccocontrol.bmj.com/content/11/suppl_1/i110
5. Golden Holocaust: Origins of the Cigarette Catastrophe, Robert N Proctor
6. Harm reduction, BAT website, http://www.bat.com/harmreduction; Harm reduction, BAT Hong Kong website, http://www.bathongkong.com; Harm reduction, BAT website, http://www.batme.com
7. Philip Morris Wrongful Death Case Denied Review By Supreme Court, Thomas Coon Newton and Frost, https://www.tcnf.legal/schwarz-v-philip-morris/; The

intractable cigarette 'filter problem', *Research Gate*, https://www.researchgate.net/publication/51062563_The_intractable_cigarette_'filter_problem' and https://www.ncbi.nlm.nih.gov/pmc/articles/PMC3088411/
8. The role of litigation in tobacco control, https://www.scielosp.org/article/spm/2006.v48suppl1/s121-s136/; Tobacco timeline, Dayton University, http://academic.udayton.edu/health/syllabi/tobacco/history2.htm
9. Ibid
10. Ibid
11. https://www.smokefreeworld.org
12. The Philip Morris-funded Foundation for a Smoke-Free World: tax return sheds light on funding activities, *The Lancet*, https://www.thelancet.com/journals/lancet/article/PIIS0140-6736(19)31347-9/fulltext
13. A billion dollar lie: We must not take our eyes off big tobacco, Vital Strategies, https://medium.com/vital-strategies/a-billion-dollar-lie-we-must-not-take-our-eyes-off-big-tobacco-beaebb76f759
14. Foundation for a Smoke Free World, *Tobacco Tactics*, http://www.tobaccotactics.org/index.php?title=Foundation_for_a_Smoke-Free_World
15. Ibid
16. Tobacco industry interference with tobacco control, *WHO*, http://apps.who.int/iris/bitstream/10665/83128/1/9789241597340_eng.pdf
17. Research into the impact of tobacco advertising, Stanford University, http://tobacco.stanford.edu/tobacco_main/images.php?token2=fm_st090.php&token1=fm_img2312.php&theme_file=fm_mt017.php&theme_name=Movie%20Stars&subtheme_name=Movie%20Stars%20-%20Menhttp://tobacco.stanford.edu/tobacco_main/images.php?token2=fm_st412.php&token1=fm_img12465.php&theme_file=fm_mt006.php&theme_name=Filter%20Safety%20Myths&subtheme_name=Kent%20Classic

23. INCONVENIENT TRUTHS
1. South Africa, Tobacco Atlas 6th Edition 2018, *WHO*, https://tobaccoatlas.org/country/south-africa/
2. Only around 11% of that is from corporate income tax, the rest is actually paid by consumers; The contribution of British American Tobacco South Africa to the South African economy, BAT website, http://www.batsa.co.za/group/sites/bat_a2elad.nsf/vwPagesWebLive/DOA2LJ7R/$FILE/medMDAG2LAG.pdf?openelementt
3. Global cost of smoking, Tobacco Atlas 6th Edition 2018, *WHO* http://www.tobaccoatlas.org/news/wntd-2017-global-costs-of-smoking/; Global economic cost of smoking-attributable diseases, Mark Goodchild, http://tobaccocontrol.bmj.com/content/early/2017/05/02/tobaccocontrol-2016-053305; From illegal markets to legitimate businesses: the portfolio of organised crime in Europe, *Transcrime*, https://www.int-comp.org/media/1997/ocp-full-report.pdf
4. Ashes to ashes: How BAT avoids taxes in low and middle income countries, *Tax Justice Network*, https://www.taxjustice.net/wp-content/uploads/2019/04/Ashes-to-ashes_How-British-American-Tobacco-Avoids-Tax-in-Low-and-Middle-Income-Countries_Tax-Justice-Network_2019.pdf
5. Importance of tobacco to a country's economy, Kenneth E Warner, https://www.ncbi.nlm.nih.gov/pmc/articles/PMC1759416/pdf/v004p00180.pdf
6. The contribution of British American Tobacco South Africa to the South African

economy, BAT website, http://www.batsa.co.za/group/sites/bat_a2elad.nsf/vwPagesWebLive/DOA2LJ7R/$FILE/medMDAG2LAG.pdf?openelement
7. The company went bust after the story broke that they had invented and planted the whole 'white monopoly capital' narrative to seed discontent and contribute to the de-stabilisation of South Africa
8. Research into the impact of tobacco advertising, Stanford University, http://tobacco.stanford.edu/tobacco_main/images_body.php?token1=fm_img0526.php

24. PEBBLES FOR GOVERNMENT'S DAVID
1. www.tobaccofreeportfolios.org
2. Thirteenth Child, Patricia Wrede, https://www.amazon.com/Thirteenth-Child-Frontier-Magic-Patricia/dp/0545033454
3. Research into the impact of tobacco advertising, Stanford University, http://tobacco.stanford.edu/tobacco_main/images.php?token2=fm_st002.php&token1=fm_img0102.php&theme_file=fm_mt001.php&theme_name=Doctors%20Smoking&subtheme_name=20,679%20Physicians

25. TOO BIG TO FAIL?
1. Reinet's tobacco holding falls below 50%, Marc Hasenfuss, https://www.businesslive.co.za/bd/companies/industrials/2019-01-23-reinets-tobacco-holding-falls-below-50/
2. Interview with source, Pretoria, August 2019
3. Tobacco wars turn deadly, *Moneyweb*, https://www.moneyweb.co.za/news/south-africa/tobacco-wars-turn-deadly/
4. Governments made more money from smoking than the companies they're suing for damages, *Financial Post*, https://business.financialpost.com/opinion/terence-corcoran-governments-made-more-money-from-smoking-than-the-companies-theyre-suing-for-damages https://tobaccotrial.blogspot.com/2019/06/tobacco-companies-ask-for-further-6.html.

CONCLUSION
1. Van Loggerenberg, *Tobacco Wars*

ADDENDUMS
1. WHAT PROJECT HONEY BADGER WAS INVESTIGATING
1. Project Honey Badger letters sent to FITA and TISA, November 2013 and 29 April 2014

2. WHERE THE QUOTED INTERNAL INDUSTRY DOCUMENTS COME FROM
1. www.tobaccotactics.org; https://bat.library.ucsf.edu; www.documentcloud.org; https://www.library.ucsf.edu/archives/tobacco/; https://www.industrydocumentslibrary.ucsf.edu/tobacco; Philip Morris: Corporate Affairs Approach, https://www.documentcloud.org/documents/3892762-2014-Corporate-Affairs-Approach-and-Issues.html; www.tobaccoarchives.com/docbasic.html; www.cdc.gov/tobacco/industrydocs/ docsites.htm; www.tobaccodocuments.org; www.tobaccodetectives.com; www.ctr-usa.org/ctr; www.rjrtdocs.com; www.bw.aalatg.com; www.lorillard-

docs.com; www.hlth.gov.bc.ca/guildford and http://galen.library.ucsf.edu/tobacco; https://www.tobaccocontrollaws.org/files/live/litigation/596/US_United%20States%20v.%20Philip%20Morris_1.pdf
2. Colombian Governors v. Philip Morris Companies, Inc. et al., U.S. District Court, Eastern Distr. Of New York, Docket No. 00 Civ. 2881 (NGG), filed 08 November 2000
3. BAT memo 'Visit Notes, Colombia Meeting', BAT Bates No. 503891629
4. https://twitter.com/espionageafrica
5. www.icij.org
6. https://www.icij.org/investigations/big-tobacco-smuggling/tobacco-companies-linked-criminal-organizations-lucrativ
7. Philip Morris accused of smuggling, money-laundering conspiracy in racketeering lawsuit, *International Consortium of Investigative Journalists*, https://www.icij.org/investigations/big-tobacco-smuggling/philip-morris-accused-smuggling-money-laundering-conspiracy-racketeering-lawsuit/
8. https://www.icij.org/investigations/big-tobacco-smuggling/cyprus-big-tobaccos-favorite-smuggling-hub-uk/
9. Africa: Disguising BAT's involvement in cigarette smuggling, *International Consortium of Investigative Journalists*, https://www.icij.org/investigations/big-tobacco-smuggling/africa-disguising-bats-involvement-cigarette-smuggling/
10. https://www.icij.org/investigations/big-tobacco-smuggling/latin-america-big-tobacco-partners-money-launderers-smugglers/
11. https://www.icij.org/investigations/big-tobacco-smuggling/philip-morris-mafia-connections/
12. https://www.icij.org/investigations/big-tobacco-smuggling/bat-finds-partner-asias-most-notorious-criminal-organization/
13. https://www.icij.org/investigations/big-tobacco-smuggling/global-reach-tobacco-companys-involvement-cigarette-smuggling-exposed-company-papers/
14. http://www.publicintegrity.org/investigations/tobacco
15. https://www.reportingproject.net/underground/index.php?option=com_content&view=frontpage&Itemid=9

3. COUNTERFEITS
1. Although PMI itself has suggested this may be as low as 2%, see e.g. http://www.tobaccoatlas.org/topic/illicit-cigarette-trade/
2. Illicit trade: Converging criminal networks, *OECD*, http://dx.doi.org/10.1787/9789264251847-en http://www.keepeek.com/Digital-Asset-Management/oecd/governance/charting-illicit-trade_9789264251847-en#page153 OECD Task Force on Countering Illicit Trade (TF-CIT), *OECD*, http://www.oecd.org/gov/risk/oecdtaskforceoncounteringillicittrade.htm
3. The determination of whether a pack is counterfeit or not is done by the manufacturer. They have a tendency to overstate the prevalence of counterfeits, because they do not have to make seizure payments on counterfeits. https://www.securingindustry.com/pharmaceuticals/cigarettes-and-toys-top-eu-customs-seizures-in-2016/s40/a5124/#.WdTAFUyQ1E4; https://assets.kpmg.com/content/dam/kpmg/pdf/2016/06/project-sun-report.pdf
4. China's Marlboro country, Organised Crime and Corruption Reporting Project,

https://www.reportingproject.net/underground/index.php%3Foption%3Dcom_content%26view%3Darticle%26id%3D9%26Itemid%3D22
5. The world's most widely smuggled legal substance, *International Consortium of Investigative Journalists*, https://www.icij.org/project/tobacco-underground/worlds-most-widely-smuggled-legal-substance
6. https://www.reportingproject.net/underground/index.php?id=9&option=com_content&view=article
7. https://bzdww.com/article/5671/; 'China's Marlboro country', Organised Crime and Corruption Reporting Project, https://www.reportingproject.net/underground/index.php%3Foption%3Dcom_content%26view%3Darticle%26id%3D9%26Itemid%3D22
8. https://bzdww.com/article/5671/
9. https://s3.amazonaws.com/www-s31.icij.org/uploads/2017/10/tobacco underground.pdf
10. Illicit cigarette trade helps pay for North Korea's nukes, *New York Post*, https://nypost.com/2017/11/01/illicit-cigarette-trade-helps-pay-for-north-koreas-nukes/

4. ILLICIT WHITES
1. Reducing the illicit trade in tobacco products in the ASEAN Region: a review of the Protocol to Eliminate Illicit Trade in Tobacco Products, Sou and Preece, https://worldcustomsjournal.org/Archives/Volume%207%2C%20Number%202%20(Sep%202013)/07%20Sou%20and%20Preece.pdf; http://www.wcoomd.org/en/media/newsroom/2016/july/millions-of-cigarettes-seized-during-operation-gryphon-ii.aspx
2. Project Sun, KPMG, https://assets.kpmg.com/content/dam/kpmg/pdf/2016/06/project-sun-report.pdf
3. Smuggling, the tobacco industry, and plain packs, Luk Joossens, https://www.cancerresearchuk.org/sites/default/files/smuggling_fullreport.pdf
4. Ibid
5. Made to be smuggled, The Centre for Public Integrity, https://publicintegrity.org/health/made-to-be-smuggled/
6. Project Sun, KPMG, https://assets.kpmg.com/content/dam/kpmg/pdf/2016/06/project-sun-report.pdf

5. A SHORT HISTORY OF TOBACCO SMUGGLING
1. The more distant history of tobacco – and trying to regulate it – is referenced throughout this book. The various storylines were woven together from http://thepirateempire.blogspot.co.id/2017/10/tobacco-part-ii-pirates-stealing-and.html; https://ofhistoryandkings.blogspot.co.id/2011/02/that-obnoxious-weed-colonial-tobacco.html; https://ofhistoryandkings.blogspot.co.id/2011/02/tobacco-trade-part-two-bideford.html; http://archive.tobacco.org/History/colonialtobacco.html; http://www.kislakfoundation.org/prize/200101.html; The lure of the devil's weed; https://en.wikipedia.org/wiki/History_of_tobacco; https://warwick.ac.uk/fac/arts/history/ecc/emforum/projects/disstheses/dissertations/spence-caroline.pdf; https://tobaccofreelife.org/tobacco/tobacco-history/; http://archive.tobacco.org/History/Tobacco_History.html

6. TRANSCRIPT: BBC'S 'THE SECRET BRIBES OF BIG TOBACCO'
1. The Secret Bribes of Big Tobacco, *BBC*, https://www.youtube.com/watch?v= wETSRZyUTeE; https://www.bbc.co.uk/news/business-34944702; https://www.bbc.co.uk/news/business-34944702

7. BIG TOBACCO'S ROGUE'S GALLERY – ADDITIONAL DETAIL
1. Philip Morris to Help Colombia Halt Cigarette Smuggling, E Souder, *Dow Jones News Service*, 2000
2. The multi-million dollar trade route, *International Consortium of Investigative Journalists*, https://www.icij.org/investigations/big-tobacco-smuggling/multi-million-dollar-trade-route/
3. Big tobacco, *The Nation*, https://www.thenation.com/article/big-tobacco/
4. Ibid
5. Tobacco's Other Secret, *CBS 60 Minutes*, http://www.nsra-adnf.ca/english/imptob/Imperial%20Tobacco%20 smuggling.html
6. Controlling Illicit Tobacco Trade: International Experience, Hana Ross, https://tobacconomics.org/wp-content/uploads/2015/05/Ross_International_experience_05.28.15.pdf
7. Tobacco's Other Secret, *CBS 60 Minutes*, https://www.cbsnews.com/news/tobaccos-other-secret/
8. Italian prosecutors accuse Philip Morris of tax evasion, *The Wall Street Journal*, https://www.wsj.com/articles/SB836775941251927000 http://articles.latimes.com/1997/oct/28/business/fi-47481
9. International business rival asserts PMI smuggles in South Africa, *The New York Times*, http://www.nytimes.com/1997/11/22/business/international-business-rival-asserts-philip-morris-smuggles-in-south-africa.html
10. Hong Kong Tobacco Exec Gets 3-Year Jail Term for Bribery; *Reuters*, HK Top Court Restores Ex-Tobacco Exec's Conviction
11. https://www.icij.org/investigations/big-tobacco-smuggling/global-reach-tobacco-companys-involvement-cigarette-smuggling-exposed-company-papers/
12. Industry Lobbying of the Public Sector and other Tactics, Yusuf Saloojee for *WHO*, https://www.who.int/tobacco/media/en/YUSSUF2000X.pdf
13. Illegal pathways to illegal profits, *Tobacco Free Kids*, https://www.tobaccofreekids.org/assets/global/pdfs/en/Illegal_profits_to_illicit_profit_en.pdf; The tobacco industry rallies against illicit trade but have we forgotten about its complicity?, *The Conversation*, http://theconversation.com/tobacco-industry-rallies-against-illicit-trade-but-have-we-forgotten-its-complicity-38760; Tobacco giant implicated in global smuggling schemes, *The Guardian*, https://www.theguardian.com/uk/2000/jan/31/kevinmaguire.duncancampbell
14. Tobacco firms used suspected drug traffickers, EU lawsuit claims, *International Consortium of Investigative Journalists*, https://www.icij.org/investigations/big-tobacco-smuggling/tobacco-firms-used-suspected-drug-traffickers-eu-lawsuit-claims/
15. The tobacco industry rallies against illicit trade but have we forgotten about its complicity?, *The Conversation*, http://theconversation.com/tobacco-industry-rallies-against-illicit-trade-but-have-we-forgotten-its-complicity-38760
16. http://3pk43x313ggr4cy0lh3tctjh.wpengine.netdna-cdn.com/wp-content/uploads/2015/03/TA5_2015_WEB.pdf

17. New documents link Clarke's firm with smuggling of cigarettes, Industry Documents Library, https://www.industrydocumentslibrary.ucsf.edu/docs/#id=qphp0219
18. Dubai diplomat accused of smuggling BAT cigarettes, *The Guardian*, https://www.theguardian.com/uk/2001/dec/17/britishamericantobaccobusiness.smoking
19. Progress in combating cigarette smuggling: controlling the supply chain, Luk Joossens, https://tobaccocontrol.bmj.com/content/17/6/399
20. UK Parliament, Public Account – Minutes of Evidence, Hearings into tobacco smuggling involving UK companies, http://www.publications.parliament.uk/pa/cm200203/cmselect/cmpubacc/143/2061901.htmm
21. Tobacco giant, British American Tobacco, caught in intensive smuggling, corporate espionage, *Premium Times*, http://www.premiumtimesng.com/business/5939-investigation-tobacco-giant-british-american-tobacco-caught-in-intensive-smuggling-corporate-espionage.html; BAT-sucked in alleged industrial espionage, *Full Disclosure*, http://www.full-disclosure.co.za/wp-content/uploads/2013/08/bat-sucked-in-alleged-industrial-espionage.pdf
22. The tobacco industry rallies against illicit trade but have we forgotten about its complicity?, *The Conversation*, http://theconversation.com/tobacco-industry-rallies-against-illicit-trade-but-have-we-forgotten-its-complicity-38760
23. Britain: Clarke's evidence on BAT to be investigated for 'contradictions', *Corpwatch*, http://www.corpwatch.org/article.php?id=12679; The multi-million dollar trade route, *International Consortium of Investigative Journalists*, https://www.icij.org/investigations/big-tobacco-smuggling/multi-million-dollar-trade-route/
24. The multi-million dollar trade route, *International Consortium of Investigative Journalists*, https://www.icij.org/investigations/big-tobacco-smuggling/multi-million-dollar-trade-route/
25. Tobacco giant, British American Tobacco, caught in intensive smuggling, corporate espionage, *Premium Times*, http://www.premiumtimesng.com/business/5939-investigation-tobacco-giant-british-american-tobacco-caught-in-intensive-smuggling-corporate-espionage.html
26. http://www.cbc.ca/news/canada/tobacco-giants-to-pay-up-to-1-15b-over-contraband-sales-1.701089
27. Tobacco giant, British American Tobacco, caught in intensive smuggling, corporate espionage, *Premium Times*, http://www.premiumtimesng.com/business/5939-investigation-tobacco-giant-british-american-tobacco-caught-in-intensive-smuggling-corporate-espionage.html
28. Tobacco giant, British American Tobacco, caught in intensive smuggling, corporate espionage, *Premium Times*, http://www.premiumtimesng.com/business/5939-investigation-tobacco-giant-british-american-tobacco-caught-in-intensive-smuggling-corporate-espionage.html
29. Ibid
30. Ibid
31. Africa: Disguising BAT's involvement in cigarette smuggling, *International Consortium of Investigative Journalists*, https://www.icij.org/investigations/big-tobacco-smuggling/africa-disguising-bats-involvement-cigarette-smuggling/; British American Tobacco and the 'insidious impact of illicit trade' in cigarettes across Africa, E LeGresley, https://tobaccocontrol.bmj.com/content/tobaccocontrol/17/5/339.full.pdf
32. Assessment of the European Union's illicit trade agreements with the four major

Transnational Tobacco Companies, Luk Joossens, https://tobaccocontrol.bmj.com/content/25/3/254
33. Smuggling, the tobacco industry, and plain packs, Luk Joossens, https://www.cancerresearchuk.org/sites/default/files/smuggling_fullreport.pdf
34. The tobacco industry rallies against illicit trade but have we forgotten about its complicity?, *The Conversation*, http://theconversation.com/tobacco-industry-rallies-against-illicit-trade-but-have-we-forgotten-its-complicity-38760
35. Tobacco giant, British American Tobacco, caught in intensive smuggling, corporate espionage, *Premium Times*, http://www.premiumtimesng.com/business/5939-investigation-tobacco-giant-british-american-tobacco-caught-in-intensive-smuggling-corporate-espionage.html
36. Ibid; BATUKE letter, Bates No. 301626956
37. Tobacco firms used suspected drug traffickers, EU lawsuit claims, *International Consortium of Investigative Journalists*, https://www.icij.org/investigations/big-tobacco-smuggling/tobacco-firms-used-suspected-drug-traffickers-eu-lawsuit-claims/
38. Ibid
39. Ibid
40. Philip Morris accused of smuggling, money-laundering conspiracy in racketeering lawsuit, *International Consortium of Investigative Journalists*, https://www.icij.org/investigations/big-tobacco-smuggling/philip-morris-accused-smuggling-money-laundering-conspiracy-racketeering-lawsuit/
41. EU Probes Cigarette Deal That May Have Aided Syria, *The Wall Street Journal*, https://www.wsj.com/articles/SB10000872396390444233104577595221203321922; Smuggling, the tobacco industry, and plain packs, Luk Joossens, https://www.cancerresearchuk.org/sites/default/files/smuggling_fullreport.pdf
42. Tobacco firms used suspected drug traffickers, EU lawsuit claims, *International Consortium of Investigative Journalists*, https://www.icij.org/investigations/big-tobacco-smuggling/tobacco-firms-used-suspected-drug-traffickers-eu-lawsuit-claims//
43. BAT-sucked in alleged industrial espionage, *Full Disclosure*, http://www.full-disclosure.co.za/wp-content/uploads/2013/08/bat-sucked-in-alleged-industrial-espionage.pdf
44. BAT's Russia branch accused of massive tax fraud, *RAPSI News*, http://www.rapsinews.com/news/20130521/267481534.html
45. British American Tobacco 'bribed' Kenyan politician Martha Karua to stop action against cigarette smuggling, *The Independent*, http://www.independent.co.uk/news/uk/crime/british-american-tobacco-bribed-kenyan-politician-martha-karua-to-stop-action-against-cigarette-a6779236.html
46. BAT's tactics to influence track and trace tender, *Tobacco Tactics*, https://tobaccotactics.org/index.php?title=Kenya-_BAT's_Tactics_to_Influence_Track_and_Trace_Tender
47. BAT fined for oversupplying tobacco in low-tax European jurisdictions, *The Guardian*, http://www.theguardian.com/business/2014/nov/16/bat-fined-for-over-supplying-tobacco-in-low-tax-european-jurisdictions; The tobacco industry rallies against illicit trade but have we forgotten about its complicity?, *The Conversation*, http://theconversation.com/tobacco-industry-rallies-against-illicit-trade-but-have-we-forgotten-its-complicity-38760; Tobacco industry lobbying: the scandal of the century, *EU Observer*, https://euobserver.com/opinion/131592

48. The tobacco industry by the numbers, *The Mail and Guardian*, http://mg.co.za/article/2012-05-18-the-tobacco-industry-by-the-numbers
49. Philip Morris ordered to defend fraud suit over US military vendors, *Reuters*, https://www.reuters.com/article/usa-court-tobacco/philip-morris-ordered-to-defend-fraud-suit-over-u-s-military-vendors-idUSL1N0QW15B20140826
50. SARS wars: massive data leak alleges British American Tobacco SAS role in bribery and corruption, *Daily Maverick*, https://www.dailymaverick.co.za/article/2016-08-16-SARS-wars-massive-data-leak-alleges-british-american-tobacco-sas-role-in-bribery-and-corruption/
51. BAT's smoke and mirrors war on rivals, *Times Live*, http://www.timeslive.co.za/local/2014/03/30/bat-s-smoke-and-mirrors-war-on-rivals1; SARS smoking out big tobacco, *Fin24*, http://www.fin24.com/Economy/SARS-smokes-out-big-tobacco-20150516; BAT-sucked in alleged industrial espionage, *Full Disclosure*, http://www.full-disclosure.co.za/wp-content/uploads/2013/08/bat-sucked-in-alleged-industrial-espionage.pdf
52. BAT's smoke and mirrors war on rivals, *Sunday Times*, https://www.pressreader.com/south-africa/sunday-times/20140330/282299613130796/TextView
53. Tobacco giant Philip Morris faces US2.2 billion Thai tax fine, *Straits Times*, http://www.straitstimes.com/asia/se-asia/tobacco-giant-philip-morris-faces-us22-billion-thai-tax-fine; Philip Morris International Inc. Could Face a $2.2 Billion Fine for Tax Evasion, *The Motley Fool*, https://www.fool.com/investing/general/2016/01/21/philip-morris-international-inc-could-face-a-22-bi.aspx
54. Philip Morris, BAT fined $260 million for illegal cigarette hoarding, *The Korea Times*, http://www.koreatimes.co.kr/www/tech/2017/02/694_223714.html Philip Morris, BAT Korea Face Multi-billion Fine for Tax Evasion, *Business Korea*, http://businesskorea.co.kr/english/news/industry/16760-tax-evasion-philip-morris-bat-korea-face-multi-billion-fine-tax-evasion
55. US court fines UPS $247 million over illegal cigarette shipments, *CNBC*, http://video.cnbc.com/gallery/?video=3000622173, http://www.cnbc.com/2017/05/26/u-s-court-fines-ups-247-million-over-illegal-cigarette-shipments.html
56. Gravísima denuncia contra Philip Morris por fraude, *Periodico Tribuna*, http://periodicotribuna.com.ar/18065-gravisima-denuncia-contra-philip-morris-por-fraude-.html;https://whyitisbad.wordpress.com
57. Thailand Slaps Philip Morris With More Tax Evasion Charges, *The Wall Street Journal*, https://www.wsj.com/articles/thailand-slaps-philip-morris-with-more-tax-evasion-charges-1487090584
58. Where there's smoke there's fire and lots of illegal cash, *New Matilda*, https://newmatilda.com/2017/08/02/exclusive-where-theres-smokes-theres-fire-and-lots-of-illegal-cash/
59. The Serious Fraud Office is investigating British American Tobacco for bribery, *Business Insider Singapore*, http://www.businessinsider.sg/british-american-tobacco-bribery-charges-serious-fraud-office-inquiry-2017-8/?r=UK&IR=T

8. EMAIL FROM JTI MANAGER ON DOING NOTHING

1. Email from David Reynolds to JTI, dated 10 April 2010, https://www.reportingproject.net/troubleswithbigtobacco/documents/OCCRP_tobacco_10.pdf
2. Ibid

9. EXTRACTS FROM AFFIDAVITS ON BAT'S ESPIONAGE RING IN SOUTH AFRICA

1. Affidavits by Daniel Francois van der Westhuizen, dated 2 February 2016, https://drive.google.com/file/d/0B6h7NrhWigQ7VjRaeWZ1bmJ1UkE/view; https://drive.google.com/file/d/0B6h7NrhWigQ7emFYWDBOdkZ2anc/view; https://drive.google.com/file/d/0B6h7NrhWigQ7WmQxemdLVk8wd2M/view; https://drive.google.com/file/d/0B6h7NrhWigQ7aUNxS1BEX1ZGQ2c/view
2. Ibid

Index

Adriano Mazzotti, 98, 143, 152
Altria, 24, 83, 137, 139, 276
Amalgamated Tobacco, 28, 29, 140-142, 200, 300
American Tobacco Company, 22-23
Andorra, 57
Anna Gilmore, 55, 62, 272, 275, 278, 279, 281, 284
Anton Rupert, 24
Argentina 102, 121, 253
Aruba, 47, 242, 246, 247
Astroturfing, 101, 107, 109
Australia, 32, 53, 65, 67, 93, 94, 107, 132, 146
Avoidance, 29, 36, 82, 193-201
Barbara Curson, 220
Belarus, 31
Belgium, 52, 72
Belinda Walter, 8, 9, 151-189
Bots, 11, 102, 113
Botswana, 66, 67, 97, 146, 181
Brazil, 23, 57, 93, 99, 194, 196
Bribery, corruption, 6, 17, 32, 39, 44, 50, 51-53, 84, 92, 130, 133, 135, 137-139, 142, 143, 150, 158, 160, 164, 165, 174, 181, 187, 219, 225, 240, 241, 243, 248, 251, 253, 261
British American Tobacco, 6, 8, 9, 12-14, 16-18, 21, 24-25, 27-32, 36-41, 43, 46-59, 62, 67, 73, 75, 84, 90-91, 95-97, 100, 102-109, 112-113, 115-116, 118-121, 128, 130, 133, 137, 139, 143-148, 150-189, 194-196, 199-200, 209, 211, 213, 216, 219-221, 226, 230, 231, 235, 240-254, 257-263
Buck Duke, 7, 21-23
Cameroon, 247, 248
Canada, 17, 33, 38, 50-52, 92, 173, 221, 243-244, 247-249
Capture, 75, 78, 121, 125-134, 147, 149, 150, 188, 199, 206, 214
Carnilinx, 27, 29, 36, 143, 152, 155, 161-165, 177-179, 183, 185, 188, 200, 257-263
Cheap whites (also illicit whites), 27, 44, 55, 97, 234, 235
China, 13, 15, 24, 32, 36, 38, 44, 46-50, 97, 232, 233, 236, 237, 243
Codentify, 53, 74, 75, 109-112, 147, 253
Colombia, 38, 50, 51, 52, 71, 92, 173, 197, 242, 245, 246, 249
Corné van Walbeek, 115, 278
Counterfeits, 27, 32, 42, 44, 46, 54, 55, 65, 96, 97, 162, 164, 232, 233, 157, 257, 259
David Reynolds, 60, 255, 256
Democractic Republic of Congo, 54, 62, 252
Economic hitmen, 18, 134, 149, 170, 206, 210

Index   301

Euromonitor, 97
Europe, 7, 12, 16, 25, 33, 51, 60, 63, 66, 72, 75, 78, 83, 90, 97, 126, 127, 137, 165, 173, 198, 210, 234, 236, 238, 245, 246, 248, 250, 251, 256
Exaggerate size / prevalence of illicit tobacco, 94-99, 131
Excise, 16, 25, 29, 43, 54, 65, 91, 92, 108, 128-133, 148, 162, 169, 193, 194, 196, 199, 225, 248, 257, 258
Fair Trade Independent Tobacco Association (FITA), 31, 38, 45, 48, 51, 57, 83, 84, 98, 99, 137, 152, 166, 178, 188
Fictitious transactions, 44, 82, 197, 227
Forensic Security Services (FSS), 95, 96, 131, 148, 153-167, 172, 174, 176-185
Framework Convention on Tobacco Control (FCTC), 25, 121, 132, 254
France, 31, 33, 72, 194, 238, 239
Francois van der Westhuizen, 151-154, 159-162, 231, 257, 262
Gallaher, 51, 61, 235
Gambia, 31
Geneva, 21, 51, 245, 255
Ghost writers, 101, 106
Gold Leaf Tobacco, 28, 29, 36, 142, 143, 200
Greece, 32
Hana Ross, 75, 266, 269, 275, 295
Harvest Mark, 77
Hennie Delport, 170-174
Hong Kong, 17, 50, 93, 94, 104, 173, 243
Illicit Trade Protocol, 25, 70, 106, 110, 145-147, 149
Illicit whites (see cheap whites)
Imperial Tobacco, 11, 12, 15, 21, 22, 38, 41, 51, 52, 54, 59, 107, 140, 145, 194, 195, 221, 243, 245-248
Inexto, 75, 110-112, 253
Institute of Economic Affairs, 103
International Consortium of Investigative Journalists, 231

International Tax and Investment Centre, 104
Interpol, 30, 146-149
Invoices, 155, 157, 158, 176, 180, 199, 200, 227
Ipsos, 114-117
Iraq, 72, 93, 153, 155
Ireland, 33, 92, 96
Italy, 17, 50, 92, 131, 239, 243
Jacob Zuma, 8, 141, 142, 188
Jacques Pauw, 7, 30, 35, 140, 142, 158, 185
James Bonsack, 21, 22
Japan Tobacco International (JTI), 15, 18, 21, 25, 36, 39, 41, 52, 54, 60-62, 74, 108, 109, 119, 135, 136, 155, 194, 198, 211, 221, 235, 243, 248-250, 255, 256, 273
Johann van Loggerenberg, 7, 9, 27, 30, 39, 142, 143, 182-186, 189, 223
Jordan, 32
Kenya, 53, 75, 112, 130, 132, 139, 150, 196, 241, 251, 254, 271, 275
Know your customer, 43, 71, 80, 210, 214
KPMG, 61, 93, 105, 166, 173, 187
Law enforcement, 10, 34, 63, 65, 75, 84, 120, 125, 128-134, 143-175, 183, 193, 210, 211, 232, 233, 257, 259-261
Lobby, 90, 100, 102, 103, 106-108, 126, 127, 135-140, 205, 206, 214, 241, 244
Lonrho, 178, 179
Luis Pestana, 151, 152, 166, 231
Media, 29, 50-52, 57, 75, 84, 90, 94, 102-105, 108-110, 113, 115, 116, 137, 165, 166, 249, 251, 254
Michael Eads, 75, 112
Middle East 52, 71, 248, 252, 265, 267, 272
Mitch McConnell, 136, 137
Money laundering, 14, 39, 44, 51, 52, 82, 104, 142, 163, 165, 173, 174, 181,

189, 199, 200, 215, 219, 221, 226, 227, 231, 249, 253
Monsanto, 78
Montenegro 31, 32, 60
Nigeria, 51, 58, 92, 99, 145, 247, 248
North Korea, 32, 233
OLAF European Commission's Anti-Fraud Office, 54, 165, 221
Paraguay, 31
Procter & Gamble, 78, 79
Paul Hopkins, 53, 150, 231, 240, 241, 251
Philip Morris International (PMI), 17, 21, 24, 25, 36, 38, 39, 41, 49, 50-54, 57, 64, 72, 74, 76, 83, 89, 91, 92, 97, 99, 102-104, 107, 109, 110-111, 118, 121, 126, 127, 137-140, 146, 147, 194, 197, 202-206, 216, 231, 242, 243, 245, 249-253
Philippines, 53, 119, 140, 252, 253
Poland, 99
Political patronage, 18, 135-143
Prevalence of illicit, 90-96, 115, 128, 189, 215
Profit, 8, 9, 13, 14, 21, 29-33, 37, 38, 45, 47, 48-51, 57, 61, 64-69, 79, 80, 82-85, 92, 98-100, 104, 118, 132, 137, 141, 173, 178, 193, 195-197, 200, 201, 206, 214, 235, 237-239, 245, 248, 250, 253
Project Honey Badger, 14, 15, 30, 65, 172, 181, 189, 196, 225-229
Project Star, 103, 105
Project Sun, 61, 103, 105
Proxies, 102, 103, 106, 107, 113, 125, 206, 215
Public relations firms, 89, 95, 99, 102, 105, 113, 120, 205,
'Reduced-risk' products, 202-206
Rembrandt, 24, 243
RJ Reynolds, 15, 16, 18, 22, 23, 50, 52, 54, 57, 58, 60, 90, 106, 136, 138, 139, 198, 204, 243, 245, 248-250

Russia, 29, 52, 53, 60, 194, 234-237, 244, 248, 250, 256
Settlements, 17, 51, 52, 74, 103, 109, 194, 220, 231, 237, 246, 248
Silent coup, 84, 123-134
Simon Rudland, 142
Smuggling, 7, 13, 17, 19, 29-32, 36-39, 42, 44-72
Somalia, 37, 252
South African Revenue Service (SARS), 7, 9, 10, 12, 14-16, 30, 39-40, 43, 64, 65, 75, 76, 97, 102, 103, 109, 115, 128, 133, 140, 141, 142, 148, 151, 152, 157, 162, 168-189, 195, 196, 198, 199, 220, 221, 225, 226, 227-229, 258-263
South Korea, 53, 72, 139, 194, 253
Spain, 52, 57, 70, 92, 126, 238, 239, 249
Spies, 9, 123, 150-167, 172, 184
State Security Agency (SSA), 141, 143, 145, 149, 152, 153, 156, 169, 171, 177-179, 181-189
Sudan, 51, 247
Supply chain, 10, 13, 33, 43, 50, 62, 66, 68-80, 85, 99, 103, 108, 112, 130, 134, 145, 147, 195, 206, 201, 211, 214, 216, 219
Switzerland, 23, 58, 197, 198, 200, 236
Terrorism, 51, 79, 132, 154, 174, 275
Thailand, 53, 119, 139, 140, 252, 253
ThisFish, 77
Tobacco Free Portfolios, 216
Tobacco Institute of Southern Africa (TISA), 31, 39, 40, 54, 93, 95-97, 108, 109, 114, 115, 131, 146, 148, 156, 161, 170, 176, 177, 181
Tobacco Task Team, 172, 176, 177, 178, 181, 185, 263
Tobacco Wars, 7, 23, 39, 40, 223
Tom Moyane, 10, 142, 188, 189
Traceability, 73, 75, 76-78, 100, 102, 103, 110-112, 132, 133, 145, 147, 210

Index 303

Umbrella operations, 44, 57
United Arab Emirates 36, 44, 46, 97, 234
United Kingdom, 11, 18, 50, 51, 53, 58, 61, 71, 72, 84, 92, 94, 98, 103, 139, 154, 155, 158, 160, 162, 163, 165, 183, 184, 194, 195, 196, 197, 219, 221, 231, 235
United States of America, 7, 24, 38, 70, 91, 106, 108, 137, 209, 243, 244, 251, 253
Uzbekistan, 75, 93, 130
Vintage tobacco advertisements, 81, 122, 190, 207, 212, 218
Wastage allowance, 199, 226
Whistle-blower, 53, 56, 110, 146, 165, 179, 182, 231, 240, 247, 251, 254
Yussuf Saloojee, 39, 116, 273, 278, 284, 285, 295
Yusuf Kajee, 28, 140, 141-143, 157, 179
Zimbabwe, 36, 45, 46, 97, 142, 167, 181, 226, 250

About the author

TELITA SNYCKERS is an international management consultant focusing on making tax and customs agencies smarter. Before becoming a well-seasoned traveller, she held down a position as an executive at the South African Revenue Service, and as a compliance manager with the tax agency in Singapore (some way from where her journey started as a prosecutor in musty Court 6 of the Johannesburg Magistrate's Court).

Having worked in more than 25 countries around the world – from Cape Town to Canberra; from Singapore to Serbia – she knows a thing or two about spotting a smuggler, not wearing your best shoes in Kosovo, and connecting dots where none seem obvious.

She has written several articles on supply chain security relating to tobacco, and on tobacco industry tactics, but fell into this book by accident, uncovering a story that just had to be told – one that ties together divergent lines about honey traps, lipstick on pigs, moral fig leaves, jam on faces, economic hitmen, toothpaste, and big tobacco.

She pretends to enjoy dangerous exploits like scuba diving with tiger sharks and climbing Kilimanjaro, but is actually a bit of a nerd and is at her happiest curled up alone with a book.

She has a master's degree in constitutional law, as well as diplomas in exchange control and the combating of money laundering.

When word got out about this book, the tobacco industry offered her a job. She turned them down.